Local Area Networks

Networks

4th Edition

Also available from Continuum:
Anthony Lewis: Wide Area Networks
Colin Ritchie: Relational Database Principles
Colin Ritchie: Operating Systems

Local Area Networks

Networks

4th Edition

Peter Hodson

continuum
LONDON • NEW YORK

Continuum

The Tower Building
11 York Road
London SE1 7NX

370 Lexington Avenue
New York
NY 10017-65503

First published in 1992 by Letts Educational
Reprinted in 1994
Second edition published in 1995
Third edition published in 1997
Reprinted in 1998
Fourth edition published in 2003

British Library Cataloguing-in-Publication Data
A catalogue record for this book is available from the British Library.

ISBN: 0-8264-5866-1 (paperback)

Typeset by YHT Ltd, London
Printed and bound in Great Britain by MPG Books Ltd, Bodmin

Contents

Contents

Contents

Preface

The educational sector is experiencing significant changes in the way in which courses are delivered. Increasingly, courses are being modularized to enable students from a wider range of educational backgrounds to study individual modules that were previously available only on particular programmes. Courses are also being run with significantly reduced lecturer contact time, and therefore texts are needed that are provocative and interactive.

1. Aim of the book

The aim of this book is to provide the course text for the networking element required by most degree and Edexcel Higher National courses in computing.

It has been developed by the author over a number of years whilst presenting courses to both students and practising professionals. The first chapters cover simple concepts and principles of communication that may be revision for some students. The rest of the book deals with issues relating to LANs and their interconnection and internetworking.

2. Approach

The book provides a framework for understanding key concepts in local area networks. Additionally, the more practical issues of cabling structures and interconnections of networks are discussed. By covering key concepts and practical issues, the text provides a blend of material based on the traditional concepts of solid *technical* content coupled with the *real issues of relevance in practice*. In this way the book can be used as

a) a core text to support courses which are delivered through traditional lectures;

b) a text allowing self-learning on part, or the whole, of courses where lecturer contact time is limited.

Important issues are repeated in several chapters, allowing individual chapters to be free-standing whilst reinforcing the learning process when the book is read as a whole.

3. Questions

The author has developed an extensive range of questions which have been successfully tried on students over several years. Questions are divided into two main levels: short in-text questions and longer, end of chapter questions.

Short questions

The short questions occur at frequent intervals in the text and encourage students to apply their understanding of the preceding text without halting them for too long in their progression through the topic. Answers to these questions are given at the end of the chapter.

Further questions

These end of chapter questions are graded in difficulty from simple tutorial questions to partial or full examination style questions. Approximately half of these questions (indicated with an asterisk) have answers at the end of the book; the others have answers in the Lecturers' Supplement only.

4. Lecturers' supplement

A supplement is available to lecturers. It contains suggested answers to those chapter end questions that do not have answers in the book (approximately half). It also contains larger versions of about 50 diagrams in the book for use as OHP masters. It is available free from Continuum to lecturers adopting the book as a course text – you will be required to give details of the course title, student numbers and book supplier – or for a charge of £3 to any lecturer applying on college headed paper.

Notes on the 4th edition

The fourth edition has updated the material on network standards and common LAN standards that are now in use. Over recent years there has been an increasing emphasis on Ethernet implementations, and this is reflected by the heavier treatment of Ethernet compared with other LANs. Equally, the evolving standards have led to changes in LAN designs. The text has been updated to reflect the current position, especially in relation to switches. The rapid emergence of wireless networks has also been captured in the text and given some prominence.

Throughout the text k is used to represent 1000 rather than K representing 1024. This makes arithmetic calculations somewhat easier, but it should be noted that in other texts K is used to represent 1000. Technically, K is degrees Kelvin, so this text remains true to the correct use of k.

Peter Hodson
January 2002

Acknowledgements

I am grateful to my friends and colleagues who have helped at various times in the compilation of this fourth edition. Also to past students, on whom various iterations of the developing text were tested, and from whom I have gratefully received feedback. In particular, I would acknowledge the help and kind permission for the use of vendor material from a number of organizations. Each organization is acknowledged as appropriate where their material appears.

Finally, to my family Liz, Cerys, Hannah and Nicholas who have patiently let me have the time needed to put this text together. I thank them for supporting my indulgence.

1 Basics of data communications

1. Introduction

Effective use of computer systems demands that the user has the ability to move data between devices reliably. In a very simple example we must be able to print from a PC to an attached printer without any errors occurring as the data is transferred. This can be considered as a two stage activity. Firstly the data must be correctly sent and received. Secondly, the sending device must know that it has been correctly received. If, during this second stage, the sender is informed that it has not been correctly received and the transfer was unsuccessful, then an attempt to put matters right and recover from the error is made. The whole concept of data communication is based on these basic principles of sending data, checking its correct receipt and confirming how successful the transfer was. The designs which have evolved to manage this approach are known as protocols, i.e., who says what and when!

At the simplest level there may be two devices that are directly connected using a short piece of wire. At more advanced levels they may be connected either by a telephone line or a complete data communications network and be separated by thousands of miles.

In this first chapter we will explore some of the basic elements of achieving data transfer.

2. Data transfer and asynchronous transmission

To transfer data between two devices there are a few fundamental points which need to be clear. To help clarify these points let us consider a connection between two devices, which could be two computers or a computer and a peripheral device such as a printer.

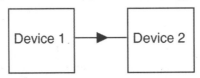

Fig. 1.1 Simple serial connection

In Fig. 1.1, device 1 is the sending or transmitting device. A frequently used notation to represent the transmitting device is Tx. Similarly, device 2 in Fig. 1.1 is the receiving device, or Rx. To pass information between the two devices we need to be able to send signals. Historical signalling techniques between humans have included smoke signals and semaphore flags. Of course, the information in a computer system is held in binary format, and so it is convenient to communicate with digital signals between the Tx and Rx devices. The connection between the two devices can range from a simple direct connection to a much more complex combination of relays and links.

We will start at the simplest case where Fig. 1.1 represents a simple connection between two adjacent devices. Each binary digit, or bit, is sent across the connection and represented as a signal on the transmission medium.

If this connection is a single copper wire connection, then exchange of data can only be by a serial sequence of bits flowing along the transmission medium. Technically, this single connection consists of two conductors or copper wires to make up an electrical circuit, but we call it a single connection. Data can only flow in one direction at any instant in time along this single connection. We will see later that the bits are grouped together to represent a character (i.e., a letter of the alphabet, a number or a symbol such as an '!'), typically 8 bits at a time. Each bit is usually represented on the copper wire as a voltage level. To ensure that each device is capable of sending or receiving digital information to/from other devices, international standards have been established. These were intended to persuade designers not to create their own signalling representations for their devices. This would have created havoc, with possibly hundreds of different approaches and with there being little real prospect of being able to connect devices supplied by different vendors. The interface standards (which include signalling conventions) that are most commonly found on devices are the RS232C standard and the V.24 interface standard. The RS232C standard has been developed by the Electronics Industry Association (EIA) in the USA. RS stands for Recommended Standard and C is the revision level. The V.24 standard is released by the CCITT, which is part of the International Telecommunications Union, set up by the United Nations. Using RS232C conventions, a 0 bit is represented by a positive voltage and 1 is represented as a negative voltage. The more recent X.21 standard has been in place for quite a while, but migration to this has been slow. Fortunately, transition arrangements between X.21 and RS232C have been introduced to accommodate this slow migration.

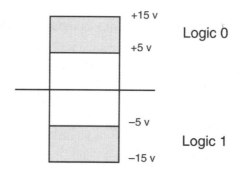

Fig. 1.2 RS232C voltage levels

Normally the voltage levels used in RS232C signalling are +12 V and −12 V, although voltage levels between +5 V and +15 V will be interpreted as a 0 and, equally, a 1 will be interpreted from a signal in the −5 V to −15 V range. A voltage level in the shaded areas of Fig. 1.2 should be recognized as a signal representing a bit. Using this standard, the bit stream 01010 can be represented by the signal levels in Fig. 1.3.

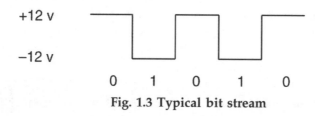

Fig. 1.3 Typical bit stream

Question 1.1   Draw the signal levels that would represent the bit stream 10100 using the RS232C standard.

Question 1.2   In answering Question 1.1, were there any particular difficulties in representing the last two bits?

An important issue to be resolved is how long the signal for each bit should last. For example, in RS232C, each bit needs to be represented for a given length of time at the required voltage level on the copper wire. The length or duration of the signal has to be sufficient for the receiving end to recognize the incoming signal and record it accurately. If each change of signal occurred after 10 ms (milliseconds) such that every bit took this length of time, then in a 1 s (second) period we could send 100 of these signals. This is usually stated as 100 bit/s (or 100 bps) (i.e., bits per second). How did we calculate this? Let's do the calculation in the way in which you would normally attempt it. If we signal at 100 bit/s, i.e., we send 100 bits in 1 s, then each bit will last 1/100 s, or 10 ms. The number of bits per second that we are able to send between devices is known as the data rate. In RS232C signalling, where each signal represents 1 bit, the signalling rate (measured in hertz) and the data rate (bit/s) have the same value, e.g., 100 Hz and 100 bit/s.

Question 1.3   If the data rate were 1600 bit/s, what would the duration of each signal level be?

Hopefully you will see that the faster you want to send data between two devices, the shorter the duration of each bit signalled on the transmission medium must be. A problem now arises at the receiving end of any data transfer. How does the receiver know when data is about to be sent and how will it know the rate at which the sending device will be transmitting? To recognize the incoming data and recover or capture the data accurately, the receiver needs to read or sample the signal on the cable or transmission media at the same rate as the speed at which the data is being transmitted.

Let us first look at the situation where everything is idle, i.e., the quiescent state, and examine a simple case where we want to send a character of data across the connection. To alert the receiver that a character (8 bits) of data is about to be transmitted, a start bit is additionally sent at the front of the character. Conventionally, we also send a stop bit at the end of the character. These start and stop bits also act as delimiters on the character so that the boundary points of any character being transmitted will be understood by the receiver. Thus the stop bit is an important check for the receiver that the end boundary point of the character frame has been correctly reached. Hence, a typical transfer of a character in asynchronous mode would look like Fig. 1.4.

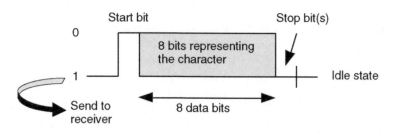

Fig. 1.4 Asynchronous character representation

The eight data bits representing the character are signalled at whatever the level is to represent the bit sequence. The first bit sent after the start bit is the least significant end of the character. The last bit sent is the parity bit. As an example, the ASCII representation of the letter 'A' is 1000001. If we use an even parity checking approach, the 8 bit representation is 01000001. (ASCII codes and parity settings are explained later in this chapter.) The bit stream sent across the connection is shown in Fig. 1.5.

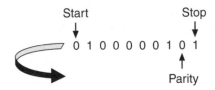

Fig. 1.5 Sequence of bit transmission

This will sometimes be seen in other textbooks or journals as shown in Fig. 1.6. Both formats show exactly the same sequence of bits over the transmission line.

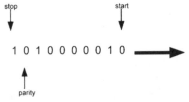

Fig. 1.6 Alternative representation of bit sequence

Figure 1.5 is better when you consider the layout of a string of characters to be sent. You would start with the characters, e.g., THE MESSAGE, then form the bit representation and send the bits. If we used the representation in Fig 1.6 then we would need to lay the characters out as EGASSEM EHT.

Question 1.4	Draw the asynchronous representation of the character frame for the eight bits 01011010.

Some systems may need more than one stop bit and a character will be terminated by one and a half or two stop bits. This is usually for slower devices, typically with slow mechanical components, and is becoming less common. If we send two stop bits to a receiving device that only requires one, it won't matter since the second stop bit will just appear to be the start of an idle signal level.

The form of transmission discussed above is known as *asynchronous transmission*. The receiver doesn't know when the next character is going to arrive and awaits the arrival of the next start bit. There is no information within the character about the speed at which it is being sent, and so there is no 'timing' information (i.e., there is nothing to tell the receiver how quickly it needs to sample the incoming signal in order to recover the transmitted data). To clarify how important it is that the receiver should sample the transmission at the correct rate we will consider a simple example. A device is transmitting the character 01011010 at 100 bit/s (i.e., the duration or time cell of each bit is 10 ms) and the receiver tries to recover the data by sampling every 20 ms. Let's see what happens.

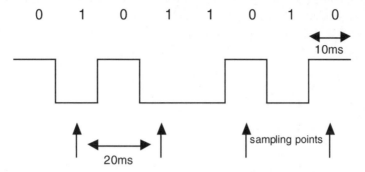

Fig. 1.7 Sampling the transmission incorrectly

A receiver incorrectly sampling the transmission as shown in Fig. 1.7 would read the data sent as 1100. Clearly this is not what we want. The receiver needs to sample the line at the same rate as the sender is transmitting the data. To achieve this, the Tx and Rx interfaces of each device have internal clocks, which are, to a reasonable level of accuracy, both 'clocking' at the same rate. Devices sending data to each other know the data rate between themselves because the data communications designer will have established the speeds at one of the standard rates at which data should be exchanged. So the arrival of the start bit at the receiver starts its interface clock and instructs the receiver's interface to sample the incoming signal. Provided that the sender and receiver clocks are running at the same rate, the data should be received successfully. We hope that the accuracy of the clocks is such that they maintain synchronization and the receiver continues to clock near the midpoint of a time cell. If they are not accurate it is possible that the receiver's clock will drift out of synchronization with the transmitter's clock and will try to sample at some point off the middle of the time cell and potentially misread the signal.

Fig. 1.8 shows the offset of two clocks not in synchronization. The sampling point is drifting away from recovering the signal at the midpoint of the time cell where the clearest indication of the signal level is. At the edges of the time cell, because changes of signal level aren't instantaneous, it is less clear what the signal level is intended to be. Indeed you could easily misinterpret the signal and receive the 'wrong' data. For relatively short lengths of data (in this case a character), the accuracy between the Tx and Rx clocks is normally sufficient for such drift not to be an issue. The faster the data rate and the greater the number of bits sent in one 'burst', the more acute this issue becomes.

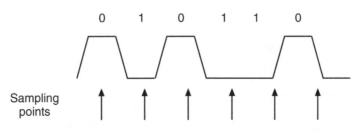

Fig. 1.8 Delayed sampling effect

As a check within the asynchronous protocol, the receiver insists on seeing a stop bit in the tenth (and possibly eleventh) bit position. If that isn't present, and there isn't a stop bit in the character position where there should be one, then there has been an error. In a typical character transfer, successive characters will have a short gap between them, as shown in Fig. 1.9. It is possible for this inter-character time gap to be nothing or very small, especially when the sender is transmitting at its maximum rate.

Fig. 1.9 Successive character transmissions

Consider a case where there is no 'lost' time between each character sent, i.e., a start bit for one character follows immediately behind the stop bit of the previous character. If 200 characters are sent down a transmission line at a rate of 1200 bit/s we can now calculate the time it takes to transfer the data.

$$200 \text{ characters} = 200 \times 10 \text{ transmission bits}$$

(assuming one stop bit and one start bit).

$$\text{time to transmit} = \frac{\text{number of bits sent}}{\text{speed of transmission}}$$

$$\text{time to transmit} = \frac{200 \times 10}{1200} \text{ s}$$

$$= 1.66\text{s}$$

Question 1.5   If we assume that characters could be sent without a delay between them, how long would it take to send 100 characters down a line asynchronously at 2400 bit/s?

Typical transfer rates and their respective character rates are shown in Table 1.1.

Transfer rate bit/s	Character rate character/s
110	10
300	30
600	60
1,200	120
2,400	240
4,800	480
9,600	960
19,200	1,920

Table 1.1 Typical transfer rates and character rates

The odd entry in Table 1.1 is the first entry. That is because devices receiving data at the slow rate of 110 bit/s are those which need two stop bits (i.e., 11 bit characters).

An important feature to note here is how many extra or redundant bits we have to transmit in order to achieve a successful transmission using this technique. Effectively, for each 8 bit character we send a 10 bit sequence, i.e., there is a 25 per cent overhead, or two extra bits for every eight we need to send.

If we reconsider the example above where we sent 200 characters in 1.66 s, we had 200 × 8 bits of 'real' data. Because the transmission time was 1.66 s, the effective data rate is (200 × 8)/1.66 bit/s = 963.86 bit/s. Of course, as users of the system, we cannot alter this and we must simply accept that to carry data there are associated overheads. The higher the overheads are, i.e., the larger the number of extra bits in comparison with the data element that are carried during transmission, the lower is the effective throughput of the intended data transfer.

3. Data representation and parity checks

There are several different bit representations of a character, two of which are the ASCII and EBCDIC representations. The Appendix gives the ASCII representation, which is the most widely used, especially outside the IBM user base. It should be noted from this table that we only use 7 bits to uniquely represent the range of characters. The eighth bit is used as a parity bit to help ensure that the character transfer has been successful. Fig. 1.10 shows a transmission in which one bit has been corrupted. This alteration of the original data will be detected by parity checking techniques.

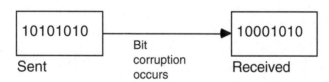

Fig. 1.10 Serial bit corruption

Parity for each character is a simple technique, but unfortunately several variations of parity settings are in use. The most common of these are odd and even parity. In the case of odd parity, the parity bit is set to ensure that the total number of 'ones', including the parity bit itself, is an odd number. Even parity ensures that the total number of 'ones' in a character is even. Both of these parity modes are commonly used. Frequently, even parity is used in asynchronous transmission and odd parity settings are used in synchronous transmission. Other methods such as space, mark or null parity, are less prevalent. Fig. 1.10 shows an even parity setting.

On receipt of a character, a check is made to see if the parity is correctly set. If it is incorrect, the character transfer is assumed to have been corrupted and is discarded. A retransmission of the corrupted character is required. The first step of this process is known as error detection, i.e., when the parity check is made. The second is known as error correction, i.e., when the retransmission request is made.

The installer of the data communications equipment is responsible for ensuring that the correct parity setting has been established between installed devices under his or her control. The suppliers or vendors of each item of equipment will identify the required parity setting for the individual interface, i.e., will state whether odd or even parity is required.

Consider the ASCII representation for 'A', which is 1000001. Using odd parity, this would be represented as 11000001. Using even parity, it would be represented as 011000001. The parity, bit is placed in the most significant bit position, and it is the last bit to be sent in a character transfer, since we start the transmission by sending the least significant bit of the character first.

Question 1.6   What would the parity bits be for the ASCII code of 'B' and 'E' using odd parity setting? What would they be for even parity setting?

This technique is good for detecting single bit errors, but if two bits were corrupted it would not detect the problem. Fig. 1.11 shows this situation. Parity checking is fine at detecting those error conditions where the number of bits that have changed are odd, but it cannot detect the case where an even number of bits have changed. Hence, 1, 3, 5 or 7 bits corruptions will be detected. However, 2, 4, 6 or 8 bit corruptions will not be detected.

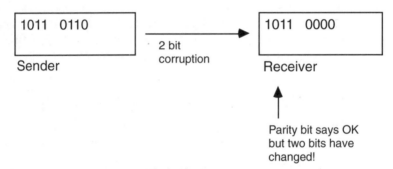

Fig. 1.11 Multiple bit corruption

It will not surprise you to learn that more sophisticated techniques of error detection have been implemented. It is critical that corrupted or erroneous data be detected. We are slightly less concerned about data being corrupted than we are about making sure we know when it is wrong, although we clearly strive to achieve error free transfers. At least action can be taken to put it right when we know it is wrong. Undetected errors can create enormous problems because we probably believe the corrupted data is right and continue to use it afterwards.

Question 1.7   Suggest an example where an undetected error in a data transfer would be problematic.

---

4. Synchronous transmission

The approach to data transfer using serial lines with asynchronous transmission works well when the volume of data to be transferred is low. However, sending large volumes of data at low data rates is time consuming. A start and stop bit for every character is quite an overhead, but most importantly we are relying on the receiver station sampling (or clocking) the data at the same rate as the sender. To send data at higher rates we use a different technique known as synchronous transmission. The basis for this change stems from the difficulty we experience in keeping two clocks synchronized, i.e., the sending device's clock and the receiver's clock.

At low speeds this synchronization isn't too critical given that the time cell or duration of the signal for each bit is reasonably wide, and the total period to keep it synchronized is only 10 bits 'clocked' across. After 10 bits, the opportunity to resynchronize clocks on receipt of the next start bit is available.

At higher speeds, the time cell for each bit obviously decreases. To speed up the effective transfer rate, only the 8 bit ASCII code (or equivalent) is sent, without the start/ stop bit sequence. Characters are 'blocked' together to form a character sequence.

To permit the receiving device to synchronize its clock with that of the sender, each block of characters is preceded with a few synchronization (SYN) characters, as shown in Fig. 1.12.

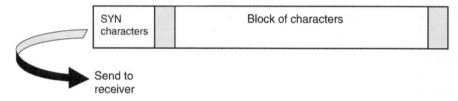

Fig. 1.12 Synchronous transfer

When such a frame of information arrives at the receiving device, the receiver's clock uses the SYN characters to lock onto the sender's signal. Once this synchronization has been achieved the remainder of the frame is sampled at the correct signalling rate and the data transfer is completed. This approach to data transfer is called synchronous because the 'block' contains the timing information (in the SYN characters) to allow the synchronization to occur.

Of course we still need to know at the receiving end when the block has come to an end. To manage this aspect (amongst others), the detail of how we construct the block so the receiver understands the detail of the block structure is known as the protocol. Some protocols exist where there is no fixed length to the number of characters in such a block. Hence, we need to have indicators to show where the start and end occur. Several ASCII characters are designated control characters, and two of these control characters are used to help define the boundary points. They are STX (start of text) and ETX (end of text). The flexibility of using a protocol which implements variable length blocks is quite useful, rather than being constrained by fixed size blocks for all transmissions. These control characters are often known as delimiters.

Question 1.8   Can you devise another technique to establish the exact length of a variable length block, other than the approach just outlined?

The exact structure of such a block and how many special characters are placed at the front and back is protocol dependent. Several different protocols exist and the variations within each of these protocols makes world-wide integration of all such systems just that little bit more difficult. At this stage we are not going to look at the detailed structure of a particular protocol standard. We will use the structure shown in Fig. 1.13 as representative of a synchronous protocol, and we will compare it with the asynchronous version from an efficiency point of view .

Fig. 1.13 shows a possible protocol which has placed three additional characters at the front of a block and one character at the end. Consider a transfer in which the data comprises 50 characters in a single block. To send 50 data characters requires a transmission of 54 characters. Assuming the efficiency to be (useful data/total data) × 100 per cent, the efficiency of this system is (50/54 × 100) per cent = 92.5 per cent.

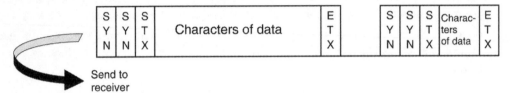

Send to
receiver

Fig. 1.13 Example of long and short blocks

In comparison, the asynchronous case has an efficiency of 8 in 10 bits being data, i.e., 80 per cent.

Question 1.9 If data were transmitted synchronously using the protocol outlined in Fig. 1.13 and the block size was 100 data characters, what would the efficiency of such a protocol standard be?

The efficiency of synchronous transmission is variable and it depends on the block size and exact structure of the protocol overheads, but it is normally much better than for the asynchronous methods. In addition, higher transmission speeds can be used for the synchronous case because the receiver is given help in synchronizing with the sender (using the timing signal, i.e., SYN characters) prior to capturing the data component.

Consider a possible scenario where the protocol outlined in Fig. 1.13 always has data blocks containing 50 data characters, and a transmission line with a speed of 9600 bit/s is used. The time taken to transmit one block is as follows:

$$\frac{(\text{total number of data characters} + \text{number of bytes of overheads}) \times 8}{\text{speed of line (bit/s)}} = \frac{(50 + 4) \times 8}{9600}$$

$$= 0.045 \text{ s}$$

$$= 45 \text{ ms}$$

Question 1.10 If data were transmitted synchronously using the protocol outlined in Fig. 1.13 and a maximum block size of 100 data characters, what is the shortest time it would take to transmit 2000 characters over a line with a speed of 9600 bit/s?

What assumption have you made in this calculation?

Question 1.10 has introduced an important idea. If we have a large unit of data to transmit to the receiver, how should we go about it? What should the maximum block size be? In any transmission there is always the probability that an error may occur. In fact, the only thing we can guarantee is that an error will occur at some time. Errors in transmission may occur because of noise being picked up on the transmission line from crosstalk, thermal noise, impulse noise or jitter and peak. The larger the size of a block, the greater is the probability of an error occurring during the transmission of that block.

In Chapter 2, we will consider how reliable data transmission can be achieved.

Further questions

(There are answers to the questions marked with an asterisk at the end of the book.)

1. *What would the parity bits be for the ASCII codes of 'D' and 'F' using odd parity setting? What would they be for even parity setting?

2. *If we assume that characters could be sent without a delay between them, how long would it take to asynchronously send 200 characters down a 9600 bit/s line?

3. Outline the basic differences between asynchronous and synchronous mode.

4. What techniques may be used for delimiters for a block of data in synchronous mode?

5. A 4 kbyte file is sent across a 9600 bit/s synchronous mode link which supports a maximum block size of 200 bytes. Assuming each block requires four control characters, what is the shortest time it would take to transmit the data?

6. A communications line supports data at the rate of 9600 bit/s. What is the shortest time it will take to carry a 100 kbyte (or 100 kB) file? State any assumptions you have made.

Answer 1.1   The signal levels are shown in Fig. 1.14.

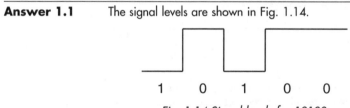

1   0   1   0   0

Fig. 1.14 Signal levels for 10100

Answer 1.2   Perhaps the only difficulty is knowing where the boundary point between the two 0s is located, or how long to make the signal level. Of course if all binary values are drawn for a fixed length of time, this is not really a problem.

Answer 1.3   At 1600 bit/s each signal level or binary value lasts for 1/1600 s (or 0.625 ms or 625 micro seconds).

Answer 1.4   Fig. 1.15 is drawn with the right hand side representing the first bits sent. You may have drawn the diagram in the reverse order, which is perfectly correct as long as you know the order in which the bits are sent.

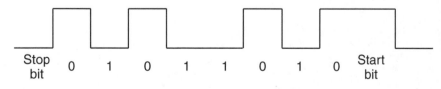

Stop   0   1   0   1   1   0   1   0   Start
bit   bit

Fig. 1.15 Asynchronous representation for 01011010

Answer 1.5 100 characters = 10 × 100 bits = 1000 bits

To send 1000 bits at 2400 bit/s would take

$$\frac{1000}{2400} = 0.41\,s$$

Answer 1.6 B is 42_H or 11000010 with odd parity

01000010 with even parity

E is 45_H or 01000101 with odd parity

11000101 with even parity

Answer 1.7 Any data transfer which contains an undetected error is a problem. Obviously some errors are more critical than others. Your answer could have identified many areas, but typical examples could be a manufacturing system, e.g., a robot cell, or an aircraft control system.

Answer 1.8 Fixed length blocks aside, a variable length block could have a field (i.e., a pointer) at the front of the block which states how long this block will be.

Answer 1.9 100 data characters in a (100 + 4) overall block gives an efficiency of

$$\left(\frac{100}{104} \times 100\right) \text{per cent} = 96.15 \text{ per cent}$$

Answer 1.10 The transmission of 2000 characters using a protocol of 100 data character blocks needs

$$\left(\frac{2000}{100}\right) = 20 \text{ blocks}$$

total bits transmitted = 20 blocks (each of (100 + 4) characters) × 8 bits

If the line speed is 9600 bit/s,

$$\text{time to transmit} = \frac{20 \times (100 + 4) \times 8 \text{ s}}{9600}$$

$$= 1.734 \text{ s}$$

The assumption made here is that there is no delay in sending each block and every block is successfully transferred without an error occurring.

2 Reliable data transmission

1. Introduction

Chapter 1 introduced some of the fundamental issues of data transfer. In this chapter we will be looking at the techniques which are used to ensure that data is transferred successfully. Designers always strive to ensure error free transmission, but of course errors do occur and a number of possible opportunities for error exist. The data may get corrupted before it arrives at the receiver, it may not ever arrive at the destination, or the response from the receiver back to the sender may suffer from either of these problems. If the transfer is not successful then an attempt must be made to put the problem right. Effectively, the two stages are error detection and error correction. The larger the size of the data component being transferred, the greater is the risk of an error occurring. We begin by looking at how data communication systems have evolved to manage this situation.

2. Size of data transfer

If a signal is sent over a long distance without its strength being boosted, we see that the quality of the signal deteriorates as it is propagated along the transmission medium. If the distance is too great (further than the maximum distance allowed by accepted standards), then the signal may be unrecognizable and attempts to read the data are either inaccurate or unsuccessful. Fig. 2.1 shows how a good-quality digital signal introduced at one point on a transmission medium may be seen as a poor-quality signal at a more distant point.

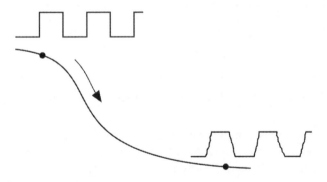

Fig. 2.1 Signal deterioration

If we assume that the probability of an error occurring is fixed, then a few simple calculations can be attempted. Error probabilities are often stated in the following format: one error bit will occur in every n thousand bits transmitted, e.g., the error probability may be one error bit in every 10,000 bits transmitted, which is the same as saying 1:10,000, or an error rate of 10^{-4}. Keeping the concept simple, if the size of the block of data being transmitted is small, then the probability of an error occurring is also small. The larger the size of the block of data is, the greater is the probability that an error will occur. The problem is that we don't know in advance how big an intended data transfer being sent from any user will be. It could be that the user only transmits small units of data, or it could be that a whole database is being transmitted and many megabytes of data need to be sent.

Given this 'probability of error' problem, it is normal to fix a maximum block size for any attempted transfer. This maximum block size is fixed with a few criteria in mind. It shouldn't be too small, because the overheads of the protocol (and the bits used for synchronization and additional header bits, etc.) will reduce the efficiency. Neither should it be too large, since it increases the chance of an error occurring during the time it takes to send the block of data. When an error does occur, we have to resend the data. The larger the unit of data to be resent, the longer is the proportion of time spent in resending data as we attempt error recovery. The overall efficiency of the transmission can be decreased if the maximum block size is set wrongly, but we are trading off one problem characteristic against another.

Packet switching

Assuming the designers have got it right and have set a maximum block size that is a good compromise, then under normal conditions any large unit of data is broken up into a number of smaller blocks. So the original unit of data is fragmented into a number of blocks, each of which are the maximum size set by the designer of the protocol. Typically, protocols refer to these blocks as packets of data. In the technique known as packet switching a sequence of blocks is sent across the transmission medium and reassembled at the destination. We will see later that a standard that is frequently used has a maximum data component, or packet size, of 500 bytes plus header bytes.

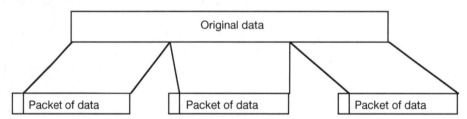

Fig. 2.2 Breakdown of large message into packets

Fig. 2.2 shows the original data or message being broken down into smaller data blocks before transmission. Each unit, element or block is frequently referred to as a packet. Fig. 2.3 shows the smaller blocks or packets being transmitted to their destination.

Question 2.1   If 1800 bytes of data needs to be sent for a particular message, and the largest block size that may be transmitted is 500 bytes, how many blocks of data will be sent?

At the receiving end we need to reassemble the packets back into the structure of the original data or message. To ensure that this is correctly achieved, each packet is identified with a packet number or packet ID. This ID is a part of a small header that is added to each of the packets of data that are created as a result of the fragmentation of

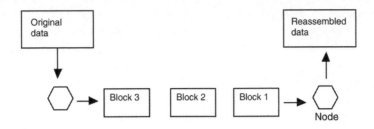

Fig. 2.3 Fragmentation

the original message. Fig. 2.2 shows fragmented packets with a header placed at the front of each of them. We will see later that these headers also contain some routing information which identifies how they should get to the destination address. If one out of a sequence of packets arrives with an error, then the packet ID will allow the receiver to be clear which packet it is and commence corrective action.

Question 2.2   A message of 2000 bytes is to be sent across a connection that operates with a maximum packet size of 500 bytes. How many packets are likely to be sent? What extra information is needed to be certain that this answer is correct? Are you making any assumptions in stating your answer?

---

3. Datagrams and virtual circuits

Once a decision to fragment a large message and send multiple smaller packets across the network has been taken, a further decision on how to route these packets across the network needs to be made. In a small self-contained Local Area Network (LAN), routing isn't an issue, since packets will always reach the destination station by virtue of the design. As we will see in Chapter 8, this is because every station hears the traffic of every other station. In a large, more complex LAN or a Wide Area Network (WAN) this needs more consideration and, since LANs interconnect with WANs, we must understand these issues and select the appropriate option.

To send a series of packets across a network, there are two major approaches. One option is to open a connection or route across the network (or series of joined networks) and then send all the data across that route. At the end of the transfer, the connection is closed. This approach is known as connection-based or a virtual circuit. The circuit is not dedicated solely to this traffic and each physical link shares its capacity with other virtual circuits. The important point is that a logical route is initially established when all the routing decisions are taken. Data just follows that pre-established route, using the logical route numbers that were determined when the virtual circuit was established. Hence, at any intermediate node, the data is forwarded on a pre-established onward path based on the logical circuit number. The data packet does not carry the final destination address; it only carries the logical circuit number.

In the alternative option, no route is pre-established and each packet transfer is free standing and independently routed. This is known as a connectionless or datagram service. Each packet is required to carry the full address of its destination and may be forwarded at the various intermediate routing stations via a different route from the other packets in the sequence. If the intermediate routing station has a set of routing tables which remain static, then the route will be the same for all packets. If the information held by the routing station is periodically updated or changed dynamically on the basis of the prevailing conditions, then different routes may be followed by individual packets. Hence, the potential exists for datagrams to arrive at the destination out of sequence. The receiving station must have the ability to resequence the packets.

IBM have historically favoured a connection-based approach across LANs, whereas other network communities have been content with either approach, depending on the application that needs to be supported, or the protocols which are implemented.

4. Error detection

Error management is viewed as a two stage activity. Initially we will consider the error detection stage. This may be as simple as 'echo checking' with the user performing the second stage of error recovery. Echo checking simply involves the user viewing his or her monitor to ensure that any data displayed is the same as that which was intended to be keyed in. This is helpful because the monitor displays the character that has been seen by the host and has been sent back to the monitor. There is not a direct connection between the monitor and the keyboard. Hence, if the display is what the user intended to happen, then it is almost certain that this is the data which is held by the host machine. We will, of course, have parity checking working on these transfers. In the event of a discrepancy, the user makes the appropriate corrections with the use of the delete key or editor. This approach to error detection works well for slow-speed manual keyboard entry. However, as the size of the data component becomes greater and the speed of the transfer increases, more automated and sophisticated approaches are needed.

Should a data packet accidentally become lost or corrupted during transmission, the receiver must be able to detect the situation and request that the missing packet be resent. As suggested earlier in this chapter, there are more sophisticated error detection techniques than parity bit checking. If a packet is corrupted in any way during transmission it is important that this is detected so that retransmission can take place to correct the problem. An international standard approach to error detection is to protect the data with a checksum or Cyclic Redundancy Check (CRC), as shown in Fig. 2.4.

Question 2.3 A data packet arrives at a destination and the checksum (or CRC) indicates that the data has been corrupted. What action is likely to be undertaken by the receiver?

The calculation of the checksum or the CRC is normally a hardware operation at the transmission interface, and the CCITT standard 16- or 32-bit CRC is frequently adopted. The CCITT is an international committee which establishes telecommunications standards. A CRC is generated using a predetermined (fixed) polynomial generator which is a 16- or 32-bit fixed sequence of bits. The polynomial generator is divided into the data to be transmitted and the remainder determines the CRC:

$$\frac{\text{data}}{\text{polynomial generator}} \rightarrow \text{remainder}$$

The method of division uses modulo 2 arithmetic which is effectively 'exclusive ORs'.

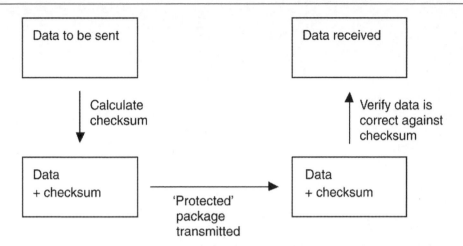

Fig. 2.4 Protection of data

The generation of the CRC is implemented by the hardware and uses the internationally agreed polynomial generators. In LAN environments the CRC is generated on the network adapter card, e.g., on an Ethernet card. The polynomial generators are designed to detect a very high percentage of all error patterns, including most error conditions below 16 bits. Typically, 99.997% of all error conditions will be identified.

To demonstrate the technique let's use a simplified example. Assume that the abbreviated polynomial standard is $x^4 + x^2 + 1$. A bit pattern representing the presence or absence of each power position is determined. There is a power 4 position, but not a power 3 position, etc., This results in a digital representation of 10101 (see Fig. 2.5).

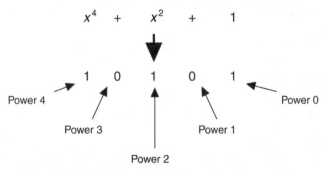

Fig. 2.5 Digital representation of polynomial

The digital representation of the polynomial (the divisor) is now divided into the data to be transmitted (let's say for simplicity that this data is 11011). Before we do the division (see Fig. 2.6) we add as many 0s to the end of the data as the highest power of the polynomial, which in this example is 4. There is a mathematical basis for this, but again for simplicity we'll just demonstrate the techniques and not provide the theory. This makes the data or dividend 110110000. When attempting modulo 2 arithmetic, the fact that the divisor is numerically larger than an element of the dividend does not matter, provided that there are the same number of significant bits. Remember that each stage of the division is an exclusive OR.

```
                         1 1 1 0
          1 0 1 0 1 | 1 1 0 1 1 0 0 0 0
                      1 0 1 0 1
                      ─────────
                      1 1 1 0 0
                      1 0 1 0 1
                      ─────────
                        1 0 0 1 0
                        1 0 1 0 1
                        ─────────
                          1 1 1 0 0
                          1 0 1 0 1
                          ─────────
                            1 0 0 1
```

Fig. 2.6 Polynomial division

The remainder is 1001, which becomes the CRC.

The CRC is appended to the original data, and thus the transmitted data stream becomes 110111001.

The CRC CCITT standard 16 bit polynomial is $x^{16} + x^{15} + x^5 + 1$, and the 32-bit pattern is even more complex. Hence the use of a simple example!

Question 2.4	If we use the same polynomial generator that we used in our example, what would the CRC be if the original data component was 10111?
Question 2.5	With the same polynomial generator, the following input has just been received: 111010001. Has the transmission occurred without error?
Question 2.6	What is the digital representation of the polynomial (the divisor) if the polynomial standard is $x^{16} + x^{15} + x^5 + 1$?

Clearly, the CCITT standard is a complex arrangement for error detection, and sometimes (e.g., when fragmentation of a packet into smaller units is required because individual networks *en route* have smaller packet size capabilities) it is necessary to provide simpler checks. Typically, 'ones' complement checks are then implemented over a specified number of bytes (perhaps just the header bytes).

Question 2.7	If a packet is fragmented and only the header checked with a 'ones' complement check, how can we be certain that the body of data will be correct when delivered to the destination host?

5. Error recovery or error correction

Once an error has been detected, then error recovery or correction techniques are required. In the simplest format, shown in Fig. 2.7 and Fig 2.11, only one packet is sent and no further packet is sent until a response or timeout occurs. An ACK is sent by the receiver to the sender to ACKnowledge correct receipt of the data, whilst a NAK or Not AcKnowledged response indicates that a retransmission is required. If nothing is received back by the sender, presumably something has got lost (either the data sent or the reply). To recover from this, the sender only waits for a predetermined amount of time; then it times out and tries to send the data again. Normally, only a few reattempts after successive timeouts are tried before the sender gives up.

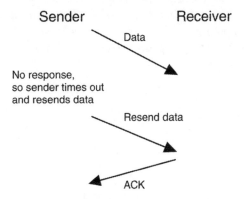

Fig. 2.7 Timeout mechanism

In most cases, however, a response is received, usually without a timeout and resend activity. For those limited number of occasions where a resend is necessary, a variety of protocols exist which determine how long we wait and how we react to these responses.

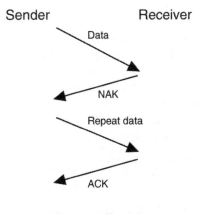

Fig. 2.8 Idle RQ

Fig. 2.8 shows a simple arrangement with the sender waiting for a response once it has sent a packet. Whilst it is waiting, the sender remains idle and does not attempt to send any more data. Equally, the transmission line is idle for the period while the receiver is determining the response to make. If the response is an ACK, the sender transmits the next data packet in the sequence. If, however, the response is a NAK, then it resends the last data packet again. This is known as Idle RQ, or idle repeat request. Idle RQ is grossly inefficient and so techniques to make better use of the line capacity are utilized. Rather than the sending station remaining idle whilst we wait for a response or timeout, more than one packet is dispatched. Fig. 2.9 shows the scenario when three packets have been sent. Other protocol standards exist where the number is established, or the 'window' is established, of how many packets may be sent before a response is received. These protocols also allow flow control to be established, i.e., protocols which prevent the sender station from sending data faster than the receiver station can cope and therefore control the rate at which data is sent. This approach is known as Continuous RQ and there are two techniques for error recovery using this approach. To ensure the receiver correctly identifies the packets arriving, each packet is given an ID or sequence number.

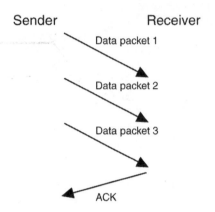

Fig. 2.9 Sequenced data packets

Each data packet may be separately acknowledged or a group acknowledgement can be sent. If the single ACK shown in Fig. 2.9 indicates that the receiver has successfully received data packet 3, then it is assumed that data packets 1 and 2 have also been received without error. As a point of detail, this ACK normally contains a field indicating which data packet(s) it is acknowledging. In this example the ACK would contain a field would indicating an ID of 4, meaning that all packets up to data packet 3 have been received and the next expected packet to be received should have an ID of 4.

If, however, it is determined that one of the packets has an error, then an error recovery process is required. In the example shown in Fig. 2.9, if data packet 2 had been incorrect on receipt, by the time the error was recognized, data packet 3 (or more) would probably have been dispatched.

The NAK that was returned to the sender would contain information indicating that data packet 2 was in error and needed retransmitting. The protocol could now follow one of two options: restart the data transmission from packet number 2 and then carry on with data packets 3, 4, etc., or selectively resend data packet 2 and then continue by sending the next un-transmitted packet. In the example of Fig. 2.9 this would be packet number 4. The first technique is known as Go-Back-N, and, although it sends more data across the network, this approach is frequently implemented because it is simple. The receiving end does not have to hold and store the correctly received data packets with the higher IDs or sequence numbers, and it is not required to slot the retransmitted data packet into its correct sequence position within the data packets already held at the destination. Of course, it does require the retransmission of some packets that have already been correctly sent. The alternative technique, known as selective retransmission, has the reverse properties. In outlining how selective retransmission operates, we assumed that the NAK for data packet 2 arrived after data packet 3 had been dispatched. It is equally possible that data packet 4 had also been dispatched, in which case the recovery would involve sending data packet 2 and then returning to send the original sequence of data packets 5, 6, and so on.

Question 2.8 If the data packet has three bits in the header to indicate the sequence number or ID, how many unique sequence numbers are there?

Question 2.9 Is there a possibility of a wraparound of the sequence number or ID if an ACK is not received and the transmitter continues sending?

Question 2.10 Is it true that each packet of data being transmitted may consist of an element of the original message plus an ID representing its sequence number, plus a checksum, plus synchronization characters, plus start and end limiters of the frame?

To implement these error recovery strategies there is a full range of file transfer programs and systems available in the marketplace so, as a user, you do not need a detailed knowledge of the mechanisms involved. Many are embedded in sophisticated application programs or high-level services such as EDI (electronic data interchange). At a simple level, a file transfer can be actioned between two connected PCs, as shown in Fig. 2.10, running public domain software such as Kermit. (Public domain software is software that is freely available, often on the Internet, and for which there is no charge, although sometimes a small fee is requested. Basically, it is not sold: it is available for anyone to use. On the negative side, the software may not be very well documented or supported.)

Fig. 2.10 Simple file transfer

In our error recovery strategies so far, there is an implicit requirement to send data back from the receiving device to the sending device as a means of acknowledging correct or incorrect receipt of data.

There are also error correction codes in existence that do not rely on this response back to the sender, but include additional information embedded in the original data transmission sent. If an error occurs, this additional embedded data can be used by the receiver to determine what the error is and put it right. A number of limited situations exist where the expense of always sending the additional data is considered to be worthwhile, such as satellite link connections. These techniques are known as Forward Error Correction (FEC) methods and are more widely used in systems areas other than data communications, such as memory access. A typical example of a FEC technique is the use of Hamming codes.

6. Flow control

As we have developed our data transfer concepts, we have assumed that the destination is capable of receiving the data at whatever rate it is sent. In reality, of course, this may not be true. At a simple level, a personal computer is capable of generating and sending data much faster than a printer can handle it. For short bursts of data this can be managed by having a receiver memory or buffer to store incoming data until it can be handled. If data is sent more quickly than the receiver can manage, including the use of any buffering capability it may have, then data overflow occurs and data loss will result. It wouldn't be very useful to many users if only half the text sent to a printer was successfully output and the rest was lost! To prevent overflow occurring and the sender swamping the receiver by sending data more quickly than its capacity can handle, we need to introduce the idea of flow control.

We have seen a model developed that has an easy to implement flow control technique capability. Consider the positive acknowledgement system, shown in Fig. 2.11, where further data will only be sent on receipt of an ACK from the receiver.

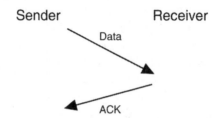

Fig. 2.11 Positive acknowledgement (PAR)

If the receiver wants to exert flow control at this level, we need an additional response to indicate that the packet has been received OK, but not to send any more packets until a future response indicates a state of readiness to receive more. The RNR (Receiver Not Ready) response, shown in Fig. 2.12, is such a response.

A Ready Indicator (RI) response notifies the sender that the receiving device is now ready to continue and data flow can be resumed. At the receiving end, the time delay between sending the RNR and the ready indicator permits the receiving device to 'catch up' with the processing of the information flow. Once it has emptied its buffers and is ready to resume receipt of the flow, it sends the ready indicator response.

Fig. 2.12 is a simple example. Of course multiple packets determined by the window size could be sent. This alternative flow control technique presets the maximum amount of data that can be outstanding before a response is made, i.e., the window size is preset. If, for example, the window size is set to 3, then once these packets have been sent, no more data will be sent until an ACK is received. Control of the window is implemented utilizing the sequence number ID.

When the connection between the two devices is a simple RS232C interface, the complexities of the flow control protocol outlined above can be reduced. RS232C uses two of the control lines within the interface to signal the flow control. When the sender has data to send, it signals RTS (Ready to Send). If the receiver is ready to accept data, it responds with CTS (Clear to Send). At any time when the receiver changes the CTS

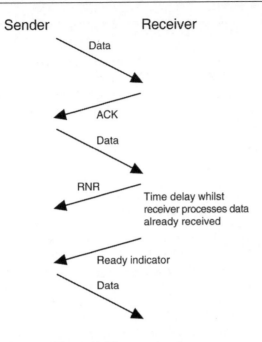

Fig. 2.12 Flow control

signal because it can't cope with more data just now, the sender stops. As soon as CTS is signalled again, data flow may be resumed. The RTS and CTS signals are separate signalling control lines as shown later in Fig. 3.6.

Question 2.11   Since the RS232C flow control technique is so simple, why don't we use it for all data transfers rather than the more complex protocol using additional response codes such as RNR?

Further questions

(There are answers to the questions marked with an asterisk at the end of the book.)

1. *Using a simple polynomial generator of $x^5 + x^3 + 1$, calculate the checksum needed for the data stream 101101.

2. A range of packet numbers have been despatched (ID = 1, ID = 2, ID = 3, ID = 4 and ID = 5) but the receiver detects an error in ID = 3. Assuming that the receiver could get a NAK to the sender before any further packets were despatched, what would the packet send sequence expected be if:

   a) selective retransmission were implemented;

   b) Go-back-N retransmission were implemented.

3. *A 10 kbyte file is sent across a packet switched network operating at 64 kbit/s and capable of carrying 512 byte data packets. The response from the receiver is a 128 bit packet (ACK or NAK) and Idle RQ is the acknowledgement technique. If the end-to-end propagation delay is 2 ms, what is the minimum time for transmission? Explain why this is the minimum time.

4. Why does the propagation delay have a greater impact in Idle RQ than Continuous RQ?

5. A particular network has a maximum packet size of 128 bytes and a maximum timeout for PAR of 30 s. If an 8-bit sequence number is used, what is the maximum data rate per connection that can be achieved? (Assume there is no window to restrict data flow and the full range of packets available with an 8-bit sequence ID are sent before timeout).

6. Discuss the trade-offs which have to be considered in fixing the maximum message length within a communications system.

Answer 2.1	The first three blocks will carry 1500 bytes of data and a fourth block will be partially full and carry 300 bytes of data. Hence four blocks will be carried. We have made an assumption in answering this question that no errors occurred and retransmissions are not necessary. Hence the answer may be modified in the light of further information later in the chapter.
Answer 2.2	If we send 2000 bytes of data in 500 byte blocks or packets, it would seem that four blocks would be necessary. However, what is not clear is whether the maximum packet size is 500 bytes of data plus header bits, or whether the 500 byte maximum includes header bits, making the data component less than 500 bytes.
	A frequently used standard has 500 bytes of data plus header bits. If this standard were used then we could still carry the message in four packets. However, we must be clear in our own mind what the standard is before calculating the answer.
	Of course we are still assuming that each packet was received correctly and no retransmission of the data is necessary.
Answer 2.3	It is probable that the protocol being used would send a NAK (Not AcKnowledged response) to the sender indicating that a retransmission was required.
Answer 2.4	1010
Answer 2.5	If 111010001 has just been received, the data component is 11101 and the CRC component is 0010. If we calculate the CRC from the data component, we get 0010. Hence the data has been correctly delivered.
	An alternative approach to checking the accuracy is to divide (using modulo 2 arithmetic) the CRC into the bit stream received and ensure there is no remainder.
Answer 2.6	11000000000100001 (Remember that anything raised to the power of 0 is 1)
Answer 2.7	Once the original message has been reassembled, this complete message which started with an overall CRC can now be checked, i.e., the original message had a CRC as part of its data before fragmentation.
Answer 2.8	Three bits represent 0 to 7, i.e., eight unique IDs.
Answer 2.9	Wraparound is where the cycle overtakes itself. In this example we could use IDs 0, 1, 2, 3, 4, 5, 6, 7, 0, 1, . . . So yes, theoretically, we could get wraparound. We need to provide other controls to make sure this possibility doesn't occur. If we don't provide such controls, then if the above scenario occurred and an ACK for packet 1 was returned, we wouldn't be sure if this related to the first or second packet with an ID of 1 that was sent.
Answer 2.10	Yes, it may seem like a lot of extra bits of overhead, but it is typical of what happens.
Answer 2.11	Many connections do not have the range of separate wires offered by the RS232C standard and have to use the normal transmit and receive pair of connections to use in-band flow control techniques. RS232c is typically used over short distances

for local connection, where multiple separate wires in a connection are cost effective. The control signalling of CTS and RTS are on separate wires and are known as out-of-band signalling. The terminology represents the situation where the signals are in the bandwidth of the data signalling, i.e., they may or may not use some of the capacity of the data signalling line.

3 Connections and interfacing

1. Introduction

In all our considerations so far we have assumed that the transmission medium is a single circuit that handles serial transmission. In this chapter, we need to extend this to consider a range of serial and parallel connections. Not all connections are between two adjacent devices. Hence the principles of both local and remote connections will also be established such that the distance between two devices isn't a barrier to connection. Of course, to connect over long distances will require interconnection to the long haul facilities of a telephone company or carrier.

2. Serial and parallel connections

In Chapters 1 and 2, we concentrated on connections where only one transmission circuit is in place. In such an arrangement, at any one instant in time, data can only be sent in one direction in a serial fashion, i.e., a stream of bits is sent sequentially only in one direction. This is known as a *simplex system* (see Fig. 3.1).

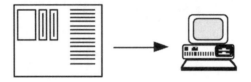

Fig. 3.1 Simplex system

Half-duplex operation

There is a slightly more sophisticated model that is known as half-duplex operation. This enables, for example, the ACKs (acknowledgements) or NAKs (not acknowledgements, i.e., not received OK) sent as responses from the receiver back to the sender to be handled. In a half-duplex arrangement the data flow is in one direction or the other, but not in both directions simultaneously. Hence we still only need a single copper circuit or an equivalent transmission medium. Electrically, we need a second wire to complete the circuit and act as a reference point, but for the purposes of signalling we can discount this. Half-duplex operation is analogous to a single lane stretch of road controlled by traffic lights allowing traffic through in one direction or the other, but not in both simultaneously – otherwise we have a conflict of interest! Another example is a radio link, where an ACK is the statement 'roger' and the release of control in one direction to the other direction is the statement 'over'. Therefore a half-duplex system needs a protocol in place to ensure that the transmissions are only in one direction at any instant.

Full-duplex operation

In a third approach we could introduce more than one circuit between the devices, allowing data flow in both directions simultaneously. This mode of operation is known as full-duplex. Indeed, the RS232C interface which was introduced earlier permits the flow of data and signals in both directions simultaneously. In practice, of course, we would need more than two separate wires because we need to send control signals, etc., However, in Fig. 3.2, for the sake of clarity, the system is represented as a two channel circuit. The connection cable or ribbon used in systems can have up to 15 or 25 separate wire circuits within one cable, although fewer wires in a single cable is more the norm.

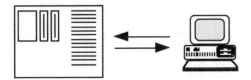

Fig. 3.2 Duplex transmission

Parallel connection

The serial transmission approach is perhaps the most frequently used technique. However, it does have the disadvantage that each byte of information needs at least eight time slots to be transmitted. Over relatively short distances (e.g., between a PC and its attached printer) it is possible to have eight separate wires, and so we could send each bit of a byte simultaneously. Each wire carries one bit of the character. This approach is known as parallel transmission. Fig. 3.3 shows four characters being transmitted across a parallel connection.

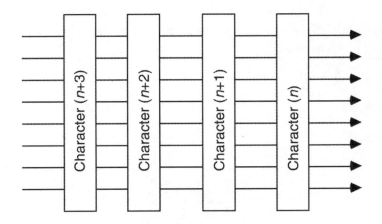

Fig. 3.3 Parallel transmission

Because each individual wire has slightly different properties, there is a possibility that data could travel at marginally different speeds over each of the wires. This introduces the problem of skew (see Fig. 3.4), where the signal for each bit of the character arrives at the destination at a marginally different time from the others.

Ideally, we need to clock all eight transmission lines at the receiving end simultaneously, so we cannot allow any significant skew to develop. Hence, we tend

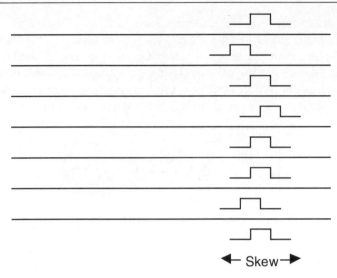

Fig. 3.4 Skew

to keep the length of parallel transmission fairly short. Higher costs are also associated with the cabling and interfacing of the parallel approach. Consequently, parallel transmission is normally only used over short distances between two devices where the advantage of speed over the serial transmission technique may be desirable.

Question 3.1   If you assume that the transmission speed of a parallel connection is 800 byte/s, what is the shortest time taken to transmit 3200 bytes of data?

Question 3.2   What assumptions have you had to make in answering the previous question?

3. Connectors

D-connectors

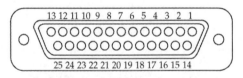

Fig. 3.5 RS232 25-pin connector

The V.24 and RS232C interfaces were originally designed to connect digital equipment to Data Communications Equipment (DCEs) such as modems. If we are connecting two devices together without using a modem then an RS232C connection typically uses a 25-pin D-type connection (see Fig. 3.5), and it can only be used to interconnect over short distances, normally less than 15 m (50 ft). Remember that it is normal to only use a subset of the 25 wire connections and the connecting cable would almost certainly have fewer than 25 wires. D-types smaller than 25-way connectors exist, and they are especially useful where space on the back of the device is an issue and not all the pins are required. You can often operate a connection quite successfully using only four or five wires. A typical connection layout is shown in Fig. 3.6.

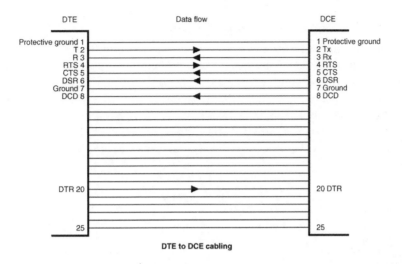

Fig. 3.6 V.24/RS232C connection

RJ-45 modular connections

Local area networks have rapidly migrated towards the use of modular cable connections with RJ-45 modular plugs and jacks. These connectors are used to plug into the hubs or access units.

Both token ring and some Ethernet implementations use the EIA/TIA 568 standards for 100 Ω category 3, 4 or 5 cable. The recent 100VG-AnyLAN network is also based on Unshielded Twisted Pair (UTP) four-pair cable. Chapter 6 discusses the detail of cable classification used in LANs. Each of the LANs requires a different pin connection combination within the plug. This is shown in Fig. 3.7.

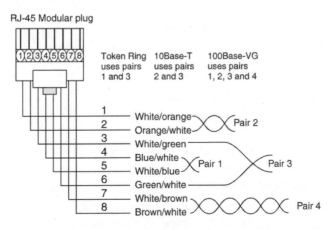

Fig. 3.7 EIA/TIA 568B specification

The pair usages are as follows:

a) Token ring networks use pairs 1 and 3;

b) 10baseT networks use pairs 2 and 3;

c) 100baseVG networks use pairs 1, 2, 3 and 4.

4. Modem connection and signalling

In designing the network interface, it was recognized that, to interconnect devices that were more than 50 ft apart, existing telephone circuits could provide the supporting infrastructure and the connecting links. The only difficulty was that old telephone circuits operated with analogue signals because they were designed to handle voice traffic. These older style analogue telephone circuits have been replaced with digital circuits over the last decade or so. Today, the vast majority of telephone circuits in the UK are digital. A typical connection of a digital device to an analogue network is shown in Fig. 3.8.

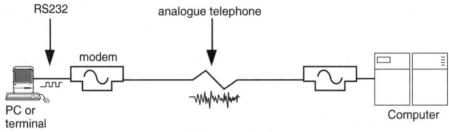

Fig. 3.8 Modem link

Even though the telephone networks are now largely digital, the interface into the network remains analogue for many users unless their organization has subscribed to a digital interface. Fig. 3.9 shows how a digital network interface brought into an organization's premises can either interface directly to TE1 digital equipment or, alternatively, to older equipment using an adapter.

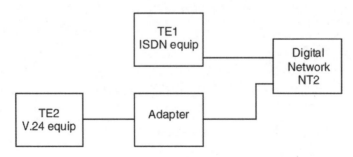

Fig. 3.9 Digital network connection

Connection to analogue networks

For those users with an analogue interface, because that is the service available from the PTT, such as British Telecom, the issue is resolved by using a modem. A modem converts the digital output of the computing device into an analogue signal for the network and then provides the reverse at the other end (see Fig. 3.10). Through the introduction of a carrier signal which could be modified to represent the digital signal that was to be transmitted, the concept of modulation was born. Modems are MOdulation and DEModulation devices.

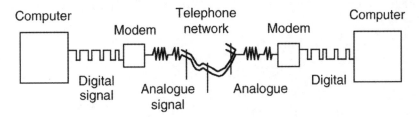

Fig. 3.10 Signalling on a modem link

Standard names were given to the devices in this arrangement: DTE (Data Terminal Equipment) and DCE (Data Circuit-terminating Equipment), as shown in Fig. 3.11.

Fig. 3.11 DTE/DCE representation of link

To carry the digital information, an analogue carrier signal is modulated or modified in some predetermined manner to represent the digital information to be conveyed. A typical carrier signal is shown in Fig. 3.12.

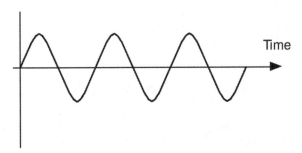

Fig. 3.12 Carrier signal

Depending on the application and the type of modem used, one of the physical properties of the waveform shown in Fig. 3.12 would be modified to carry or represent the digital signal.

Question 3.3   The carrier signal has a number of physical properties. Can you identify them?

The modulation of the carrier signal, by modification of one of the physical properties, is shown in Figures 3.13, 3.14 and 3.15. In each case the particular property for that technique is modified whilst an attempt is made to keep the other properties constant. From these figures, it can be seen that alteration of one property does in fact have an impact on others, but the modems will ensure that this is correctly handled.

In frequency modulation, the frequency of the carrier is modified while the amplitude is kept constant. One frequency is assigned to represent a digital 0 and another frequency represents a 1.

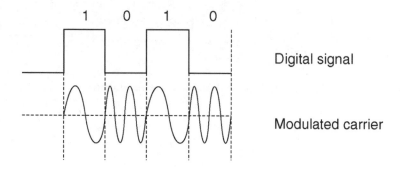

Fig. 3.13 Frequency modulation

In amplitude modulation, the amplitude of the carrier signal is modified to represent the digital data. As you might expect, 0 and 1 are assigned different amplitudes.

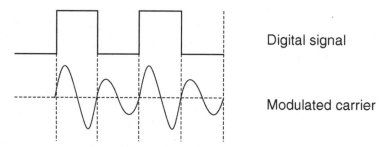

Fig. 3.14 Amplitude modulation

Phase modulation modifies the phase of the carrier, which affects the frequency while the amplitude remains constant. Typically, a signal's phase is measured relative to the previous signal.

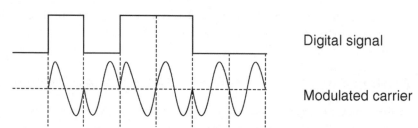

Fig. 3.15 Phase modulation

Question 3.4	Sketch the resulting signal to carry 10011 using the three modulation techniques described above.

Because there are a number of approaches to modulation, it is important that you know which approach is to be used across a link between any two devices. Modems are manufactured to a range of standards which fix the bit rate, baud rate and the modulation technique. The internationally used standard from the CCITT is known as the V series, e.g., V.21.

Let us look at this standard in just a little more detail. It uses frequency division of the bandwidth to represent digital information. The rate at which we change the signal is fairly slow and is fixed at 200 to 300 baud. The modem works by using fixed frequencies to represent a 0 and a 1. To achieve full-duplex operation, a different frequency pair is used to signal in the opposite direction. Hence, the standard states that, for the two modems, the frequencies used to send to the other end are as shown in Table 3.1.

	0	*1*
Initiate mode (i.e. modem making the call) (Hz)	980	1180
Answer mode (i.e. modem receiving the call) (Hz)	1650	1850

Table 3.1 V series modem standard

The V.21 standard sends one bit on each signal change, and so it operates at 300 bit/s, which is quite slow by today's norms. To achieve higher speeds it is common to see the three different approaches to modulation combined. Hence in any signal time cell we could differentiate between several signal levels with the result that more than one digit could be sent in that time, e.g., 00, 01, 10, 11. In such a scenario, if the signalling rate were 300 baud, the data rate would be 600 bit/s.

Increasing the baud rate is quite difficult, since we need to be able to clearly identify the signal at the remote end; such techniques typically achieve 2400 baud. Hence, quite a bit of emphasis has been given to carrying multiple signal levels in each time cell to achieve the higher bit rates.

A common example is Quadrature Amplitude Modulation (QAM), which is based on changing the amplitude and phase. If we use two amplitude levels and four phase shifts, then, combining the two, we can generate eight different levels. With eight levels, three bits can be sent on each signal change as shown in Table 3.2, where $A1$ and $A2$ are the two amplitude levels and $P0$ to $P3$ are the four phase levels.

With this approach, the bit rate is three times the baud rate. Also, because each signal has a better differentiation from other signals, it is possible to increase the baud rate to higher levels and still recover the signal accurately. Coupled with good correction mechanisms, such as Trellis-coded modulation, relatively high bit rates can now be offered over modem links.

The latest V90 modems operate at 33,600 bit/s in one direction and up to 56,000 bit/s in the other, but we still need error correction because the lines do not provide 'perfect' error-free connections.

Bit representation	Amplitude	Phase
000	A1	P0
001	A2	P0
010	A1	P1
011	A2	P1
100	A1	P2
101	A2	P2
110	A1	P3
111	A2	P3

Table 3.2 Quadrature amplitude modulation

Connection to digital networks

Fig. 3.9 showed the arrangement for connecting digital equipment to digital networks such as ISDN. Of course, much of the traffic that is carried across a digital network is voice traffic, which is analogue. We then have the opposite problem to the one which modems resolved. Analogue signals are converted to digital signals using CODEC devices.

This is achieved by sampling the analogue signal and representing the level of signal as a digital signal. Typically, each sample is represented by an eight-bit sequence, so the number of different sample levels can be 2^8. This is not a linear scale either, with a coarser scale at the ends of the frequency spectrum. By sampling 8000 times a second, the supporting digital channel required to carry voice traffic is:

$$8000 \quad \times \quad 8 \quad = \quad 64 \text{ k bit/s}$$

8000		8		64 k bit/s
↑		↑		↑
Samples		Number of		Channel
per second		bits in		capacity
		each sample		

Significant reductions in the 64 kbit/s channel requirement can be gained through compression techniques and modified forms of representation, without significant loss of quality. However, 64kbit/s was the 'building block' of digital network channels. This sampling approach is called Pulse Code Modulation (PCM).

Recent developments in digital services include ADSL (asymmetric digital subscriber line). This is covered in more detail in Chapter 4.

5. Summary of links

As a very simplistic summary, we could consider the following guidelines as a starting point. If the distance between two communicating devices is very short (a few metres), then a parallel connection can be considered. Fig. 3.16 shows the typical type of parallel ribbon cable used.

For distances up to 15 m, RS232C connections may be considered. To extend beyond that point, we could use services such as the telephone network and interconnect via modems or network terminal points. Alternatively, if the connection is totally within

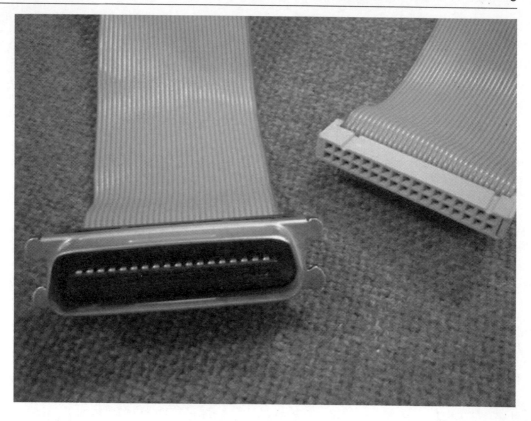

Fig. 3.16 Parallel ribbon cable

our building and we wish to extend the 15m limit, we could use line drivers. However, what is now more popular when a number of devices requiring such connections exist within an organization is to connect these devices internally within each building using a local area network. The LAN can then be equipped with a single interconnection to the PTT services, to provide the ability to communicate over extended distances (see Fig. 3.17).

Telephone networks are provided by national carriers or telecommunications agencies, known as PTTs or PTOs. In the UK, British Telecom is one of the major PTTs.

Question 3.5   Do any of these examples show how you would connect a home PC to the Internet?

Further questions

(There are answers to the questions marked with an asterisk at the end of the book.)

1. Sketch the waveforms resulting from frequency, amplitude and phase modulation techniques which represent the data 110101.

2. In Chapter 2 we discussed the use of the signals RTS and CTS. Is such an approach to flow control acceptable for parallel transmission?

3. A duplex connection between two devices supports a data rate of 9600 bit/s. Both

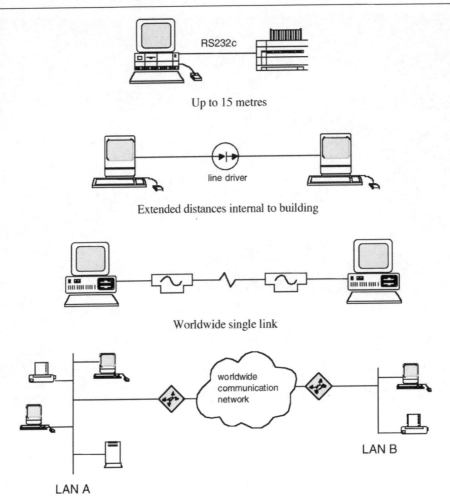

RS232c

Up to 15 metres

line driver

Extended distances internal to building

Worldwide single link

worldwide communication network

LAN B

LAN A

Worldwide interconnection

Fig. 3.17 Range of connections

devices have a 4 kbyte file which they need to send to the other device. What is the shortest possible time in which this exchange may occur?

4. In answering Question 3, what limitations may alter your answer?

5. *Can we connect two devices which are 20 m apart with a parallel circuit?

6. *Is an RS232C connection normally simplex, half-duplex or duplex?

Answer 3.1	In parallel transmission we transmit one byte at a time, in this case at 800 byte/s. To receive 3200 bytes will take 4 s.
Answer 3.2	There is no delay between each byte, and there are no error(s) which require retransmission.
Answer 3.3	The carrier has frequency, amplitude and phase properties.
Answer 3.4	The resulting signal is shown in Fig. 3.18.

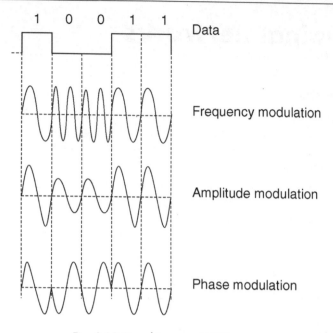

Fig. 3.18 Signal to carry 10011

Answer 3.5   Not exactly. At home you would use your PC and modem to establish a connection to an Internet Service Provider (ISP). They provide the connection to the worldwide communications network shown in the bottom example of Fig. 3.17.

4 Terminal networks

1. Introduction

In the early days of computing there was little opportunity for users to 'talk' directly to the mainframe computers. Jobs were submitted in batch format, prepared on paper tape or punch cards, and a relatively small range of peripheral devices existed that were directly connected to the host machine.

As systems evolved, the opportunity to permit direct terminal connection to the host machine was established. With the growing demand for terminal access, it was no longer feasible to provide each user with a direct connection as shown in Fig. 4.1.

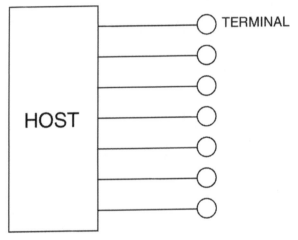

Fig. 4.1 Direct connection

Direct connections require individual ports on the host machine for each connected device. This became expensive both in terms of physical cabinet space and cost as the number of direct connection requirements grew. Equally, poor utilization of the system for the volume of data carried by each connected station was experienced, especially when many of the terminals could be inactive for significant periods of time. It was from this early scenario that the requirements for multiplexing emerged. Further developments occurred as remote terminals needed access to host machines with connectivity across PTT services.

2. Multiplexing

To overcome the problem of so many direct terminal connections, each potentially carrying low volumes of traffic, the concept of channelling multiple data inputs into one connection was developed (see Fig. 4.2). The main requirement is that each input can be separately identified and handled on arrival.

At the host end of the connection or 'pipe' of mixed data inputs is a single connection, but each individual station's data flowing down the pipe must be separately identified

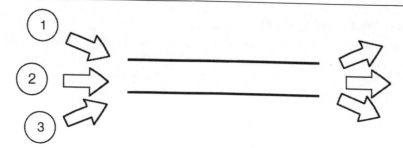

Fig. 4.2 Channelling

and managed by routing it to the appropriate 'process' or 'operating system socket' within the host machine, as shown in Fig. 4.3.

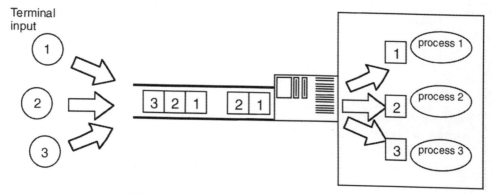

Fig. 4.3 Data flow in a multiplexer

The clever bit of this design is how a particular input is identified and filtered through to the correct destination point or process at the host end. The intention is to emulate the original structure of direct connection (see Fig. 4.4).

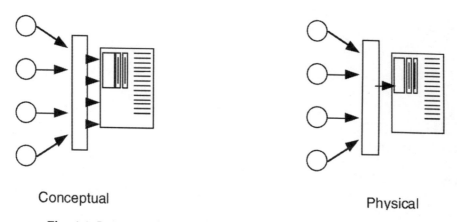

Conceptual

Physical

Fig. 4.4 Conceptual and physical multiplexer arrangement

Time Division Multiplexing (TDM)

The approaches used to implement multiplexing were initially based on dividing the pipe or communications channel into either time slots or frequency bands. In the first approach, each connected station is allocated, in turn, a time slot to forward any data it has to send to the multiplexer. Effectively, this is like polling each device, asking it if it has any data to send. A station with no data to send leaves an empty slot in the pipe. This approach is known as time division multiplexing.

Consider a typical situation where four consecutive 'polls' resulted in the attached terminals having the need to send data as indicated in Fig. 4.5.

	Poll 1	Poll 2	Poll 3	Poll 4
Terminal 1	✓	✓		✓
Terminal 2	✓		✓	✓
Terminal 3	✓	✓	✓	

Fig. 4.5 Typical poll outcome

Such a poll outcome would result in the sequence of data flowing in our multiplexed channel as shown in Fig. 4.6. The data element, especially in the early range of Time Division Multiplexers (TDMs), could be either a bit or a character, and the channels were called bit or character interleaved channels.

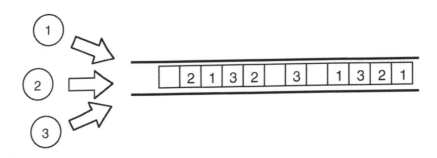

Fig. 4.6 Typical multiplexed data flow

When a character is sent using asynchronous transmission, the start and stop bits are removed and only the eight bits are sent. These start and stop bits are of course restored at the receiving end.

Question 4.1   Why are there empty slots in Fig. 4.6? Why didn't we just bring forward the next active station's transmission into the empty slot space?

A multiplexer provides us with the opportunity of remote connection on a cost effective basis (see Fig. 4.7). Only a single communications channel is required rather than a separate link for each station. This is especially helpful where a significant number of

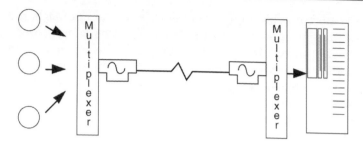

Fig. 4.7 Remote connections via multiplexer

stations are geographically distant from the host machine. The interface between the two multiplexers could be a synchronous modem working at 2400 to 19,200 bit/s, a wideband modem working at up to 168 kbit/s, or a digital link on kilostream or megastream. The high speed links provide X.21 connections at 64 kbit/s. X.21 is the common interface between DTEs and DCEs for synchronous operation on public data networks.

Question 4.2   If most of the time slots are not used, how could we ensure that the receiving multiplexer stayed in synchronization with the remote multiplexer when using asynchronous mode?

As the technology of TDMs has changed to utilize high speed digital links between multiplexers, we have seen the introduction of high speed TDMs linking over 50 channels or input devices. Each channel can support either asynchronous or synchronous protocols with V.24 or RS232C interfaces.

Frequency Division Multiplexing (FDM)

In the time slot or time division multiplexing arrangement, the data signal in each time slot occupies the full frequency range or capacity of the transmission link. Alternatively, it is possible to divide the frequency range or spectrum of the cable up into a number of separate channels or ranges using the concept of frequency division multiplexing.

Question 4.3   If TDM is the abbreviation normally used for time division multiplexing, what abbreviation is assigned to frequency division multiplexing?

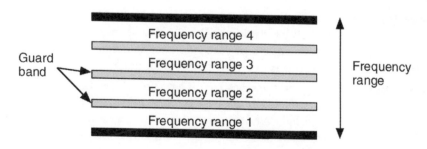

Fig. 4.8 Frequency division of transmission medium

Frequency division multiplexing is the basis of a second approach, using an analogue line for the connection, and it is most suited to supporting asynchronous traffic. Each connected or active terminal is allocated to one of the frequency channels and becomes dedicated to that device for the duration of the connection. At the interface, the multiplexer converts the signal into the frequency range for the allocated channel (see Fig. 4.8). Because each frequency channel is only a fraction of the whole frequency range of the transmission link, the data rate for each individual channel will also be a fraction of the total data rate achievable if the whole bandwidth were available (as in time division multiplexing).

However, the advantage for any terminal here is that the frequency channel is dedicated and always available to that station. There is no waiting 'your turn' to send. A small disadvantage is the loss of some of the frequency range to act as a guard band. These guard bands are necessary to ensure that there is a clear separation of each of the frequency channels defined. Fig. 4.9 shows how the transmission link carries all the input frequencies in what appears to be a complete mixture of all the inputs. The hardware at the receiving end has to pick out each frequency channel from the 'mixed' signal received and pass the digital signal for each of the inputs to the destination host.

This ability to select a particular frequency within the mixed frequency transmission is the same approach as we use when we tune into a radio station from one of the many that are transmitted on the airwaves.

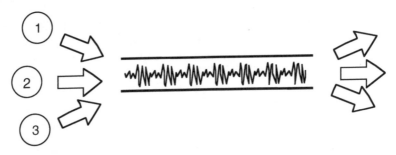

Fig. 4.9 Signalling with frequency division multiplexing

Both the TDM and Frequency Division Multiplexing (FDM) approaches have the disadvantage that there is wasted capacity whenever the input stations have nothing to send.

Question 4.4 How is wasted capacity in TDM and FDM seen on the transmission medium?

Question 4.5 A transmission link offers a fixed bandwidth of 3000 Hz and can carry 19,200 bit/s using V.21 signalling. If we have 18 stations, each sending two characters per second, what utilisation have we made of the link if TDM is operating in asynchronous mode?

Question 4.6 Using the same link as in Question 4.5, we now implement FDM with 18 channels (each of 120 Hz bandwidth), each providing a 110 bit/s capacity. What is the utilization of the transmission link in this arrangement assuming asynchronous transmission, with each station still sending two characters/s?

Performance improvements

To improve on this performance, the multiplexer developments included Statistical or Intelligent TDM (STDM or ITDM). This development changes the sending algorithm from a polled or round robin approach to a first come, first served basis, i.e., as soon as a station has something to send it is placed in the next free slot. Since slots are now randomly ordered, to assist the receiving end in identifying which station that has sent the data, each slot needs to be larger than the data element so that it can also carry the sending station's ID. Because more than one station could generate an input at the same time, the multiplexer must also have an input storage buffer to hold data until the next free slot is available.

Question 4.7   Assume that 16 bits per time slot is implemented for a given STDM. Using the same scenario as in Question 4.5, what is the utilization of the transmission medium now?

When we implement STDM with asynchronous protocols we can normally assume that, if the total traffic across a link is less than the aggregate of that of each of the stations working at capacity, then the provision is adequate. Indeed, the higher the number of devices connected, the greater is the probability that some devices will be idle at any particular moment. In such situations it is normal to design for up to four times the maximum input capacity.

For example, if the multiplexer is providing a 9600 bit/s connection, we could connect devices with an aggregate asynchronous traffic of 4 × 9600 bit/s, i.e., 38,400 bit/s.

Question 4.8   If we had a 9600 bit/s STDM connecting asynchronous stations each requiring 1200 bit/s connections, how many stations could be permitted to connect to the STDM?

---

3. ADSL

It was recognized that the requirement for many subscribers was a digital service that provided a small bandwidth for outbound traffic and a much wider bandwidth for inbound traffic. This was originally conceived as a requirement for services such as video on demand, where the outbound traffic was small amounts of data to select the service and the inbound data was the video service. Whilst this potential consumer demand has not materialized, this technology provided the ideal solution for Internet users where typically only short messages are sent but large volumes of web page material are received.

Hence, this asymmetric requirement of the bandwidth led to the provision of ASDL, asymmetric digital subscriber line. It builds on the frequency division multiplexing, FDM, to use the 1 MHz bandwidth available on the twisted pair wires. The typical breakdown of the bandwidth is:

Frequency	Use
0–20 kHz	Telephone
25–200 kHz	Outbound traffic
250–1000kHz	Inbound traffic

Table 4.1 ADSL bandwidth utilization

The voice traffic is carried in the 0–4 kHz range of the lower band, with the remaining bandwidth acting as a guardband to prevent crosstalk with the higher bandwidth traffic. The other bands carry the outbound and inbound traffic. Both of these bandwidths operate as a series of 4 kHz channels and implements FDM to carry the traffic. It builds on a technique called Discrete Multitone (DMT). With DMT techniques, each of the 4 kHz channels are tested for signal-to-noise ratio and, depending on the results, will be designated to carry between 0 and 60 kbit/s. FDM then uses each of the channels to carry the total traffic.

With current designs, we could have up to 256 channels on the inbound side, giving us a theoretical maximum capacity of 256 × 60 kbit/s, i.e., 15.36 Mbit/s. In practice, much lower rates, typically 1.5 Mbit/s, are implemented, but clearly these are big improvements in throughput compared to other local subscriber services. Depending on the distances involved and the quality of the line, data rates of 9 Mbit/s are frequently achieved.

4. Packet assembly and disassembly

The packet assembly and disassembly approach, known as PAD, is primarily a wide area network issue, and it is outside the scope of a local area network text. However, we will briefly address the issue to give a picture of alternative approaches for the connection of remote character terminals to host machines which support X.25.

A range of terminals are available, each with slightly different characteristics. For example, how do you delete the last character typed – using a backspace or a left arrow? Also, the interface from the terminal or PC with terminal emulation is typically character-based with RS232. To improve on the performance, we connect the remote terminals to a local PAD. This allows us to use our existing non-X.25 devices and still be part of an X.25 network (see Fig. 4.10).

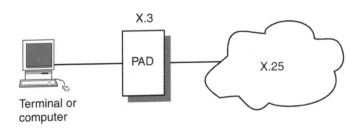

Fig. 4.10 PAD connection

The PAD accepts input from one or more terminals and assembles the characters into a packet for that terminal. It can also translate any of the different characteristics outlined above into a common standard. Once the packet has been assembled, the PAD can send it across the public network as though it is an X.25 device sending the data. Equally, packets arriving at the PAD are disassembled and forwarded as characters to the terminal. The protocols between the terminal and the PAD are defined by X.28, and within the PAD X.3 defines the operational parameters.

Further questions

(There are answers to the questions marked with an asterisk at the end of the book.)

1. Is STDM likely to be more beneficial when you have a small number of low-activity terminals or a large number of low-activity terminals?

2. A 3000 Hz bandwidth transmission medium has channel widths of 240 Hz and guard bands of 240 Hz. What percentage capacity is lost in allocating guard bands?

3. Is TDM suited to digital circuit connection between multiplexers?

4. *Why are many of the examples based around transmission media with a 3000 Hz bandwidth or 64 kbit/s capacity?

5. *A typical poll sequence for a TDM based system resulted in the following outcome. Sketch the expected data flow across the multiplexed channel.

	Poll 1	Poll 2	Poll 3	Poll 4
Terminal 1	✓			
Terminal 2	✓	✓	✓	✓
Terminal 3	✓		✓	✓

6. A multiplexer connects 50 remote stations. Half of the stations will generate a base load of 2 character/s for an 8 h working day. The other half are more intelligent devices (e.g., remote sensors), and generate 240 bytes of data every 2 min throughout the 24 h period. What kind of connection should be considered between the multiplexers?

Answer 4.1	The algorithm used to send the data (round robin) by polling around the stations is also used at the receiving end to separate the 'mixed' data into the original inputs. If we avoided sending empty slots by filling them with the next data to send, the receiving end would have difficulty in identifying which traffic was which. If such a modification were to be preferred, then we would have to send some form of ID with each slot. This wouldn't be simple TDM, but a more complex approach, which is introduced later.
Answer 4.2	In asynchronous mode we send the data between the multiplexers without the start bits because they are 'stripped off'. To ensure there is synchronization between the two, it is common to send null or synchronization characters in empty slot positions to retain a data flow.
Answer 4.3	It is known as FDM.
Answer 4.4	In TDM, wasted capacity is seen as an empty slot. In FDM, wasted capacity is seen as an idle channel.

Answer 4.5   One station sends 2 character/s or 16 bit/s. Eighteen stations send 18×16 bit/s = 288 bit/s. Hence the utilization is

$$288/19{,}200 \times 100 \text{ per cent} = 1.5 \text{ per cent}$$

Answer 4.6   If we ignore the lost capacity of the guard bands, and have all eighteen channels working at a rate of 16 bit/s over the 110 bit/s channels, then the utilization of each channel is

$$16/110 \times 100 \text{ per cent} = 14.5 \text{ per cent}$$

Of course, the overall utilization of the transmission medium is the same as in Answer 4.5

Answer 4.7   In this mode, we are sending twice as many bits down the transmission medium as we did in Question 4.5. The utilization of the line is therefore twice as high at 3 per cent. We should note that we haven't got any more data through the system though. We have simply used 8 bits in each slot as an identifier.

Answer 4.8   The first calculation is to determine how many stations we could support if each one were working to capacity.

One station can send 1200 bit/s. A 9600 bit/s channel can support 9600/1200 stations, i.e., eight stations.

Of course, not every station would be working at capacity, and we have seen that designers often work on a $4 \times$ factoring. If this were applied then we could support up to 32 stations. We should treat this as a maximum and use a figure somewhere between eight and 32.

5 Network applications

1. Introduction

It has already been seen that connectivity of devices, even where they are geographically distant, can be achieved using network services. The devices considered for connection in the previous chapters have mainly been dumb terminals. However, the 1980s saw the introduction to the marketplace of both the personal computer and local area networks. A range of new applications based on network technology emerged. In this chapter we will initially review some of these applications. Of course, some of the applications were technology driven and were created because we were then able to do something new that hadn't previously been achievable. Other developments were considered primarily on the basis of business needs and implemented because the technology was available.

2. Network uses

At a simple level, a microcomputer user will wish to have the ability to send data to a printer. When that printer is relatively expensive (e.g., colour laser), it may not be possible to provide one for each user and so the resource will have to be shared. This can be achieved by interconnecting all the devices requiring access to the shared facility via a network. The network provides an intelligent switching capability between the devices that need to print, and there needs to be a facility within the network to provide a very big print buffer. This allows data to be sent from any device to this buffer, which in practical terms is a queue, called a print server queue.

Other examples of situations in a typical office environment where connections between devices are required include e-mail service, terminal access to central computing facilities (e.g., a mainframe), access to external or remote systems or devices, and access to a central database. These requirements will be explored in a little more detail later in the chapter.

Other environments where connection is required include the following:

a)   point-of-sale tills in retail outlets;

b)   sensor devices connected to a central control mechanism (e.g., heating thermostats and time clocks);

c)   automated teller machines (ATMs) connected to a bank's central computers;

d)   process control devices or robot cells connected in a manufacturing environment.

Before the PC became a popular workplace tool, computer systems usually consisted of central mainframes. Suites of programs were written to handle particular applications and this often resulted in multiple occurrences of data. For example, a customer's name and address might exist in files associated with several application program suites. Amendment of data required multiple updating, and this frequently led to discrepancies or variations between the various occurrences of the data. Providing a solution to this problem led to the central database developments that we now see as the more appropriate approach. PCs introduced another problem in the 1980s with users developing their own independent application programs and creating their own, local data. Hence we reintroduced the problem that mutually incompatible multiple data sets might coexist. Data was frequently created within organizations which possibly only one or two individuals knew existed. Applications were developed that were locally produced, were frequently undocumented, and did not conform to organizational standards. These systems might use a range of different software across the organization (e.g., Lotus 1–2–3, Excel, Quattro Pro), and even the same products were frequently at different version levels. These incompatible standards reduced the ability to easily move information between one PC and another, and made it more difficult to share the information.

Thus, the PC developments created and supported, in some circumstances, an unprofessional approach to IT; companies in this situation frequently had no clear IT strategy. The widespread introduction of LANs as an interconnection mechanism supporting central facilities, offered an opportunity for organizations to regain control. Data and software products could (and should) be co-ordinated and be recognized at central points in the system, and private copies of data could (and should) disappear. By private data we simply mean data collected by individuals to assist in their local environment. If correctly structured and shared, this may be of benefit to others in the same organization when it is made available. This is not normally confidential information, and everyone should recognize that information is a corporate asset and should be shared. Typically, the central point at which to store both data and software in a networked solution is a file server (see Fig. 5.1). Just for simplicity, we draw a LAN in the following figures as a 'cloud', even though a cloud is generically used for a wide area network or public switched data network. No generic LAN symbol has been established, but we will make it clear when we are representing a LAN in this manner.

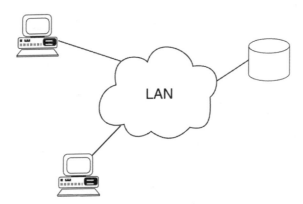

Fig. 5.1 LAN support for file server

Question 5.1   In providing a file server approach, what benefits are gained by the organization in controlling software? You may ignore the data issues for now and concentrate on the application software issues.

Central servers

The central server approach clearly offers the organization enormous benefits in creating genuine corporate data. Both data and application software can be accessed or downloaded to local workstations by authorized users as appropriate. It offers the organization the opportunity to keep control of software releases, and exercise control to act legally in terms of the number of product licences purchased (and the number of users attempting to use the product simultaneously). This approach can also avoid too great a spread of products, establishing corporate standards in various application areas (using, for example, Word 6 as the corporate word-processing package) to achieve data or document compatibility. The user gains by having access to a larger data source with better data integrity. Also, the potential exists for the availability of a wider range of supported software products that are release-compatible across the organization, plus the potential of access to other servers and services. A server is designed to give wider access to users to share the resources offered by that server. In the case of a file server, this typically consists of access to application software and associated data.

Question 5.2 What other types of server might be helpful to users?

Question 5.3 Are there any disadvantages to the server approach compared with individual workstations operating in isolation?

Question 5.4 The environment in which a file server has been described as being used so far has been biased towards an office environment. Suggest one other environment in which a central file server might be helpful.

LAN environments

A typical network within an organization is likely to provide access to its central computer facilities. This may be the repository for the main database and hold much of the corporate data. In such a situation, the network may have the features shown in Fig. 5.2.

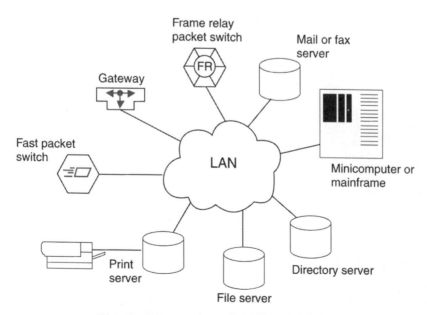

Fig. 5.2 Example of corporate network

In other environments, the services and functionality will be such that different provision and services on the network will exist. Figs 5.3 and 5.4 show a possible scenario in a manufacturing environment and a process control environment.

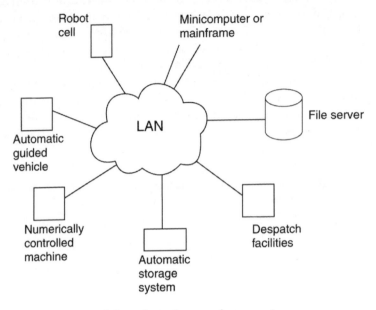

Fig. 5.3 Manufacturing environment

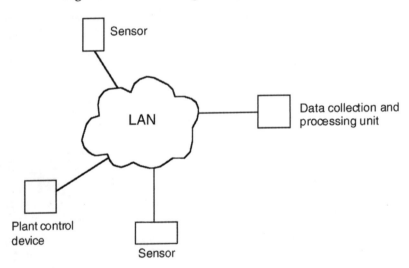

Fig. 5.4 Process control environment

Device sharing

In Fig. 5.2 and in the answer to Question 5.2, we introduced the concept that it is not only data that can be kept centrally and provided on a server basis. There are other types of device that an organization is unlikely to provide at each individual user station. For example, it is unlikely that every user will have his or her own laser printer, or at least not a quality laser printer with a variety of paper trays holding company headed stationery and A3 and A4 blank paper. It is also unlikely that each station will have its own fax or scanner.

In a networked environment with shared facilities, the organization only needs to buy a sufficient number of each type of device to satisfy the shared demand. Indeed, one of the benefits of installing a network is to provide the capability of sharing devices. In accepting that shared access is beneficial and is a correct implementation approach, we need to resolve the problem of contention where two or more stations require simultaneous access to a shared device. It isn't helpful at an individual station to find that on one attempt to use the shared facility it is seen to be available, and yet on a subsequent attempt it is seen to be unavailable or, even worse, not visible, with the user having to manually intervene to delay his or her access and reattempt it some time later. The server approach overcomes this difficulty by accepting the requests for service from stations and queuing up these requests for action on a first-come, first-served basis (or whatever other algorithm is selected). To the user such access is seen to be immediately successful, but actually the action or implementation is automatically slightly delayed until the request gets to the front of the queue.

Question 5.5	If we examine the services that could be available on a fax server, what facilities might optionally, or additionally, be provided?

Print servers

In many networks it is likely that a number of printers exist. If a user sends all printer requests to the print server (see Fig. 5.5), the option to select a specific print station for output exists. A default would normally operate if the user didn't specify or select a particular station. Hence, a user could select a particular quality printer on a print server or a directly attached printer, depending on the configuration provided.

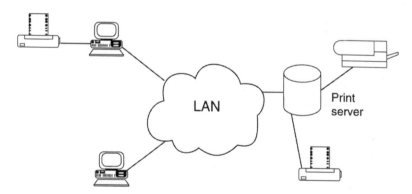

Fig. 5.5 Shared print facilities

Control of the printer server will normally be a function of the network operating system. Equally, control of individual user access to a file server will be provided within the network operating system. Network management and security issues will be covered in Chapter 14 and are important issues, since it is necessary to comply with legal requirements, such as the Data Protection Act in the UK.

Question 5.6   Is it likely that every user will know the hardware address of any other user, server or device with which they may wish to communicate, or which they may wish to select?

Question 5.7   How would a user normally identify the service he or she is seeking to use or access if using the hardware address is unacceptable?

Directory services

An example of a possible server given earlier was a directory server. Clearly users cannot be expected to know the hardware address of every device they wish to access. Using the simple printer example, the user will identify individual printers with names such as 'office laser' or 'colour printer'. The conversion between these naming conventions and the hardware addresses is carried out by the directory server. A local mechanism or procedural arrangement is needed to keep this service updated. If a hardware fault were to develop and the network interface card at a particular station were replaced, the network would need a new hardware address to be associated with the station. Using the approach just outlined, we would simply need a local mechanism to change the entry in the directory server and update the conversion to the new hardware address. One alternative would require us to inform every other station (wherever in the world that might be!) that a new hardware address existed. Such an approach would be impossibly cumbersome. There are various options for the mechanism for this service, and these are now often embedded within the network operating system.

3. Network benefits

When computer installations comprised mainframes, the opportunities for incremental growth and system evolution were sometimes restricted. For example, an increase in processing power could involve a major upgrade of the central processor. The introduction of PCs allowed additional resources to be purchased easily, but there was frequently a lack of integration into the corporate information system. LANs provided the technical capability of integrating PC based software developments to achieve a corporate entity. In comparison with centralized mainframe environments, with all processing activities taking place centrally on a 'single' host, the networked approach provided end users with improved local processing giving better response times whilst providing a systems integration capability. Additional benefits of a distributed computer system over a highly centralized approach include better overall reliability figures because single points of failure can be avoided. A multi-vendor selection option is also possible, since purchasing need not be restricted to mainframe suppliers. The reliability improvements are gained through the reduced impact of component failure and the normal capability of providing most of the services whenever component failures occur. Of course, if a major component such as a network file server were to fail, unless a backup or shadowing facility is installed, the networked service would be severely impaired.

The network infrastructure supports greater flexibility in providing connection points at various locations, especially with a structured cabling environment. This can provide the opportunity for local mobility of staff with both rapid and simple cable patching to allow reconnection to the LAN.

4. Client–servers

In this chapter we have indicated that some host machines are designated as servers. These are usually the more powerful machines which provide services to a second category of host machines known as clients. Client machines are typically end-user, desktop PCs or workstations. The relationship between the client and server machines is a simple model, with the client running client programs which make requests on the server and receive responses back. Typical client–server systems are the web, e-mail, file transfer, telnet, etc., for example, an SQL query to a database can be easily constructed using a client–server approach.

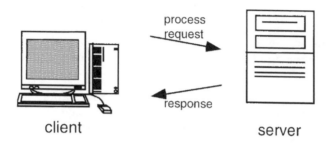

Fig. 5.6 Interaction between two cooperating processes

The distance between the client and server systems can be considerable, and hence the systems are normally considered to be distributed systems, where each task is placed on the platform where it can be handled most efficiently. The client machine is then generally able to present the end user with a user-friendly, graphical interface, and all the processing power needed to provide that front end 'image' is provided by the client process or client software.

The server is able to provide a set of shared resources to a number of clients. It is this ability to take centrally managed systems to distributed end users in a user-friendly manner that makes client–server computing distinctive. Corporate management of the information system can be maintained whilst developments continue to support an open systems standard approach. Of course, client–servers have been popularized by the availability of computer networks that are able to provide 'secure' exchange of information between two hosts.

5. Network disadvantages

Whilst the seven-layer network model (described in Chapter 7) has provided the basis of network architecture, the ability to connect any computing system to any other is not yet always easy to achieve. An interconnection at the physical layer to exchange bits is easily achievable, but the interoperability of such connections to allow a meaningful exchange of information occasionally falls short of expectations. The more complex and unique the device, the greater the difficulty in achieving seamless connections.

It is also a feature of networked systems with many small scale purchases contributing to the overall IT budget that elements of creeping escalation in user connectivity and the resource base are observed. This may be seen by some as a loss of control over expenditure. Others may see this as the freedom of local management to provide local resources as they see fit out of their own budgets. Such freedom needs to be exercised carefully if a corporate IT strategy with a coherent system is to be realized.

Unless there is a corporate network strategy, the installation may not deliver effective benefits, which in turn will make the justification for further expenditure or upgrading more difficult.

Further questions

(There are answers to the questions marked with an asterisk at the end of the book.)

1. *If you were running an email system across an organization, why might it be helpful to standardize on a single word-processing package?

2. *What benefits accrue from having the word processing package centrally located on a file server and available to be downloaded whenever a user wishes to use the application?

3. In a manufacturing environment, what types of information are likely to be sent over a LAN to a numerically controlled machine or a robot cell? Is it likely that large volumes of data will be carried, or is it likely that the emphasis will be on getting the information to the devices quickly?

4. Outline a specific example of a process control environment where a LAN may be implemented.

5. Would it be possible to replace the wiring harness in a car with a LAN such that the signals to control the traffic indicators, brake lights, etc., were carried over the LAN?

Answer 5.1   All users can download the same version of any application software. This should remove the complication of creating incompatible data or data that cannot readily be exchanged. By storing centrally controlled software on a server, we are also able to make sure that only legal software is used within the number of licences purchased.

Answer 5.2   Your answer could include the following: print servers, directory servers, fax servers, name server, mail servers, etc.

Answer 5.3   Any devices connected to an isolated, stand-alone system are dedicated and instantly available. In a server system, the devices are shared, and this potentially causes minor delays in access whilst other devices have control over the shares resource. In a free-standing system, there are potentially fewer connection or network contention problems to create difficulties. It is also possible that the number of software licences for a specific piece of application software will be insufficient for the organization at large in a server system, and if (at any given instant in time) they are all in use, then additional users attempting to access the application software will be denied access in well implemented LANs.

Answer 5.4   There are various answers, which could include hotel or holiday reservations, stock control, banking, or the finance sector.

Answer 5.5   Possibilities include the following:

a) Delay sending until a cheaper telecommunications rate or band is charged.

b) Delay sending until the end of the day. Multiple faxes to a single destination can be batched together.

c)   Use automatic retry when a busy number is detected.

Answer 5.6   Of course not. They will only know the destination by user name or the local name of a device, such as 'office laser'.

Answer 5.7   A user would normally address the service using a generic or network assigned name such as 'office laser' or 'central dbase'.

6 Network medium and topologies

1. Introduction

The physical layout of cabling in LANs has seen significant change in the last decade. Basic topologies still exist to support the individual approach that the various network standards offer. However, these basic topologies frequently exist in a physical structure that looks somewhat different from the logical structure that the standard indicates. Those changes have largely occurred as LANs have grown larger and the need to find an efficient method of managing the installation has become a necessity. In this chapter we will discuss the basic layouts and the structured layouts that are now being implemented. Chapters 8 and 9 cover the detailed design issues of the individual approaches.

2. Topologies

In connecting devices together to form a network we must consider the structure or layout of the cabling. The purpose of a LAN is to bring order and management control to what could otherwise become a difficult problem. Consider the problem of adding another node or PC to either of the layouts shown in Fig. 6.1. It is fairly clear which of the two layouts will give us the most difficulty in establishing an additional connection to all the other existing stations.

Question 6.1 In the unstructured topology of Fig. 6.1, what do you see as the major problem of adding more nodes?

Question 6.2 Why do you think the structured version is better?

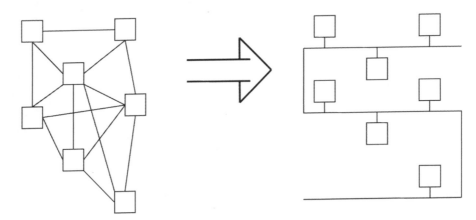

Fig. 6.1 Cable structures

Cable structure is very important, and its logical layout is a key element in supporting the different LAN approaches such as Ethernet and token ring implementations. The physical installation of the cable which represents the logical layout has been changing quite significantly over recent years. A structured cabling approach is now commonly implemented which may not resemble the logical layout we are fundamentally trying to create. Since it is important that the fundamental structures are understood, we'll use those as a starting point in describing the topologies (see Fig. 6.2).

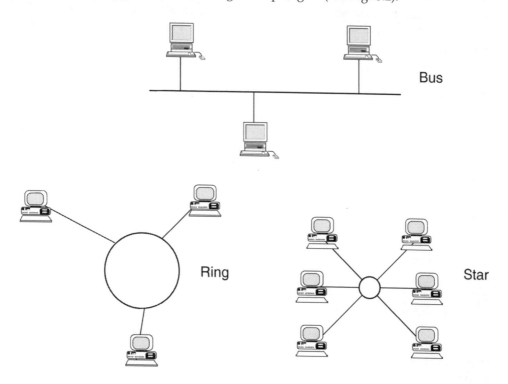

Fig. 6.2 Typical topologies

Bus

A bus topology consists of a 'single' communications channel. Each connected device is attached to the medium at an interface point and has its own unique hardware address. In fact, the hardware address is provided on the network interface card, whether the system is an Ethernet network, or some other network implementation. Data transfers between the interfaces or nodes take place using these hardware addresses.

Question 6.3 Why does each node have a hardware address which is unique as far as that LAN is concerned?

It has been common for the transmission medium to be based on copper cable, although fibre optics cable is becoming increasingly popular. The maximum permitted length of the cable depends upon a number of factors:

a) the signalling methods (e.g., digital, analogue);

b) the access method (how we share access to the shared transmission system);

c) the speed of signalling (the data rates);

d) the type of cable used (its physical properties).

Although we have represented the bus topology as a single cable run in Fig. 6.2, in all but the simplest of installations the bus will have more complex arrangements with several interconnected segments. There are precise rules on how the interconnection of segments is arranged; these will be considered in Chapter 9. A signal introduced at any point to the bus by a connected device will propagate bidirectionally and will be seen at every point on the bus structure.

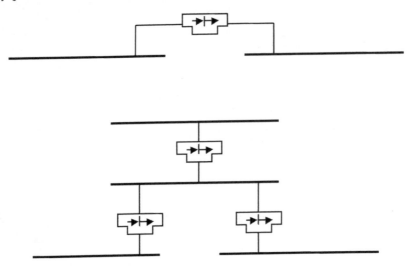

Fig. 6.3 Two examples of more complex bus structures

In the examples shown in Fig. 6.3, assume that the interconnection device is intended to be transparent to any user or connected station. It may be difficult to visualize these configurations as single bus structures, especially the second configuration. Indeed the second layout has the appearance of a tree topology, but it can logically operate as an extended bus. Remember that signals just propagate along all the segments. The interconnecting device or repeater regenerates the signal to allow a greater distance to be covered. Bus configurations can be significantly more complex in larger site installations.

The advantages of using the bus structure include the logical layout and ease of connectivity. Locating cable faults on such a topology is also relatively easy and this is an important issue for network maintainability. The topology is ideal for one-to-many data transmissions since all connected network interface cards see the traffic on the cable. Because signalling on the cable is normally bidirectional and the signal reaches all stations regardless of their position on the bus, there is a security disadvantage, since eavesdropping on other stations' traffic is possible if the network interface card is suitably configured. Also, there is no automatic acknowledgement of receipt by virtue of the topology, i.e., the signal ceases to exist when it reaches the end of the cable. Higher level protocols exist which can ensure that data is successfully exchanged on the basis of acknowledgement signals sent by the receiver to the sender.

Question 6.4 Can a bus topology easily handle broadcast messages where all stations hear the data transfer?

Question 6.5 Why might significant volumes of broadcast messages be a nuisance?

Ring

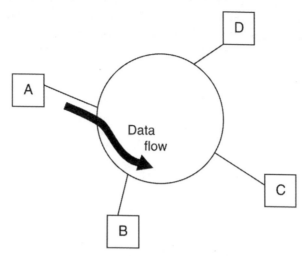

Fig. 6.4 Simple ring topology

In contrast to the bus topology, it is normal in a ring configuration (see Fig. 6.4) for the data transmission to be unidirectional. Of course, there are exceptions when dual cable rings are operating, but the simple arrangement is unidirectional. Data transmissions are passed from the device to its network interface card for onward transmission across the network. Each network interface connection has its own hardware address for identification. As in the bus topology, each interface only copies the data from the network and passes it to the device it connects to the network when it recognizes the packet's destination address as its own. When a station is not the destination address, the interface on a ring network normally acts as a simple repeater and regenerates the signal to its 'full strength'.

There are several local area network standards that are based on a ring topology. The Cambridge Ring implementation was dominant in the UK during the 1980s, but this has largely disappeared. Currently, both token ring networks and larger networks such as fibre distributed data interface (FDDI) networks are based on a ring topology.

There is one important concept which applies to most ring implementations: each network interface card allows data transmissions to pass through the interface with only a few bits delay. So, for example, in a data packet structure of, say, 64 bytes, the start of the data packet may well have circulated around the ring and arrived back at the originating station before the end of the packet has left it. In this mode, there is only one circulating data packet on the ring.

This will not be true in all ring based implementations, and very large rings may support more than one complete packets in circulation. This area is quite complex, with the FDDI topology imposing different criteria from the token ring topology. However, for the ubiquitous token ring topology, the concept that each station is only 'holding' a few of the circulating bits at any instant is an important one to recognize. The token ring topology is so named because a station cannot talk (or transmit) until it notionally holds a token that is circulating around the ring.

We have seen that each node or interface on a ring has a signal regeneration capability. Hence, to ensure the quality of the signal at any point on the ring, the critical factor is the distance between any two nodes. This must be less than the maximum distance for the standard (related to signalling, cable type, etc.) and that needed to ensure good signal recognition. Additionally, overall performance will be coupled to how many nodes play an active role in the network.

Question 6.6   Why does a ring interface introduce a delay?

Question 6.7   Why is the overall performance of a token ring coupled to the number of active nodes?

Clearly there can be no routing problems, since everyone on the ring will get the data, with the addressed node being able to copy the data. The station that generates the data and places it on the ring is normally responsible for removing the data when it returns after a complete rotation around the ring. Because the sender sees the generated packet eventually returned to itself, the opportunity to implement automatic acknowledgements can be in-built.

Larger networks may be constructed from two or more interconnected rings (see Fig. 6.5).

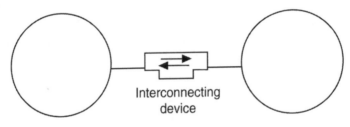

Fig. 6.5 Interconnected rings

Star

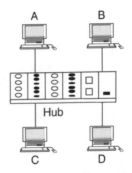

Fig. 6.6 Star configuration

Fig. 6.2 showed the way in which we conceptually view a star network configuration. However, the normal physical arrangement for a star topology includes a central switching system or hub. In Fig. 6.6, if station D wishes to talk to station B, it does so via the hub. Early implementations based on this topology include systems using a PABX (private automatic branch exchange). In the basic form shown here, the medium is not really shared, and each new device requiring connection will result in another cable run to the central point or hub. If the hub was physically close to its connected devices, then the individual cable runs would not be problematic.

Provided that the central point which enables data to be transmitted through to the destination is robust, this topology gives better overall reliability against cable faults, etc., than either of the previous two approaches. Only a single node will be unavailable in the event of a cable failure. LANs implementing the star as their logical topology are sometimes based on existing telephone wiring in the building and do not normally have high data transfer rates.

There are not many implementations of LANs which have a star topology as their underlying logical structure. However, it will be seen later that the physical layouts of many other LANs look very much like a star topology even though they are considered to be some other logical topology. These physical star topologies which are logically some other topology frequently have very high data rates and a carefully specified transmission medium.

Structured wiring systems

Each of the topologies discussed so far has advantages and disadvantages. As the network becomes a critical element in any organization and the daily business operation becomes dependent on its operability, the emphasis on the ability to maintain and manage it becomes more dominant. Weakness in the physical cable layout must be identified quite quickly.

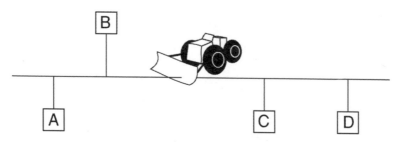

Fig. 6.7 Impact of break on bus topology

Should a break occur in a bus topology, as shown in Fig. 6.7, the network is effectively divided or partitioned. A break can occur for many reasons, including self-inflicted ones caused by building maintenance work! If all the network services, such as servers, are on the other side of the break from a station, the system is effectively unavailable for that station.

Question 6.8   Would the use of an extended bus structure using multiple segments help overcome cable breaks such as that shown in Fig. 6.7?

A ring functions by circulating bits around the network. If a break occurs, as shown in

Fig. 6.8, nothing will operate unless there is a dual circuit facility built in so that some self-healing can be achieved.

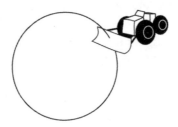

Fig. 6.8 Impact of a break in ring topology

Star topologies are slightly more robust. If the break occurs on a connection between the hub and a station, communication to and from that station is lost. As long as that connection isn't providing a central service (e.g., a server facility), only a single station is rendered useless. Of course, if a major fault develops in the central hub, a total network system crash will occur.

Trying to create a more robust cabling structure and yet maintain the logical topologies required by a LAN has been the basis of the structured approach developed over the last few years. For example, we could consider the logical layout of a ring which is physically constructed like a star. Fig. 6.9 shows a typical example. If the cable to and from each workstation to the central point was contained within a single cable sheath, then the physical resemblance to a star is much greater.

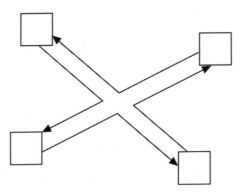

Fig. 6.9 Logical ring but physical star

If we were to add a physical connection facility at the central point to give even more management capability to the configuration, we would end up with a topology exactly like the star configuration shown in Fig. 6.6. The hub, or Multi-Station Access Unit (MAU or MSAU) (see Fig. 6.10), would have dual circuits to each connected device. The token ring implementation is now normally structured around such hubs, each of which typically support eight or sixteen stations. Hubs can be interconnected to form larger rings, as shown in Fig 6.10.

Question 6.9 Sketch the layout of a ring topology using a single hub or MSAU to structure the cabling.

Typical examples of a MAU or MSAU are the IBM 8228 and the Proteon 7202. These devices are strategically located at central points known as wiring centres or wiring closets. The location of each wiring centre is important because it determines the length of the cable runs to the individual stations that are connected. Hence the location is an important element in the design of cable structures.

Question 6.10 Why might it be important to bring wiring back to a central point or wiring centre in a token ring?

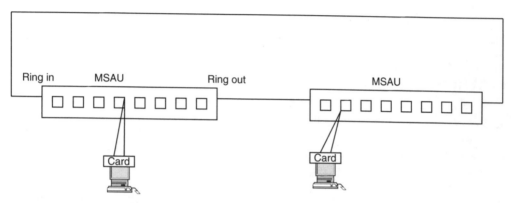

Fig. 6.10 Interconnected hubs or MSAUs

Developments have also occurred in the construction of bus topology systems. Again, it is the recognition that the arrangement of connecting individual stations to a local hub or concentrator in a star configuration offers some robustness that has been the driving force behind the changes. Provided that the concentrator has some intelligence, additional management facilities can be in-built. Typical approaches would make a bus configuration look like that in Fig. 6.11.

It is clear that the physical layout of the cabling may look nothing like the original concept behind the logical layout. In all implementations, great care is taken to ensure that the constructed network offers a convenient to manage and robust structure which can still conform to the logical structure required by the LAN technology. Because we are always striving to find ways of installing systems that can be better managed, the concept of structured wiring has received a great deal of attention over recent years. In particular, the location of hubs, concentrators or MAUs in a strategically placed location is a significant element of such designs. Just about all new bus installations have features of the star structure in Fig. 6.11.

Question 6.11 Suggest a reason why the configuration shown in Fig. 6.11 may be more robust than a physcial bus topology.

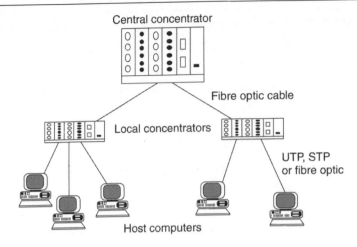

Fig. 6.11 Bus topology in a structured environment

3. Media

A range of network transmission media can be used, and the selection can be based on the application, speed requirements, cost, etc., The main transmission media used in LANs are twisted-pair cable, coaxial cable and fibre-optics cable. In wide area networks, the PTTs are continuing to install more fibre optics cable, although a significant amount of copper cable is still installed.

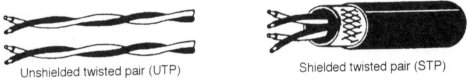

Unshielded twisted pair (UTP)   Shielded twisted pair (STP)

Fig. 6.12 Examples of twisted-pair cable

Twisted-pair cable

Twisted-pair cable consists of two wires which provide a signal path and a return path, with the wires tightly twisted into a spiral configuration (see Fig. 6.12). There are normally at least eight twists per metre. This reduces the problems of noise, crosstalk, etc., Shielded twisted-pair cable appears preferable to unshielded cable because it provides further resilience to noise problems, etc., An unshielded twisted-pair cable typically has a bandwidth of a few megahertz, and it is often used at 9600 bit/s to 64 kbit/s. In token ring LANs, it may be used at both 4 Mbit/s and 16 Mbit/s. It has been used extensively in telephone systems and the 'spare' cable pairs (since a cable may have a number of pairs) already installed in new buildings may be used for carrying data. Recent developments have seen the release of LAN standards at 100 Mbit/s and higher using a number of pairs of UTP cabling. The quality of the cable is obviously important, and a 'quality rating' system has been devised. Twisted pair cable is defined on a five level or category basis. Each cable category is rated in megahertz, which can be considered as offering the megabit per second capabilities shown in Table 6.1.

Category 1	Ordinary telephone cable or RS232 cable
Category 2	Data cable with a speed of up to 4 Mbit/s
Category 3	Data cable with a speed of up to 16 Mbit/s
Category 4	Data cable with a speed of up to 20 Mbit/s
Category 5	Data cable with typical speeds of 100 Mbit/s

Table 6.1 Twisted-pair cable categories

When implementing LANs using twisted-pair cabling (category 3 UTP has previously been the most commonly used), different vendors have their own proposals based on these categories. Currently, the emphasis is on category 5 cable installation. This is partly driven by the desire to provide the capability of supporting the higher data rates of 100 Mbit/s, 155 Mbit/s and beyond, either now or in the future. Since it is the installation of the cabling that is the significant cost element rather than the medium itself, installing the best quality cable is a sensible approach. The second driving force is the compliance with signal emission standards. The proposed European standard on signal emission limits is much stricter than existing USA standards set by the Federal Communications Commission (FCC).

One of the best known ring cable systems is the IBM cable range, the outcome of which is the IBM cable specification. A subset of this specification covering most of the LAN cabling is shown in Table 6.2. Fig. 6.13 shows examples of IBM cable.

IBM Type 1 cable	AWG 22 grade copper wire with two shielded twisted pairs (category 5)
IBM Type 3 cable	AWG 22 or 24 grade copper wire with two to four unshielded twisted pairs (originally rated category 2 but with good quality cable rated up to category 5)
IBM Type 6 cable	AWG 26 grade copper wire with two shielded twisted pairs used as patch panel cable

Table 6.2 IBM cable specification for LAN cabling

It is important to note how reliable the twisted-pair cable is in a LAN installation. Typical error rates are 10^{-6} to 10^{-7}. Twisted-pair cable is low in cost and easy to install, but can potentially give rise to static and grounding problems, and signal radiation is still a feature. Distances of up to 1.5 km can be covered without signal regeneration, although the IBM cabling scheme using Type 1 or Type 2 cable recommends maximum distances of 100 m. This will be covered in more detail in Chapter 9.

A typical twisted-pair cable is shown in Fig. 6.13.

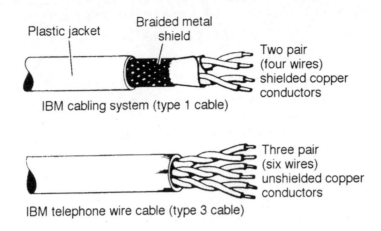

Plastic jacket

Braided metal shield

Two pair (four wires) shielded copper conductors

IBM cabling system (type 1 cable)

Three pair (six wires) unshielded copper conductors

IBM telephone wire cable (type 3 cable)

Fig. 6.13 Detailed examples of twisted-pair cable

Coaxial cable

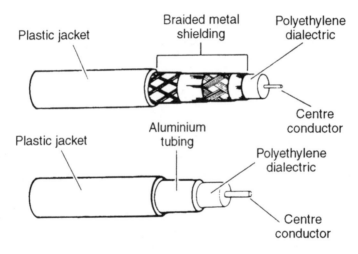

Braided metal shielding

Polyethylene dialectric

Plastic jacket

Centre conductor

Aluminium tubing

Plastic jacket

Polyethylene dialectric

Centre conductor

Fig. 6.14 Coaxial cable
(© Ungermann-Bass, reprinted with permission)

There are many different types of coaxial cable, reflecting the differing number and type of protective shields used and the two major characteristic impedances of 50 Ω (Ethernet) and 75 Ω (cable TV/CATV) (see Fig. 6.14). The 75 Ω cable is used in the broadband area where the technology used has been based on the well established CATV system. However, the 50 Ω cable used in baseband applications is the most commonly found type of coaxial cable.

The cost of cable installation is usually significantly greater than the cost of the cable itself. It should be noted that there is a European directive covering cable emissions.

Network cable comes under this directive, and the signalling frequencies on some LANs require certified cable installations. Flexible RG-58 coaxial cable, as used in thin-wire Ethernet topology, is relatively easy to install. Rigid coaxial cable, as used in the original thick-wire Ethernet topology, was more difficult to install; it normally required more careful handling or specialist skills. Data rates as high as 500 Mbit/s are supportable, although data rates of between 2 Mbit/s and 50 Mbit/s are the norm. Static and grounding problems may arise with possible signal radiation occurrences. With additional shielding, error rates may be of the order of 10^{-9}.

Typically, distances of up to 500 m can be covered without signal regeneration for thick coaxial cable, and 200 m for thin coaxial cable. It should be noted that very little coaxial cable is now being installed, although existing networks may still have coaxial cable from earlier installation work.

Fibre-optics cable

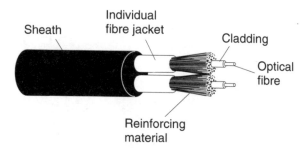

Fig. 6.15 Fibre-optics cable
(reproduced courtesy of Cray Communications)

Fibre-optics cable is often used for backbone networks, and it is the foundation medium for the 100 Mbit/s FDDI network. It consists of hair-like glass strands, covered with cladding and an outer jacket (see Fig. 6.15).

The core provides the path along which the optical signal travels through total internal reflection, by virtue of the different index of refraction of the cladding (see Fig. 6.16).

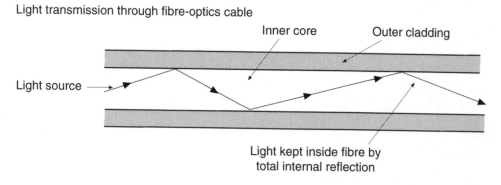

Fig. 6.16 Internal reflection of infra-red light pulses

Hopefully, most of any light source introduced at one end of the fibre will be seen at the far end. Both single-mode and multi-mode fibre-optics cable is used. The core diameter is 8 mm for single-mode cable and 50 μm to 100 μm for multi-mode cable. The achievable data rates are 100 Mbit/s upwards and regeneration is required every 2 km in current LANs. Error rates better than 10^{-10} are achievable. The narrower the core, the lower the amount of light source which becomes dispersed as it travels along the cable. It is consequently easier to recognize the signal at the far end. In Fig. 6.16 no dispersion of light is shown, but in reality at each internal reflection the beam of light is dispersed a little and becomes marginally less focused. Hence, higher speeds can be achieved over narrow core cable than over the wider core cable, where greater dispersion of the signal frequently occurs. There are additional factors that should be taken into account, such as the existence of graded-index cable. Such material is well covered in other texts.

A typical set of system components is shown in Fig. 6.17.

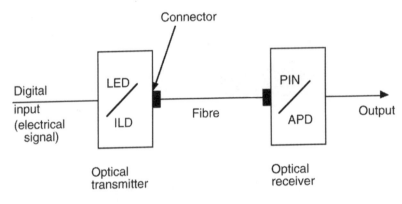

Fig. 6.17 Fibre system components

The transmitter/receiver pair is either a light-emitting diode/positive-intrinsic-negative diode (LED/PIN) pair or an injection laser diode/avalanche photo diode (ILD/APD) pair. The simple arrangement shown in Fig. 6.17 allows transmission in a single direction and a second arrangement is needed to operate in the reverse direction.

Typically, LED/PIN arrangements are used in LANs, since the risk to a user who may inadvertently 'peek' down an ILD/APD pair and damage his or her retina is too great, even though the power is low.

Two connector types are commonly used in LAN fibre-optics systems, namely 9 mm SMA style connectors and ST bayonet connectors. ST connectors have insertion losses of above 0.5 dB compared with 1.0 dB for SMA connectors. Also, there is a greater variation in loss with the SMA style, but they are a little less expensive.

Further questions

(There are answers to the questions marked with an asterisk at the end of the book.)

1. What are the differences and similarities between a logical ring topology and a physical star topology?

2. Why should there have been a current emphasis on structured cabling for LANs, whilst in the early 1980s it wasn't really a consideration?

3. *Outline three different topologies, giving at least two advantages and two disadvantages for each.

4. Consider the transfer of a file containing 1,000,000 characters from one station to another on a bus topology local network where the two stations are 1 km apart. The network has a data rate of 10 Mbit/s and a maximum packet size of 1500 bytes, inclusive of an 8 byte header. Each packet is acknowledged with an 88 bit packet before the next packet is sent. If the propagation speed on the bus is 200 m/µs, what is the total elapsed time for the transfer?

5. Why should we construct large ring LANs from two (or more) interconnected rings, rather than having one very large ring?

6. *What are the factors that determine the maximum length of any particular transmission medium?

7. What is the rationale for physically installing LAN cabling in the topology of a star?

8. Why might fibre optics be considered to be a better alternative than copper in a LAN installation?

Answer 6.1 Just in case you are uncertain, the unstructured cable layout is the version shown on the left, although it has a toplogy name of partially meshed. If we add another node, we need to add a lot of extra connections, which are costly. Each extra node adds enormous extra complexity to the cable layout, especially when the number of nodes becomes significantly large.

Answer 6.2 Provided that access points to the cable are installed in close proximity to all future connection points, any new connection is a relatively easy exercise.

Answer 6.3 Data transfers between devices identify the intended destination by its hardware address. To ensure that it is the intended destination device that gets the message and not any other station, each station or interface must be uniquely identifiable. Hence the requirement for hardware addresses that are unique as far as each network administration is concerned.

Answer 6.4 Most bus topologies operate on a passive basis, that is, each attached station's network interface card hears the data as it passes by, but plays no active role in passing it on. The analogy here is someone sitting between two other people having a conversation. The person hears what is said, but plays no active role in passing the speech onwards. Normally, the first part of any data or bit stream carries some form of destination addressing in its structure, and when a network interface card recognizes its own address, it copies the data off the network and passes it up to the attached device. In order to broadcast a message, a means of making all the stations react to the address is required. Hence, special address formats, such as all 1s in the address field or zone, are often reserved in the network architecture to indicate such a significance.

Answer 6.5 Each time a message is received at a station or network interface, the data is passed to the connected device. Note that, in this context, 'received' means that the interface recognizes that it must read the data for its attached device. If this device is busy processing, the current activity will be interrupted to note or process the incoming broadcast data. This is managed using the standard interrupt routines in the device's operating system to service this input. (We can view the network card as an input/output device in the system). Since all stations will be affected, significant numbers of broadcasts will stop all LAN connected devices and may not be 'appreciated' by the local user as its processing of local activities is slowed down.

Answer 6.6   In a ring topology, each station also operates as a repeater and regenerates the bit stream. In order to regenerate a signal as a clear 0 or 1, the node interface needs to accept each incoming bit and identify it. Bit recognition introduces a delay of at least 1 bit.

Answer 6.7   The more active nodes there are in the circuit, the greater delay there is in passing the data around, since each active node introduces a delay. Thus performance is coupled to the number of active nodes. Additionally, and perhaps more fundamentally, the more attached devices there are, the greater is the probability that a station is transmitting data at any instant in time. Since only one station can transmit at a time, there is therefore a greater probability that a station may have to wait for existing traffic to clear before it can have its turn.

Answer 6.8   The device which connects two (or more) segments together in a transparent mode simply to regenerate the signal and extend the length of the bus is known as a repeater. Hence a repeater increases the distance a signal can travel. If the repeater is an intelligent repeater in the form of a central hub, it can help overcome some cable fault situations by isolating the faulty segment, but in the structure of Fig. 6.7, it cannot significantly help. The first example in Fig. 6.3 with two segments joined with a repeater shows the problem clearly. A cable break will still effectively partition the network in two.

Answer 6.9   The layout is shown in Fig. 6.18.

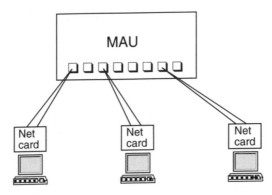

Fig. 6.18 Layout of ring topology using MAU

Answer 6.10   If the wiring in a token ring did not use a wiring centre or MAU, then presumably the cabling would run directly from station to station. Should a cable fault develop (not an unknown phenomenon!), locating the cable fault would be irksome, and bypassing the fault could take some time. If each attached device (or at least small groups of devices) is brought back to a central point, fault finding becomes simpler, and the removal of the offending section of cable from the ring becomes trivial. It can be controlled or managed from the central point.

Answer 6.11   Perhaps the simplest thing to identify is that each end device or workstation has an individual cable run or link back to the central hub or concentrator. As a result, if we get a cable break, provided that the device affected is not a central resource such as a server, then the break will only affect a single device. On a more complex level, the hub can be an intelligent device and can provide some basic recovery and intelligent repeater facilities. Both of these aspects give some additional robustness to the design approach, making it better than a physical bus to manage.

7 Standards

1. Introduction

So far in the text we have introduced a number of data communication fundamentals and principles which underpin the different LAN approaches that are available. A network purchaser can select a product from the marketplace within which the manufacturer has already implemented or preselected many of the options available. This makes the task of selecting a LAN somewhat easier. Points already raised include the transmission medium and signalling techniques. However, if we examine the problems that unfold when a meaningful dialogue is attempted between the two host machines in Fig. 7.1, other problems can be identified.

Fig. 7.1 Typical communications requirement

For example, how do we ensure that the structure of the unit of data sent is recognized at the receiving end? Are the representations of data the same on both sides, e.g., ASCII/EBCDIC? Is there a method of introducing checkpoints for recovery during a large data transfer in the event of a failure? Do we need to introduce security measures? What services do we wish to provide between the two hosts? Are there identical end to end protocols in both hosts that recover from errors in the same manner, and are the hosts both using the same addressing techniques? Are the interfaces working at the same transmission speeds?

This is by no means an exhaustive list, but it is indicative of the wide range of problems that need resolving before we can provide the optimum environment for the user. The assumption made here is that an ideal environment is one in which a user can elect to talk to any item of equipment worldwide and use each item of equipment at its most convenient location. The user should also be able to exchange appropriate information with anybody else without a major reprogramming exercise at either end.

From the user's point of view, the connection that exists between device A and device B in Fig. 7.2 should be irrelevant. It could be a simple cable, a local area network, a wide area network, or a combination of any or all of these. Effectively, what we have determined is that a form of network requirement exists with the general specification that all data input from A is delivered to B and vice versa. This specification forms an entity which we shall refer to as a communications subnet. Although we shall concentrate on the issues specifically relating to local area networks, to achieve this

Fig. 7.2 Network concept

objective we frequently need to use the interconnection services of wide area networks. Hence, we will explore these wider issues later in the text. Some of the latest network developments are beginning to blur the distinction between LANs and WANs.

2. OSI standards

The starting point in establishing OSI standards was that many standards already existed, and it was not practical to abandon these and attempt completely new drafts. It was difficult enough to get the international community to agree what was already in place (or in some cases to agree to disagree with what was already in place!).

From a practical engineering and design point of view, it is advantageous to break any large problem down into a number of smaller and, most importantly, carefully defined components. The complete model is then constructed from these individual smaller components. Network designers have followed similar engineering principles, and networks have evolved consisting of a number of functional layers. Prior to the OSI model agreement in the early 1980s, the number of layers created had been vendor dependent. Internationally, it has been agreed that the International Standards Organization's Open Systems Interconnection (ISO/OSI) Reference Model should provide the platform with which everyone should comply.

Within Europe, the majority of vendors are fully committed to implementing this model. It is also true that, even in Europe, there are networks which differ in detail within the OSI model in various aspects.

What layers have the OSI/ISO standards committee drafted? The outline is shown in Fig. 7.3.

Question 7.1 Why should we break network architectures down into a number of layers?

Layer 7	File transfer, access and management, document and message interchange etc.	Application layer
6	Data representation, transformation and security	Presentation layer
5	Dialogue and synchronisation control	Session layer
4	End-to-end transfer management (connections, error or flow control, segmentation)	Transport layer
3	Network routing and addressing	Network layer
2	Framing, data transparency, error control	Data link layer
1	Mechanical and electrical network interface definitions	Physical layer

Fig. 7.3 OSI Reference Model

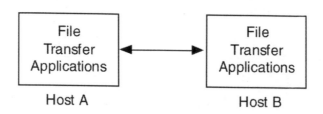

Host A   Host B

Fig. 7.4 Information flow

It is important to understand the underlying concept of information flow. A typical situation is shown in Fig. 7.4, where an application in one host machine is exchanging information with a peer application in a second host. As far as the applications are concerned, it is the two processes that are exchanging data, but in reality there is no physical connection at this level. In fact, the only physical exchange of data occurs at the bottom layer of our model, the physical layer or layer 1. In the example shown in Fig. 7.4, the activity is a file transfer. Hence the application program or process will call on the file transfer facilities within the application layer. File transfer is one of several different services provided by the application layer.

The information flow is through the application layer downwards through all the layers to layer 1, where the data bit exchanges occur, and then upwards on the receiving side.

Question 7.2   Why does physical exchange of data only occur at the bottom layer, or physical layer?

A simple analogy is that of someone writing a letter, putting it in an envelope, addressing it and giving it to the post office. When the post office delivers the letter, the recipient checks the address, opens the envelope and reads the letter. The physical transfer is the responsibility of the post office, but the writer could consider that a peer-to-peer transfer to the reader has occurred, without worrying about the detail of how the transfer physically occurred.

In the OSI model, the flow of information appears to be peer-to-peer at each level, but information is only exchanged at the physical level, as shown in Fig. 7.5.

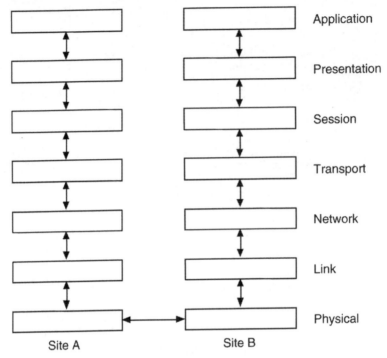

Fig. 7.5 OSI information flow

3. Description of the seven-layer model

A brief description of the functionality of each layer is given below.

Physical layer

The bottom layer of the model defines how data and control characters are physically signalled to each other. It specifies all the properties associated with the representation of a bit. The physical connection is also defined in the specification, and so the plugs and sockets are detailed in the physical layer. Detail of the media used is also described in this layer. The result is a stream of bits which are signalled from one point to another, with all of the electrical and mechanical properties of the connection being specified.

Link layer

The link layer or data link layer ensures that the bits carried by the physical layer have a structure. Where necessary, the layer assumes the responsibility for transferring blocks or packets of information between each of the connecting points, providing a point-to-point link or series of point-to-point links which contribute to an end-to-end link. Error detection and correction may be implemented at this level with the facility of retransmitting if necessary. Flow control may also be implemented within the layer.

Network layer

This level takes packet-sized data blocks from the transport level and maps the addresses to network addresses. Should routing be required, then the responsibility for routing or rerouting is also taken here on the basis of the Internet address format(s).

Transport layer

This layer provides two-way, reliable, cost effective, end-to-end exchange of data. Optimisation of the transmission is undertaken, which may involve multiplexing and resizing the message blocks if appropriate. Flow control and sequencing of the data blocks is performed at this level. Hence, regardless of whether any point-to-point connections are operating at layer 2, the layer 4 protocol ensures the two end points have a secure connection.

Session layer

The session layer establishes calls to exchange the data bit streams. It provides co-ordination between users by selecting mutually acceptable protocols, and effects checkpoints for recovery of data. It is possible for this layer to be bypassed in some implementations.

Presentation layer

This layer maps the various data formats into an external data representation (XDR) that will allow correct interpretation of the information on receipt. Encryption of data may be provided for confidentiality or security and compression of data may also be implemented.

Application layer

This layer effects the information interchange between two application processes by providing a range of service interfaces for application programs. E-mail, directory services and file transfer services are typical examples of the interfaces provided at layer 7.

4. Advantages of layering

It is important to make the advantages of this approach clear. We have promoted the idea of breaking a large complex problem down into a number of 'simpler' components as a well established engineering principle. In its application to the OSI model, the approach generates a number of benefits, including the following:

a) standard interfaces between layers allow internal developments within a particular layer to evolve;

b) alternative services may be offered at a given layer by having different options or routes through the layer;

c) internal mechanisms of each layer are invisible to the other layers;

d) layers may be completely removed if not required, or a simplified version can be used as a substitute where appropriate.

Question 7.3 Why might it be important to allow internal layer developments to evolve?

---

5. Existing standards

Prior to the OSI model being agreed, a significant amount of work on establishing LAN standards had been already undertaken. The effort of setting standards is accepted as being the price you pay for enabling there to be future and continuing growth in both interconnection and multi-vendor support. Having to conform to carefully specified standards may be viewed as a restriction on innovation, but in reality, without the standards bodies, there would be little conformity.

There are a number of standards bodies in the LAN area that have influenced the shape of the industry. They include the IEEE and ANSI (and there are also industry *de facto* standards), and much of the work undertaken by these organizations has now been incorporated into the OSI model – you can't keep on reinventing the wheel! The work on setting the standards within the IEEE area has usually been pioneered by the large organizations or groups that established the particular technology. The IEEE (the US Institute of Electrical and Electronic Engineers) established the 802 committee to examine the existing work and set the various LAN standards which have become internationally accepted. The output of the IEEE 802.x committee is the list of standards shown in Table 7.1, which covers some of the major local area network approaches.

802.3	CSMA/CD (Ethernet)
802.4	Token bus
802.5	Token ring
802.6	MAN (metropolitan area network)
802.11	Cableless or wireless
802.12	100 Mbit/s

Table 7.1 IEEE 802.x LAN standards

ANSI (the American National Standards Institute) has also established the FDDI (Fibre Distributed Data Interface) standard, since it came outside the original remit of the 802 committee by virtue of its speed of 100 Mbit/s (ISO 9314/1). Originally, the IEEE established a limit of 20 Mbit/s as the upper bound for the speed definition of a LAN, but it now recognizes the limitations of maintaining this position.

These standards from the IEEE and ANSI typically cover the functions of the lower layers of the OSI model, but unfortunately they do not correspond exactly to the OSI Reference Model. Therefore there is only equivalent functionality between the standards, and the layer boundary points of the two do not match exactly. Fig. 7.6 shows where the boundary points between the OSI and IEEE models are aligned. The IEEE 802.2 layer is responsible for the secure point-to-point delivery of the frames, performing a similar function to that provided by HDLC in the WAN world. Both connection and connectionless services can be accommodated within the IEEE 802.2 layer.

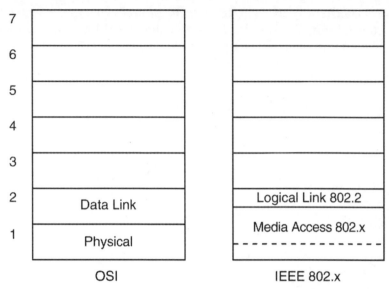

Fig. 7.6 Comparison of OSI and IEEE standards

Fortunately, the mismatch between the IEEE 802.x structure and the OSI model is not critical. Provided that there is a common interface between layer 2 and layer 3 that presents us with an access point which doesn't differentiate between the underlying network layers, the differences become irrelevant or hidden from the higher layers.

The IEEE 802.x standards are covered by equivalent ISO 8802.x standards, and so they are recognized and well understood within the network community.

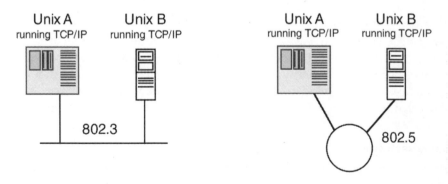

Fig. 7.7 Examples of support networks

In the examples shown in Fig. 7.7, two Unix host machines run applications which use the transport and network layer TCP/IP protocol (Transmission Control Program/ Internet Protocol). If the two machines are exchanging data, it really doesn't matter to the application program whether the data transfer between hosts is achieved over an 802.3 or 802.5 network. The important issue is that the access point to the 802.3 or 802.5

interface is able to carry the TCP/IP protocol. Basically, the user is content to accept the system shown in Fig. 7.8, with the LAN providing layer 1 and layer 2 functionality and the hosts supporting the higher layers.

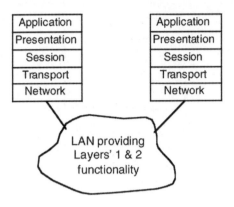

Fig. 7.8 LAN model

The functions undertaken in the LAN equivalent to OSI layer 1 and layer 2 (see Fig. 7.8) essentially resolve such issues as the following:

a) how we access the transmission medium in an orderly manner to ensure that there is no contention between individual hosts that wish to transmit simultaneously;

b) how we physically signal bits on the transmission medium;

c) how we ensure the integrity of the data at transfer.

Fig. 7.9 shows the hardware and software boundary points in a LAN.

The use of TCP/IP in Fig. 7.7 was a carefully chosen example to show the most commonly used transport layer protocol. Originally it was not part of the ISO standards but its enormous popularity as an industry *de facto* standard led to its eventual acceptance as an ISO standard. It is widely used in many Unix host machines to such an extent that it is significantly more common than the ISO TP and IP equivalent.

Further questions

(There are answers to the questions marked with an asterisk at the end of the book.)

1. *Some people would argue that standards allow real progress to be achieved. Others would argue that they hinder innovation. What are your views?

2. *The delivery of packets of data on a worldwide network requires an addressing mechanism that is accepted worldwide. How is it achieved in the seven layer model?

3. *Where in the seven layer protocol arrangement do we ensure that the destination receives the information despatched by the sender? Outline how this may have been achieved.

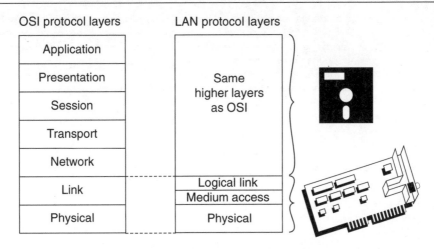

OSI protocol layers   LAN protocol layers

Application

Presentation

Session

Same higher layers as OSI

Transport

Network

Link

Logical link

Medium access

Physical   Physical

Fig. 7.9 Hardware/software boundary
(© **Learning Group International, reprinted with permission**)

4. The presentation layer has a data compression implementation responsibility. Why might we require such a facility as data compression? Where might it be useful to have data compression?

5. Do all the existing data networks have a seven layer approach? Typically, where do the differences occur and do they affect the functionality?

6. There are a number of issues which need to have been resolved when two computer systems attempt to exchange data. Identify as many of these issues as possible.

7. Outline the major advantages and disadvantages of a layered approach to designing networks.

Answer 7.1   Breaking big problems down into smaller parts so that the smaller unit may be better understood and better designed is good sound engineering practice. The same approach is used in designing software systems, where large systems problems are broken down into smaller procedures, which can then be well tested. The procedures are then linked together to form the total solution.

In a network design, if we can implement a fixed number of layers, each of which can be well defined and can talk to adjacent layers, then we have a good chance of designing a robust system. Each layer can be separately tested – indeed different versions or standards of any layer can be designed. During testing, such tests can be operated as an alternative path to the existing protocol or standard.

Answer 7.2   The physical layer is the only point in the model where the mechanical and electrical interface is defined and a signalling method is established to transmit the data stream.

Answer 7.3   Through the definition of the interfaces at each layer, the content of the layer can continue to be developed without prejudice to the rest of the model. Hence, if some new and better algorithm were developed, this could be introduced into a layer. With careful control, both versions of a layer could coexist such that testing could be undertaken on the development version whilst live data continued to be passed through the current released version. At some appropriate stage, when testing and validation procedures were complete, the new version could be switched in. Clearly, where there is worldwide use of some layers (e.g., the transport layer with TCP), then new releases are rare, since updating millions of copies worldwide to achieve continuing compatibility of connected networks is a non-trivial task. This problem now exists where version 6 of IP is replacing version 4.

8 LAN signalling and access

1. Introduction

In this chapter we will examine the differing methodologies used in LANs to implement the bottom two layers of the OSI model. The signalling and access approaches taken by the various LAN designs were fundamental to the development of the individual standards and resulting products. We will describe in this chapter the range of options open to network designers. In Chapter 9 you will see how these different signalling and access approaches were adopted in the now well established standards.

2. Signalling

In the data communications systems involving relatively low transmission speeds, signalling was typically achieved using standards such as RS232C. In these standards, to enable the receiver to recognize and lock onto a transmitted character, asynchronous transmission schemes involving the addition of start and stop bits were implemented. With the development of synchronous transmissions to support higher transmission speeds, other conventions based on control characters were used to recognize the start and end points of the data transfer.

It must be recognized that the speeds involved in local area network environments are considerably higher than those in earlier communication systems, and have been typically in the 10 Mbit/s to 100 Mbit/s range, although speeds up to 10 Gbit/s are becoming available. At these high rates of data transmission, consider the difficulty when a long string of zero bits is transmitted. It is difficult to determine the boundary points of where one 0 ends and the next starts. As noted in Chapter 1, if there is a small drift in the receiver's timing away from the sender's timing, a loss of synchronization will occur. There is a similar problem if a long string of 1s is transmitted.

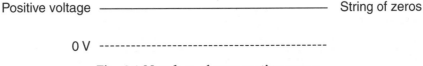

Positive voltage ———————————————————————— String of zeros

0 V --

Fig. 8.1 Number of consecutive zeros

Fig. 8.1 shows the difficulty of recognizing each of the bit boundary points, i.e., it is not clear where each 0 begins and ends. Therefore we may not know for sure at the receiving end how many 0s have been transmitted. Of course, we can make a fairly accurate estimate based on the transmission rate and duration, but we can't be absolutely certain.

Question 8.1	What would happen if the clock timing of the receiving station differed by 10% from the sending station's clock's timing, and a string of one hundred 0s was transmitted using the representation shown in Fig. 8.1?

It thus became necessary to use a signalling technique which enabled the receiver to both recognize the start of the data frame and maintain synchronization with the sending device throughout the transfer. The original techniques included sending the data signal and a 'clocking signal' as a combined or 'joint' transmission. The joint data and clock signal arrangement removes the necessity for a transmitting clock and any receiving clock(s) to try to keep in synchronization at speeds significantly higher than those previously encountered. The receiving station sees the signal change of the clocking signal and knows that there is a data signal to determine or recover. Hence, receivers lock onto the signal changes of the embedded clocking signal.

The principal signalling methods are baseband, broadband and carrierband.

Baseband

In a baseband signalling arrangement the data from the LAN interface is encoded with the clocking signal and placed onto the transmission medium. Normally this combined signal is the only signal that that exists on the transmission medium and it occupies the full bandwidth of the medium. The signalling may be bidirectional, as shown in Fig. 8.2. At the receiving interface the original data is recovered from the encoded signal and passed to the higher level protocols of that station.

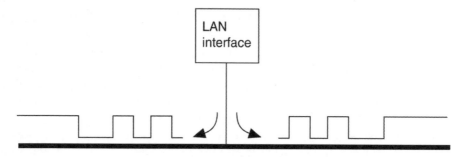

Fig. 8.2 Baseband operation

Question 8.2   Is baseband signalling likely to be a single channel or multiple channel communication on the transmission medium?

The encoding takes place within the network interface unit and takes one of the following forms.

Manchester encoding

The data to be sent is exclusively ORd (XORd) with the clocking signal to form the transmitted signal as shown in Fig. 8.3. The clocking signal is running at twice the speed of the intended data transmission rate. Hence, if we want to transmit data at a rate of 10 Mbit/s, then the clocking speed is 20 MHz.

As can be seen from the resulting signal, a 0 data bit is represented by a high to low signal change, and a 1 data bit is represented by a low to high data bit change. In the original Ethernet specification, the voltage swings were from a high of −0.225 V to a low

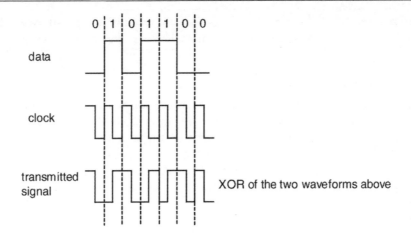

Fig. 8.3 Manchester encoded signal

of −1.825 V as nominal voltages, but a swing between both positive and negative voltages are used in the IEEE 802.3 specifications. The rise time associated with this signalling is 25 ns.

The important thing to note is that, in the time cell associated with each data bit, the signal that is transmitted always has a signal change. It is this signal change that the receiver locks onto and which enables each data item to be captured.

Question 8.3   Sketch the encoded signal for the data pattern 10011 if Manchester encoding is used.

This type of signalling is typically used in an Ethernet implementation, which will be covered fully in Chapter 9. Because the method used to access the medium means that transmissions may commence at 'almost' any time, the first part of the signal is a preamble. This preamble is intended to allow receivers to synchronize with the embedded clock and to identify the start of the data component. Hence the signal typically consists of the components shown in Fig. 8.4.

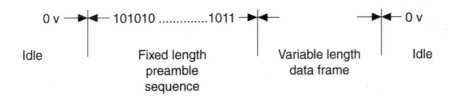

Fig. 8.4 Typical signal structure

Question 8.4   If the receiving station did not synchronize immediately with the sending station and missed the first few bits of preamble, would this matter?

Differential Manchester encoding

In Manchester encoding, if there is accidentally a polarity reversal (e.g., a twisted pair cable is connected backwards) then there is the possibility of signal misrepresentation, although in practice this would be spotted through the identification of malformed packets. With differential Manchester encoding (DME), transitions will still occur at the centre of each data bit, and hence provides the embedded clocking mechanism. However, 1s and 0s are represented by no transition at the start boundary point of the data bit for a 1, and a transition at the start boundary point of the data bit for a 0 (see Fig. 8.5).

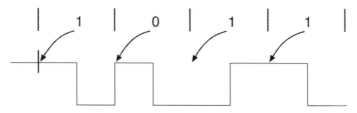

Fig. 8.5 Differential Manchester encoding

Question 8.5   As in Question 8.3, sketch the encoded signal for the data pattern 10011, but use differential Manchester encoding.

This type of signalling is typically used in token ring systems, which will be covered fully in Chapter 9. Because the token is a constantly circulating data construct, the long preamble used in Ethernet systems is not desirable or required. What is needed is a clear indication of the start and end of the data format. It should be noted from the DME waveform that there is always a transition midpoint for any bit representation that is legal. Illegal constructs could thus be envisaged which could then be utilized to provide unique identifiers to represent the start and end points of the data constructs. They are unique because they must never occur in places where we are trying to represent data.

The two possible illegal conditions or encode violations occur where no midpoint transition takes place, i.e., when the signal starts low and remains low, or when the signal starts high and remains high.

The two encode violation conditions are identified as J and K, and these are used in the leading and trailing bytes of a token ring data structure as the unique identifier. We can then be confident of knowing exactly where the structures start and end (see Fig. 8.6).

Question 8.6   Couldn't the J and K conditions accidentally occur in the middle of a long data string and consequently be interpreted as the leading/trailer bytes?

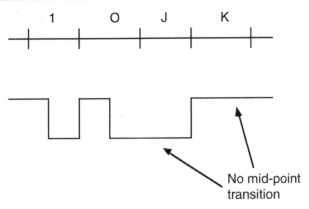

Fig. 8.6 Differential Manchester encode violations

Phase modulation

It is possible to use twisted pair cable to provide two channels, and the phase difference between the two channels may then be used to signal the data value. In this implementation a data value of 0 is represented by a signal transition in only a single channel, whereas a 1 is represented by a transition in both data channels (see Fig. 8.7).

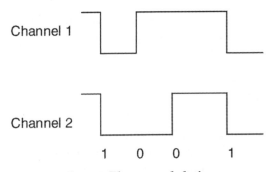

Fig. 8.7 Phase modulation

Note that, in order to balance the power load for each channel, every single channel transition (for a 0) alternates between the two channels.

Question 8.7 Sketch the encoded signal for the data pattern 11001 if phase modulation is used.

This type of signalling was typically used in Cambridge Ring systems. Because the media access method used consists of a constantly circulating slot(s), then only a single bit at the front of the data construct is needed to indicate the start condition.

4 bit/5 bit (4B/5B) encoding

As the requirements to increase network speeds up to 100 Mbit/s were being examined it became clear that the strategy of embedding the clocking signal within the data was less attractive. To recover a signal running at 200 MHz is certainly significantly more expensive than is the case at 100 MHz. However, the basic issue of recognizing the boundary points of each bit, especially in long strings of 1s and 0s, still needed to be resolved.

The simple resolution to this problem was to take each 4-bit combination and represent it as 5 bits on the transmission medium. The mapping mechanism from a 4-bit pattern to a 5-bit pattern ensured that the 5 bits will always have a signal change. For example, 0000 is represented as 11110, and 1111 is represented as 11101. No 5-bit pattern was used in the mapped version which had all 0s or all 1s. The mapping from 4 bits to 5 bits is achieved using a fixed translation or mapping table. The incoming 4 bits are taken and translated into the 5-bit encoded signal. Because the 5-bit pattern always has a change of signal, the problem of long consecutive strings of 0s or 1s being transmitted is avoided. The result is that a 100 Mbit/s data rate requires a 125 Mbit/s signalling rate. This is still considerably cheaper than 200 MHz to design and implement.

The 4B/5B signalling technique was originally specified for fibre optics systems, with light emitting diodes providing the signal representation.

5 bit/6 bit (5B/6B) encoding

The previous section outlined the developments that are required in high speed fibre optics LANs to achieve synchronization. However, this approach still needs a high frequency signalling capability of 125 MHz. To operate on copper wire transmission media such as twisted pair cable, the frequency needs to be kept low to meet the radio frequency interference and electromagnetic emission regulations of the US FCC and international CISPR regulations.

In Chapter 9 we will see how advantage can be taken of 5B/6B encoding to achieve high speed LANs which are based on copper wire cable such as unshielded twisted pair cable. The same principle as in 4B/5B encoding is employed, with an additional scrambling stage taking place (see Fig. 8.8). It is worth noting that this approach continues to be developed in other combinations such as 8B/10B for higher speed networks.

Each 5 bit quintet is mapped into a predetermined 6-bit data pattern. The 6-bit pattern is designed to ensure that sufficient transitions or signal changes occur to guarantee that synchronization can be maintained by the receiver. The 6-bit sextet data pattern contains an equal number of 0s and 1s to deliver this synchronization. Of course this offers us an additional error checking capability because we can check each delivered sextet to ensure that this balance of 0s and 1s is present. Corrupted data may be detected at this point.

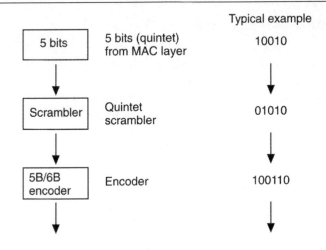

Fig. 8.8 5B/6B scrambling and encoding

Most implementations use a two level Non-Return-to-Zero (NRZ) encoding, sending one bit on each clock cycle. With a clock frequently operating at 30 MHz, the encoding of a typical data pattern is shown in Fig. 8.9.

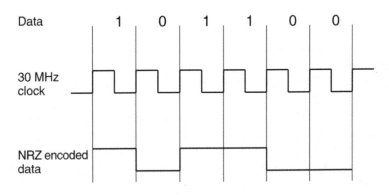

Fig. 8.9 NRZ encoding

A 30 MHz clock generates a maximum transmission frequency of 15 MHz on the transmission medium when the worst scenario data pattern of 101010 . . . is transmitted. Hence Category 3 cable upwards can support this approach.

Broadband and carrierband

The data in the broadband and carrierband approaches is placed onto the medium using a modulated carrier. Hence it is a modulated signal that appears on the medium. Frequently, phase coherent modulation is used. The result is that transmissions are normally unidirectional. Any encoding of the original data still occurs at the LAN interface before being modulated by a modem-style connection to the transmission medium (see Fig. 8.10).

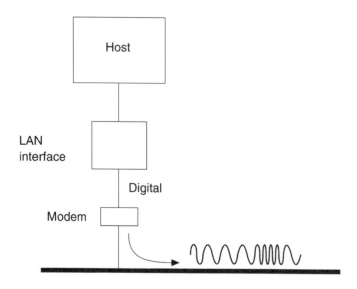

Fig. 8.10 Broadband/carrierband operation

In the case of carrierband transmission, the signal transmitted occupies the whole bandwidth of the cable and no other use is made of the cable, i.e., it is a single channel operation on the medium. This is not so in broadband operation, where multiple channels exist. Each channel has a discrete frequency range, and so we are effectively using a frequency domain multiplexing approach. Hence there is a requirement in broadband transmission to make frequency assignments to the various channels to be used. The bottom end of the frequency range can be used to carry power on the cable. Also, channels are normally 6 MHz in bandwidth, which is sufficient to carry a television channel. Several adjacent 6 MHz bandwidth channels are used to carry data at 10 Mbit/s. The US has adopted a loose standard for assigning the frequency spectrum of broadband coaxial cable into channels for specific roles.

Question 8.8 Suggest why broadband and carrierband signals are unidirectional (as shown in Fig. 8.10), whereas baseband signals may be bidirectional (as shown in Fig. 8.2).

The services that can exist or even coexist on a broadband system include IEEE 802.4 networks. It is possible to concurrently run other services such as an IEEE 802.3 LAN in other frequency channels. The physical cabling offers a number of alternative implementation styles. If a single cable system is in operation, then two way traffic is carried on the coaxial or fibre optics cable, with the frequency spectrum being split up into three zones. Inbound traffic operates in the lower frequency range and outbound traffic operates in the higher range. The terms 'inbound' and 'outbound' are relative directions to the headend device. Hence 'inbound' means 'in towards the headend'. 'Outbound' means 'away from the headend'. The headend is a special device, the function of which will be described shortly.

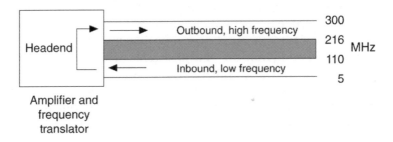

Fig. 8.11 Single cable broadband arrangement

A typical arrangement is shown schematically in Fig. 8.11 and physically in Fig. 8.12. In Fig. 8.11, we have determined that the transmission medium has a frequency range or bandwidth of 300 MHz. Of course, different transmission media will have different bandwidth capabilities. The inbound channels are using a frequency range of 5 MHz to 110 MHz and the outbound group of channels are using 216 MHz to 300 MHz. An individual service such as a LAN will be allocated a specific frequency channel in both the inbound and the outbound directions. This will be fixed at the time of installation or at the LAN standards design stage.

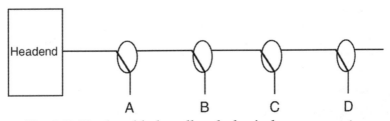

Fig. 8.12 Single cable broadband physical arrangement

In Fig. 8.12, the representation of the station attachments to the medium shows the direction of transmission towards the headend. There is high resistance in the other direction to ensure unidirectional transmission. Any in-line amplifiers will also ensure unidirectional data flow.

Note that, in this arrangement, if station C wishes to transmit to station D, it passes the data up to the headend. The frequency range of the inbound channel is translated into the appropriate frequency range of the outbound channel which is assigned to the LAN. The data is forwarded on the outbound channel and received by D, and there is no direct communication from C to D not involving the headend. The headend provides the system with an electronic control centre that amplifies signals and translates frequencies between the inbound and outbound channels. It also provides power for other amplifiers on the cable, which is carried through the cable in the bottom frequency range of 0 Hz to 50 Hz. This technology has been taken from cable television. The amplifiers which are remote from the headend are robust devices, and they are often dual-circuit for fault resilience.

A guard band provides a protection against crossover of frequencies, and it is the unusable range within the frequency spectrum.

Alternatively, a dual-cable system can be implemented (see Fig. 8.13), in which case the headend provides no frequency translation capability, and all of the frequency spectrum of the medium is available for inbound operation. Equally, all of the frequency spectrum is available for the outbound traffic on the other cable, which allows a larger number of channels to be assigned in both directions. The inbound and outbound channels for a specified function (e.g., LAN implementation) would normally be on the same frequency channel. Hence the headend in a dual-cable system is a simpler device because it does not have to undertake the frequency translation needed in a single cable system.

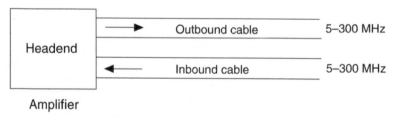

Fig. 8.13 Dual-cable broadband operation

Question 8.9	In the dual cable arrangement the headend is a cheaper and simpler device. Are there any drawbacks to a dual-cable system which make it a less attractive arrangement than the single cable layout?

Spread spectrum

The physical layer is responsible for taking the digital signal in the network interface card and sending the transmission over the airwaves. To reduce the impact of noise interference, which we sometimes experience on radio transmissions, the approach taken in wireless networks is to spread the signal over a wide band of frequencies. If other signals, which are typically narrow in bandwidth, interfere with the spread spectrum transmission, then they should only distort a small part of the transmitted signal and as a result cause fewer problems when the signal is received and demodulated. Fig. 8.14 shows how the signal frequency can be spread over a wider frequency range.

The implementation of spread spectrum may take one of two forms: frequency hopping and direct sequence. In the first approach of Frequency Hopping Spread Spectrum (FHSS), the transmission is a modulated carrier signal, and this carrier changes or hops frequency within an established frequency band of 2.4 GHz. Typically this will be

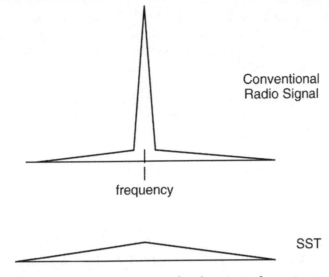

frequency

Figure 8.14 Frequency spread using spread spectrum

between 2.4 and 2.483 GHz, using a frequency band of 1 MHz or 0.001GHz during each hop dwell period. A code establishes the pattern or order in which the hops occur, usually selected from 79 frequencies within the transmission channel bandwidth. Each hop will use the frequency for up to 400 ms before moving on to the next frequency in the sequence. The period spend on each frequency is known as the dwell time. A typical hopping sequence is shown in Fig. 8.15.

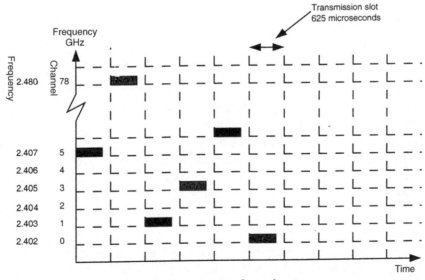

Figure 8.15 Frequency hopping sequence

Obviously, the receiver must change its reception of the frequencies in the same order of hopping as the sender, so it must be set to the same hopping code as the sender. Typical transmission speeds are 1 or 2 Mbit/s and the carrier is modulated using either a two-level or four-level (respectively) Gaussian Frequency Shift Key (GFSK) approach. For the 1 Mbit/s approach, the frequency has frequency modulation at plus and minus the current carrier frequency of nominally 160 kHz, with a higher and lower amplitude respectively representing a level 1 and 0. When operating with four different amplitude levels, then 2 Mbit/s are achievable.

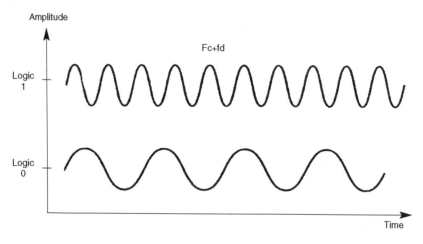

Figure 8.16 Two-level GFSK

The second alternative approach used in spread spectrum is Direct Sequence (DSSS). In this case the data to sent is combined with a bit sequence operating at a higher speed. The effect is the representation of a 0 or a 1 as a sequence of bits. The number of bits representing the signalled data bit is called the processing gain. Hence if the processing gain is set at 11, which is the minimum gain recommended by the IEEE 802.11 standard, then the number of bits transmitted to represent each data bit is 11. Most commercial systems operate with processing gains under 20, and typically a gain of 11 is implemented using the 11-bit Barker Sequence.

As an example, a 1 could be represented by a bit sequence of 00010011100 and a 0 represented by 11101100011. These representations are sometimes referred to as the chip rate of the data or as the chipping code for each data bit. DSSS also uses the 2.4 GHz bandwidth

3. Access

If a number of devices are connected to a single transmission medium, we need to define a method where only one of the devices is allowed to talk at any particular moment. Even in a simple radio communication between two people, a protocol is needed. This protocol indicates the release of the communications channel and gives permission to the other party to send in the first party's place. An example is the word 'over'. Termination of the conversation in such a protocol is achieved, for example, with the words 'over and out'. Failure to observe such a protocol could result in both parties potentially talking simultaneously. If two or more stations are 'talking' or transmitting at the same time on a single transmission medium, then clearly each of the transmissions will interfere with the other and nothing will be successfully heard or properly received. In the case of LANs, we need to define the various access methods that are currently used to control the traffic on the communications media such that a data transmission is successfully transmitted and not corrupted by other devices attempting to transmit simultaneously. There are a number of access resolution schemes in place, each of which have their individual strengths and weaknesses. Each scheme or access technique will also impact on critical issues such as delay times and data throughput rates. In this chapter, we will examine the popular schemes and identify some of the issues that relate to the users.

The major techniques used to resolve contention on transmission media are shown in Fig. 8.17. They fall into three main categories.

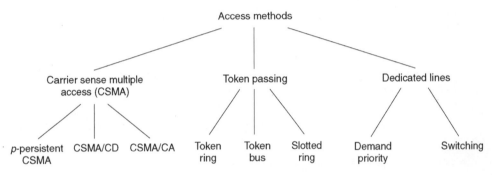

Fig. 8.17 Major access techniques

Question 8.10 What would be the result of two (or more) stations transmitting at the same time on a single transmission medium?

This section describes the access methods in the strictest sense. The detail of how these techniques have been implemented in current systems will be covered in Chapter 9. A popular technique in the LAN marketplace is based on dedicated lines to hubs. There has been particular interest in this for the Ethernet product range, and so the access techniques will also be covered in this chapter.

Carrier Sense Multiple Access (CSMA)

Within the CSMA access subgroup, the global approach for any station wishing to transmit is to listen for a carrier or signal on the medium before transmitting. Before a station transmits, it checks that it cannot hear another station talking. If it can hear another station actively transmitting data, then it waits until later. It is possible that more than one station is waiting for an existing transmission to terminate, and they may all wish to gain access simultaneously once the transmission medium becomes free. In such a situation, where multiple stations start transmitting simultaneously, their individual transmissions will collide with and corrupt each other. The three major methods of resolving contention within CSMA all start with the 'listen before you talk' technique, but they then differ in terms of the contention resolution technique adopted. They all start by sensing whether a carrier is present with multiple stations able to gain access, and hence we have the CSMA approach in each of the following developments.

p-persistent CSMA

Before sending, a station wishing to transmit senses the channel or medium. If the channel is idle, then there is no immediate transmission, but the station may transmit at each delay interval or slot time with a probability of p (see Fig. 8.18).

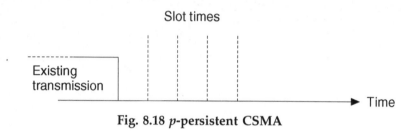

Fig. 8.18 p-persistent CSMA

If only two stations are attempting to gain access, both with a probability of 1.0 (i.e., the station will always attempt to send once an idle state is detected), then the probability of a collision occurring is 1. However, if the probability of transmitting is reduced to 0.5, under the same criteria as above the probability of a collision occurring is 0.5^2 or 0.25.

If the channel is busy, the station(s) wishing to transmit continue(s) to sense the channel and, once an idle condition is detected, transmit(s) as before (see Fig. 8.19).

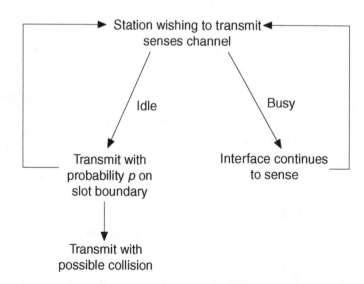

Fig. 8.19 Algorithm for p-persistent CSMA

The performance comparisons for various possible settings of p are shown in Fig. 8.20.

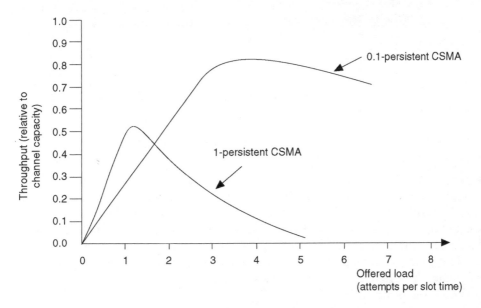

Fig. 8.20 Analytical performance

Basically, this approach trades off additional delay times before accessing the channel against a reduction in the number of collisions occurring. The average delay resulting from this approach is given by the following

$$\text{average delay} = \frac{1-p}{p} \text{ slot times}$$

The length of a slot time is a time delay that is established in any design which uses this approach. It has been implemented in radio packet switching networks.

Carrier Sense Multiple Access Collision Detection (CSMA/CD)

Using the p-persistent CSMA protocol just examined, there is still the possibility that a collision will occur. If a collision does occur, then both stations will continue to transmit and the resulting data transmitted will be corrupted and lost, and there will be wasted time associated with the transmission of corrupted data.

Rather than time being wasted in continuing to send a corrupted data transmission, an enhancement would be the ability to 'listen while you talk'. If you can't hear yourself clearly, then someone else must be attempting a transmission simultaneously. In such an event, it is sensible to stop transmitting and save the remainder of the transmission time. If we did this, at least we wouldn't waste transmission time once we were aware that a collision of data had occurred, i.e., there were multiple transmission attempts. For this to be effective, both (or all) station interfaces must detect any collision and abort their individual attempts.

Why do collisions occur? Consider the situation where a station wants to transmit, and does so as soon as the transmission channel becomes free. Fig. 8.21 shows a situation

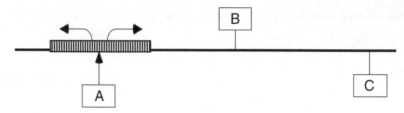

Fig. 8.21 Channel transmission

where station A has started to transmit, having determined that it couldn't hear any other transmissions.

A transmission takes a finite time to reach the other end of the medium (owing to propagation delay), so it is possible that, before the transmission from station A reaches station C, station C itself wishes to transmit. At that precise moment, station C believes that the ether or transmission medium is idle, and begins to transmit, with a subsequent collision occurring when the signals from station A and station C meet and corrupt each other. Under the worst situation, this attempted transmission occurs when the signal from station A at one extreme end of the medium has almost, but not quite, reached station C at the other end, as shown in Fig. 8.22.

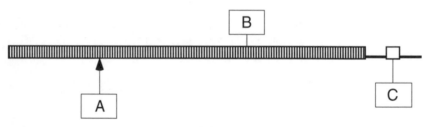

Fig. 8.22 Collision detection

Station C will abort its transmission immediately when it detects the collision, because the 'listen while you talk' function indicates the transmission has been corrupted. But station A will not be aware of the problem until the transmission commenced by station C has propagated the length of the cable and reached station A. To ensure that the collision is clearly recognized, a station detecting a collision not only aborts its transmission attempt but sends a short jamming signal as a collision indicator. This jamming signal propagates to all other stations, and any station that is transmitting, such as station A in the example above, will abort its attempt.

It is important that the transmission from station A in the case above is not completed before the collision is detected at station A. If we insist on this approach, then, when a transmission is completed by any station, we can be certain that no collisions have occurred, and that there is a reasonable expectation that the transmission will be received successfully. If a collision does occur, we know we need a retransmission. For collision detection to work successfully, there must be a maximum length of transmission medium and a minimum size of data packets for a given transmission speed. If the minimum packet size criteria was not observed, A could complete the transmission before the data and jamming signal generated at station C reached station A. Therefore, in the time it takes to transmit from one end of a transmission medium to the other end and then back again, it must not be possible to complete the transmission of the smallest-size packet of data. This means that the smallest packet size must take longer to transmit than twice the propagation delay along the longest length of the transmission medium that is established as a standard. These issues form the basic media access control techniques of the networks based on CSMA/CD.

It should be noted that collisions are not error conditions, but just a part of the contention resolution mechanism. In most networks implementing CSMA/CD, they occur quite infrequently, typically 20 to 30 times daily, although this will vary significantly under heavily loaded conditions and the conditions of different installations. If a significant number of collisions start occurring, either there is a fault on the network, e.g., an interface card is faulty and 'talking', or the network load has increased to a point where the overall load is too great and hence unsuitable for the existing LAN configuration.

Question 8.11 Are collisions more likely to occur when the size of each data transfer is normally large or when the size is normally small?

The IEEE 802.3 standard is based on CSMA/CD. It specifies the matching of transmission speeds against the maximum lengths for the various transmission media options set against the minimum frame size being transmitted. Ethernet is one such standard, and it offers a speed-length option such as 10base5, i.e., 10 Mbit/s using baseband signalling and 500 m of cable per segment, having defined a minimum frame size of 64 bytes. Other options include 10base2, 10baseT, 100baseT, etc., There are further high speed options available which are covered in detail in Chapter 9.

The important decision still to be made is that of what we do when a collision does occur and two (or more) transmission attempts are corrupted. As in all data transmissions, when we know a transfer has been unsuccessful, we determine a retransmission sequence. In the case of CSMA/CD, this involves backing off for a short time before re-attempting the transmission sequence. There is a timeout of random length at each station that is involved in the contention resolution before the transmission is retried. Each station selects a back-off period within the current 'window' of back-off time. Hence, if the current window of back-off time is 4, a station may choose to re-attempt after a delay of 0, 1, 2 or 3 back-off slot-times. In the event of further consecutive collisions, the back-off 'window' doubles in length, i.e., this is effectively a binary exponential back-off algorithm.

Question 8.12 What is a binary exponential back-off algorithm?

Because of the low number of collisions that normally occur, very few packets should ever be significantly delayed. However, there is no guarantee within the back-off algorithm that two stations attempting to transmit won't continue to collide (because they continue to randomly select the same back-off period), and hence no upper bound on access time can be guaranteed. The approach is therefore classed as non-deterministic and gives rise to concern in real-time system implementations, although maybe this concern is slightly misplaced because the issue that is really important is the probability of successful transmission. In such a case, component failures or delivery of a data packet which has become corrupted and now contains an error should equally be taken into account. In a normally operating CSMA/CD network, the probability of a component failure or corrupted data is likely to be greater than the probability of the back-off algorithm aborting its attempt because it has exceeded 216 time slot delays. This point will be raised again later.

Various collision detection systems have been implemented within CSMA/CD, and these include using both DC voltage level comparisons and Manchester encoding violations in baseband versions. Broadband collisions are usually detected by the originating station when reading data transmitted back from the headend and performing comparison checks.

Note that the maximum time to detect a collision in broadband is double that in the baseband situation. Why? Consider the situation in Fig. 8.12 where station C starts transmitting. The signal is propagated to the headend and is forwarded on the outbound channel. Consider the situation where, just before the signal reaches node D, station D wants to transmit. It senses 'idle' and hence transmits. D will know fairly soon that a collision has occurred, but station C will not know until the signal transmitted by station D has been propagated to the headend and the outbound signal reaches it. Hence the maximum time for a station is approximately four times the propagation time of the cable length, which is twice that in the baseband situation.

The situation may be further complicated when the range of a broadband cabling system is extended by placing the headend at the centre of the network.

Question 8.13 When the headend is placed at one end of the transmission medium, the longest time to detect a collision is for two stations next to each other at the other end of the cable. How does this change when the headend is placed in the middle of the cable as shown in Fig. 8.23?

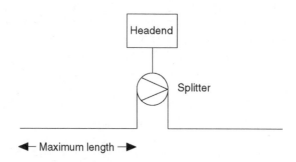

Fig. 8.23 Headend placed at centre

Carrier Sense Multiple Access Collision Avoidance (CSMA/CA)

The third category of CSMA involves collision avoidance, and several approaches are used in attempting to achieve this aim. The boundary point of what is collision avoidance and what is *p*-persistent is also a little fuzzy; many implementations utilize *p*-persistent schemes as a collision avoidance technique.

One major approach involves avoiding any collisions by calculating, for the standard being implemented, the minimum number of bits needing to be transmitted such that if a collision was going to occur, it would be during this period. The implementation then involves sending a reservation burst of this number of bits. At the end of this reservation burst, if there has been no collision, then the data can be sent with the certainty that no collision will occur. Certainly there is no major performance benefit to be gained using this approach, but there is a possible implementation gain benefit.

Another approach uses the idea of implementing slot times when the system is heavily loaded and collisions have occurred. The stations may use the slots following the end of a transmission on a strict priority base. When stations stop using their prioritized slot times the system returns to idle, and normal operations follow until the next period of heavy use is detected through multiple collisions occurring.

Finally, the most recent standard to adopt CSMA/CA is the wireless network standard of IEEE 802.11. In this environment there are no wires, and any communication between devices is based on using the airwaves as the transmission medium. A consequence of this is some devices may be hidden from others because of obstacles between them, or signal fading may result in a pair (or more) of devices never hearing each other. Because signals may not be heard by all of the devices on the network, collision detection is not an implementable option, and an alternative approach of collision avoidance has been chosen. In the IEEE 802.11 standards there are some specific terms used to describe their approach to collision avoidance, and those terms are introduced here.

With IEEE 802.11 CSMA/CA, the first stage for a station waiting to transmit is to sense if the transmission channel is idle or busy. This is the carrier sense part of the process. If it is busy, then the transmission has to back-off. If it senses that the channel is idle, then it transmits after a short delay. This delay time is specified as the Distributed Inter Frame Space (DIFS), and allows traffic of a higher priority to transmit before the data traffic on this station starts talking.

In addition to this back-off period, a station will back-off a randomly selected period. This approach is helpful, because it is just after a busy period that we are likely to have more than one station wishing to transmit. Hence, a randomly selected back-off period by each station reduces the probability of a 'clash' in the transmission. The randomly chosen period operated just like CSMA/CD. Initially the back-off is randomly chosen from either 1 or 2 slot periods, but if further clashes occur, the window of choice is doubled on each occasion so the probability of a 'clash' reduces on each re-attempt.

The station addressed in the transmission needs to make a response by sending a data link (OSI layer 2) acknowledgement back to the sender. It does this after waiting for a time which is shorter than DIFS, because responses are set at a higher priority. The delay time before the acknowledgement response is sent is called the Short Inter Frame Space (SIFS). The overall time for a station starting to transmit and receiving the response is explicitly declared in the duration field of an 802.11 frame, and is called the Network Allocation Vector (NAV). When a transmission starts, other stations hearing this transmission automatically defer their attempts to 'talk' for a period greater than the NAV time.

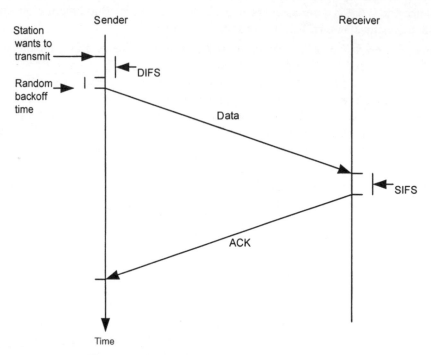

Fig. 8.24 IEEE 802.11 Data exchange sequence

Of course, when the network is busy, it will still experience transmission clashes or collisions, although individual stations do not implement collision detection circuitry, mainly because they may not be able to receive all transmissions.

Question 8.14 Why might a station not be able to hear that a collision has occurred?

In addition to NAV, the IEEE 802.11 standard also provides an additional feature to help reduce collisions. This allows reservation of access time to the transmission channel, using Request to Send (RTS) and Clear to Send (CTS) frames. The principle here is that both RTS and CTS are short frames, so the probability of a 'clash' in transmission during an attempt to make a reservation is reduced. At least part of either the RTS or CTS sequence should be heard by all stations, reducing the fading and hidden device issues identified earlier. Once the RTS/CTS exchange is complete, other stations should not transmit, ensuring that the data and ACK exchange between the two stations which made the reservation is not corrupted by other transmissions.

Additional features for priority traffic, using a point coordination function, are also defined in the standard. We simply need to know that that priority traffic can be accommodated.

Token passing

Within this subgroup, the basic approach is simply that, before a station is allowed to transmit, it must gain permission to do so. Generally, permission takes the form of a token that is passed between stations, and a station wishing to transmit must be in possession of the token before transmitting. This is effectively a speedy form of time division multiplexing without time being allocated to those stations that have nothing to say. Idle stations simply pass the token immediately on to the next station rather than holding it. The slotted ring technique is a derivative of token passing in so much as the circulating data structure or slot contains pre-established fields, one of which is the token field. All forms are logical rings, as shown in Fig. 8.25, but they may physically look like stars. In each case the bits (token or slot) circulate around the ring in one direction. The range of token passing access techniques is now considered in detail.

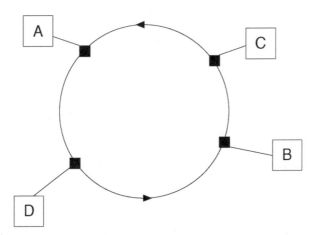

Fig. 8.25 Logical ring layout

Token ring

Although the original patent of Olof Soderblom for token ring access is fairly old, its use by IBM as its LAN architecture made this a major access technique; there are many look-alike products. The physical arrangement is historically drawn as in Fig. 8.26, but we have seen developments in Chapter 6 in which this physical representation has evolved. Thus it may be redrawn using central access boxes or hubs such as an IBM 8228 as shown in Fig. 8.27. The central points are known as multi-station access units (MSAUs or MAUs).

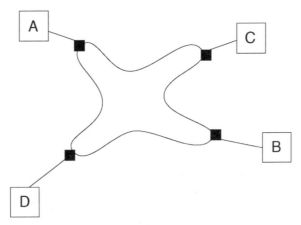

Fig. 8.26 Conventional physical ring layout

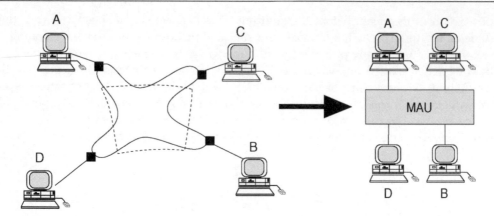

Fig. 8.27 Structured cabling approach to token ring access

Question 8.15 Why should we want to create a cabling layout that looks like that in Fig. 8.27 instead of that in Fig. 8.26?

You will note that Fig. 8.25 and Fig. 8.26 are essentially the same, although this may not be the case in other token passing techniques. Each station in the ring, unless it is powered off and effectively bypassed, introduces a delay of a few bits into the ring and plays an active role in the network. By active role, we simply mean that the station receives the bit and retransmits the value it detects, having regenerated the signal. In between the receive interface and the transmit interface of a station is a 1 bit register (see Fig. 8.28). It is this register that is inverted in value when a station is claiming a free token. (Detail on claiming a token will be covered shortly.) The combination of all this circuitry accounts for the delay of a few bits in each station.

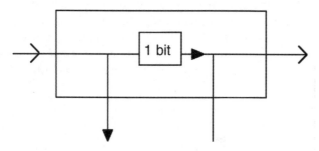

Fig. 8.28 Station listening

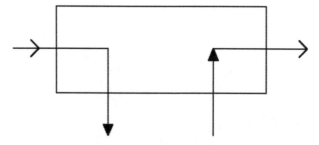

Fig. 8.29 Station talking

The ring consists of a complete circuit of interfaces with only one of the stations talking. Normally, a token is a single bit in the middle of a small data structure (typically 3 bytes). The combination of a number of bits being propagated along the medium and the summation of the number of bits delayed in the ring interface must support at least the size of the token. This requirement may need an artificial 'lengthening' to be introduced into the ring to ensure that there is a complete token support capability. For example, in a very small network the inherent delay probably won't reach 24 bits, and it is likely to be around 8 bits. The important thing to note is that each transmission has the bits spread around the ring. Indeed, it is likely that the front end of a data transmission has circulated completely around the ring and has returned to the sending station before the tail end of the transfer has even left the station. Fig. 8.29 shows how the sending station's circuits have opened to allow this condition to be supported. One station in the token ring is designated the active monitor and provides management of the ring. This station will have generated and provided any necessary lengthening of the ring in its internal buffers so that there is sufficient delay to support the token.

The token normally consists of a preamble to allow identification of the start of the data structure, some control field containing the token bit and a postamble field. The stations are kept in synchronization by the embedded clock of the differential Manchester encoding signalling method, although separate wire pairs could have been used to provide the clock.

Question 8.16 What sort of construction may the preamble in a token ring have?

At power-up, one of the interfaces becomes the active monitor and generates a token, usually the first to power up. This station continues to provide a monitoring function thereafter. Any of the stations are capable of performing this role, but only one becomes the active monitor, whilst other stations are able to stand by to assume this role should the active monitor fail or be switched off.

Thereafter, the token circulates unidirectionally around the ring, as shown in Fig. 8.30. Although this is shown as existing in a small zone of the ring, in reality it is likely to be spread much further around the topology.

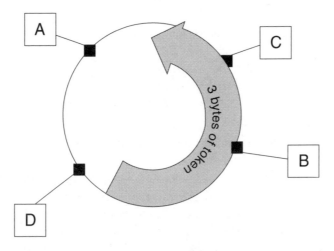

Fig. 8.30 Circulating token

Any station wishing to transmit must first claim the token. In practice, claiming the token consists of inverting the token bit in the token structure and making it unavailable to others whilst the station is transmitting. The last byte of the token (i.e., the delimiter) is held by this station. The data is then placed on the ring and circulated all the way round and back to the sender (see Fig. 8.31). The sending station places the delimiter byte back on the ring attached to the end of its data transmission. Hopefully, the intended destination is able to read the data structure as it passes through this destination station.

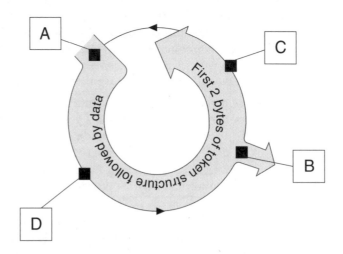

Fig. 8.31 Station A talking to Station B

On its return to the originating station, all the data is removed from the network. In the unlikely event of a failure of the originating station between the generation of the data and the data removal, the active monitor station will identify the problem, tidy up the ring and reset the token.

Question 8.17 Suggest how the monitor could identify such a failure condition.

Since the source can hold the token for a variable length of time (up to some predetermined maximum), variable length packets can be sent. Before the free token is replaced onto the network by the sender, two conditions must prevail:

a) all the data must have been sent (up to a maximum limit);

b) the start of the data must have returned to the sender (this rule is relaxed in some implementations such as the 16 Mbit/s version).

Once the conditions have been met, the free token is replaced on the ring and other stations are able to claim it. This mechanism ensures that only one token may be on the ring at any instant. Fig. 8.32 shows an example of the sending station A taking the data it has transmitted back off the ring and releasing a new token. The 4 Mbit/s implementation operates on the above rules but higher data rate token rings have relaxed the token release mechanism rules. The impact of this is that more than one

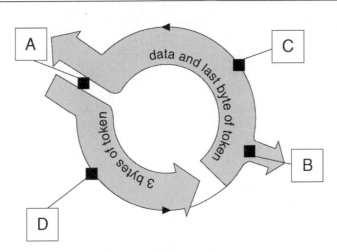

Fig. 8.32 Token release

packet of data may be circulating on the ring simultaneously, although there will still only ever be the one free token.

To provide a check on whether the data has been received correctly, a simple acknowledgement field can be introduced at the end of the data transmission (see Fig. 8.33). Automatic acknowledgement is achievable in token ring access because the sender gets the data structure back after the receiver has seen it. Hence, any bits that are added to the data structure by the receiver will be seen by the sender. This makes automatic acknowledgement possible. The receiving station can simply put a data received or station busy setting (or no response at all) into an acknowledgement field. On return to the sender this field can be examined to see whether a retransmission is needed or whether it has been received OK. Since the source station always sees the return of the data, this acknowledgement mechanism is automatic. It is certainly an advantage over the CSMA/CD LANs previously considered, although given the current reliability of LANs this may not be very significant.

Question 8.18 How many bits are needed to accommodate a range of acknowledgements to indicate received (OK or otherwise) or busy?

Priority reservation schemes can easily be introduced through the use of the control field within the token. This will allow some stations to have a higher priority of access to the ring than those stations designated as having a lower priority. As a non-free token/data structure is circulating, a reservation bid can be made by a station wishing to gain access at a priority level which is attributed to that station. A station with a higher priority can 'trump' a previous setting with its own priority if it requires access. This priority reservation bid is recognized by the station currently holding the token and, when it replaces a free token on the ring, it does so with a priority field set with any reservation priority bid if one existed. This free token with a 'high' priority setting circulates to the bidding station. Hence, the station with this high priority can get early access. After use, the station that set the priority field high must also decrease the priority back to the previous level when the token becomes free.

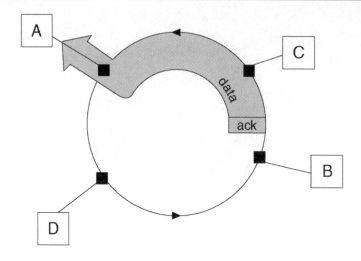

Fig. 8.33 Acknowledgement techniques

In practice, this feature is used sparingly and used for particular types of traffic. Examples are time constrained traffic such as video. One of the benefits of the token ring technique is that the system performance is stable and predictable under the heaviest loading conditions. We know in advance how long it is going to take for a token to rotate to any station even under the heaviest of loading conditions where every station claims the token as it passes around the ring. This is known as a deterministic performance.

Token bus

In the case of a token bus, there is a major distinction between the physical and logical arrangements (see Figs 8.34 and 8.35).

The control of access to the bus is handled through the use of the token, which must be held by a station before it can transmit. The token is a small data structure or packet which is passed from station to station. The order of passing is normally based upon the address number of the station interfaces. A typical logical arrangement of a token bus is shown in Fig. 8.35. Each station learns the address of the next station in the logical sequence and sets this address in the destination field when releasing the token. Hence, the token is a more complex data structure than in the token ring arrangement including a destination address.

Unlike in a token ring, where the data structure representing the token ring is spread around the ring and where each station only holds a few bits of the token at any given moment in time, the token bus stations are passed the whole of the data structure in its entirety. Once the token is held, then one or more packets of data may be transmitted. The maximum token holding time is timer based. The token is then released and passed to the next station in the address sequence. If a station receives the token and has no data to send, then it passes the token on immediately.

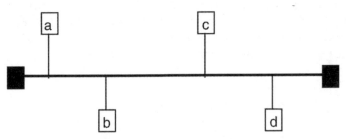

Fig. 8.34 Physical token bus arrangement

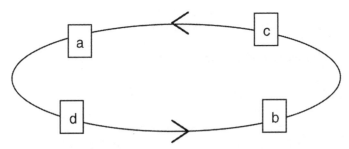

Fig. 8.35 Logical token bus arrangement

There is no central control of the operation, so each station holds the address of its predecessor and successor. Clearly there needs to be a mechanism of establishing these addresses both at initialization time and at regular periods throughout the day when stations may leave or join the network.

At initialization all stations may attempt to claim the token and a claim token frame is sent which includes a data field of a length that is dictated, initially, by the most significant two bits of the station's address. Whilst sending the claim token frame, the station listens to see if other stations are still talking after it has finished, i.e., those with a higher address in this zone of the address. Should others still be talking, this station withdraws. If this station alone is talking, it has the highest address and claims the token, but if other stations are also talking for the same duration it repeats the above process based on the next two bits of the address. This is a clever way of ensuring that the station with the highest address claims the token.

To build the logical ring, the station with the highest address that now holds the token needs to add successor stations with lower addresses in descending address order (see Fig. 8.36). The addition of successors, i.e., the addition of other stations to the ring, is achieved using a response window procedure. The station holding the token may send a solicit successor frame with an address range which starts as a narrow range but which can be widened until a response is received or it is determined that there are no other active stations. If a station is seeking to join the logical ring it waits until a solicit successor frame is broadcast with an address range covering its own address. When such a broadcast is received the station will make a bid to join.

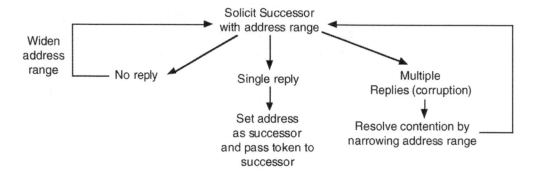

Fig. 8.36 Sequence to join the logical ring

If more than one station responds then a resolve contention sequence is entered to identify each station. If only one responds this becomes the successor and it is given the token to attempt to solicit further successors or make the ring logically complete if no further successor exists. The logical ring is now complete with all the stations linked together in descending address order.

A similar sequence is commenced when a station recognizes that it has not been passed a token within the expected time sequence and presumes that the up-line station has failed.

Typically, token bus systems are broadband systems, although carrierband is allowable. Because of the deterministic nature of the token passing performance, any delay is predictable, and hence use is made of this potential real-time characteristic in those application areas that require such predictability. The Manufacturing Automation Protocol (MAP) established by General Motors plus a number of other network and control suppliers in that sector established the standard.

Slotted ring

The slotted ring technique of controlling access was popularized by the work undertaken at Cambridge University, and the original-implementation in the UK was known as the Cambridge Ring. Although the Cambridge Ring is now essentially obsolete, the slotted ring technique is still being implemented in other network implementations. Hence the access method is covered here.

At power-up, a unique station known as the monitor station generates a slot or minipacket which circulates around the ring. As in the token ring case, the slot occupies bit positions in a number of repeaters or station interfaces and along the connecting cable runs, and hence the slot is physically spread around the ring (see Fig. 8.37). Individual repeaters typically introduce a small delay of 1 bit to 3 bits. In order to

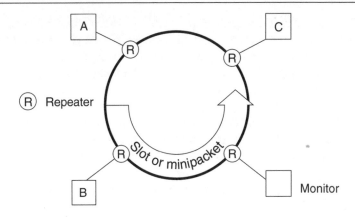

Fig. 8.37 Slotted ring

provide sufficient 'space' to hold a complete slot or minipacket structure, the monitor station will artificially lengthen the ring by providing an 'elastic' buffer.

Typically, in a small ring, only one minipacket is supported, although it is permissible to support multiple minipackets in a large ring with a large natural delay of bits in the ring interfaces. These rings are operating on twisted pair cable at 10 Mbit/s, although other media such as fibre optics are also used. On faster speed rings operating at 100 Mbit/s it is usual to see multiple packets circulating.

The slot or minipacket is a data structure that, in addition to the control fields, is designed to hold data. Hence a station wishing to talk awaits the arrival of an empty minipacket. On such an arrival, the station inserts its data and, upon return of that minipacket, will effectively remove the data by setting the packet back to the empty status. The slot is not then reusable immediately by that station. Instead, the empty slot must be passed downstream for other stations to use. It is also not usable on the next subsequent rotation.

Indeed the maximum slot utilization that a station can achieve is one slot in every $(n + 2)$ slots for an n-slot ring. The impact is that, in a 10 Mbit/s system with one slot, the maximum data throughput by an individual station is 1.3 Mbit/s, taking into account the packet structure overheads.

Question 8.19 Why do the overheads of the packet structure affect the data throughput rate?

To ensure that a slot doesn't constantly circulate around the ring in a full state because the source has become inoperable and has not removed the data, the monitor station polices the ring, using a monitor bit, to ensure that a full slot doesn't pass by twice. If that were to occur, the monitor would take corrective action to clean up the ring. This would mean that any station that was using the slot would not only change the status bit from full to empty, but also reset the monitor bit to zero. The monitor station should never see an incoming slot with the monitor bit set unless there is a problem.

To ensure that the acknowledgement protocol is efficient and simple, the circulating minipacket contains a field at the end of its data structure. This allows the receiver station to indicate receipt of data, that it is busy, or that it is currently locked on to another sender, or to provide a null response to indicate inoperability. The receiver is then in a position to know whether a retransmission is necessary. Any acknowledgement at this level simply indicates receipt (or otherwise) of the minipacket. It does not imply that the whole of the data has been received by the station or that the overall checksum is validated. Because the size of the data field in a minipacket is small, perhaps only 2 bytes, any data transfer between two stations consists of a series of 2 byte transfers until the whole transfer is complete. Overall checksum validation occurs when all the minipackets of the original packet size have been received at the destination and have been reassembled.

Dedicated lines

Demand priority

The demand priority access approach is designed to operate with LANs on an intelligent hub, based on a star topology (see Fig. 8.38).

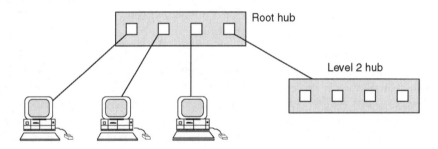

Fig. 8.38 Hub arrangement

To support sufficient node connections, the top level or root hub may have further hubs connected to it to cascade out further node connection capabilities. A station wishing to transmit will signal a request (demand) to the hub. This demand is met on a round robin scanning basis within the hub to ensure that every port on the hub has an equal opportunity to transmit. Hence the whole approach is deterministic.

When the round robin scan selects a port that has issued a demand, the node sends a data packet to the hub. This is directed from the hub only on the outbound port that is required to reach the destination. As a result, there is an in-built network security benefit, since only the hubs and the destination should 'see' this traffic. During this node selection and transfer only one packet of data is transferred.

Any lower level hub will also undertake to scan all of its ports, and can issue a demand to the higher level hub if one or more of its ports is wishing to transmit. When the node selected on a scan is a lower level hub, then more than one packet may be sent, with each port of this lower level hub having the opportunity to send the data that it had previously signalled as a request. Indeed, if this lower level hub supports n nodes, then up to n data packets could be transmitted if all the ports were active.

Consider the configuration shown in Fig. 8.39 when it is operating in normal mode. Hubs with four down-link ports are used (they would normally be 12, 24, or 48 port hubs, but we have used a four-port hub for simplicity and clarity in describing the scanning process). It is worth noting here that each hub also has an up-link port to connect to a higher level hub where appropriate, but again for clarity these ports are not shown.

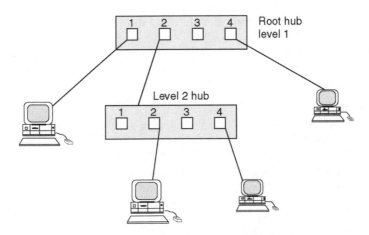

Fig. 8.39 Round robin in hub topology

In a round-robin poll, the packet service order would be 1-1 (level 1, port 1), 2-2, 2-4 and 1-4.

The demand priority access control has been designed to support LANs of high speed, typically 100 Mbit/s. It is recognized in such LANs that the bandwidth requirements of current developments in applications such as multimedia are higher than for previous LAN implementations. Indeed, some applications such as video may require priority over other traffic.

To support this, high priority and normal priority levels of access are available. An application requiring a high level service will pass this priority request to the Media Access Control (MAC) packet from the high level protocols. The demand for access is signalled to the hub using link status control tones at the appropriate level of priority. Hence the simple round robin arbitration needs modification to service the two different demand levels, taking high priority demands first. Once all these have been met, the normal priority traffic is considered.

If normal priority traffic has been delayed beyond a preset threshold (considered to be the reasonable wait time for the installation), then it has its priority level automatically raised. This ensures that no node is unduly or excessively delayed, even when there is a significant amount of other traffic on the LAN.

Each network segment can have the hubs configured to either Ethernet or token ring data packet formats. This approach of keeping the well established protocols of the

Ethernet and token ring architectures was a careful consideration. It allows existing networks based on these network architectures to evolve and grow into the demand priority approach without everything having to be changed – evolution rather than revolution! We will see later how these approaches may be integrated.

Fast switching

The current installation of 10baseT Ethernet in a star configuration, as shown in Fig. 6.11, provided the opportunity for network designers to reassess the media access approach. The original CSMA/CD concepts were based on shared media access, but the star configuration provides what is essentially a dedicated line to each device. Given the existing LAN investment in many installations in terms of both cabling and network interface cards, the requirement to protect that investment can be easily recognized. Equally, the increasing demand for additional bandwidth is now being observed. Fig. 8.19 indicated that network performance can decrease as loads increase and we will cover this issue in more detail in Chapter 13. Fast switching is designed to allow multiple sessions or circuits to be established each carrying their own traffic, which is not seen by other hosts. Such an approach makes switches scalable, i.e., we can add more switches to a network and support more hosts without having a large negative impact on the overall performance. This is because each host to switch to host connection is a separate network segment and constitutes its own collision domain. Traffic is rapidly switched between the input and output ports on the switch to create these multiple circuits, with each pair of switched input/output ports providing the full data transfer rate of the LAN.

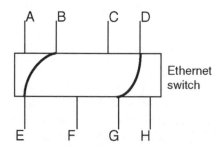

Fig. 8.40 Ethernet switch

Let us take two examples to demonstrate the technique. If station E in Fig. 8.40, which may be a PC with an Ethernet network interface card (NIC), wishes to talk to station B, it follows CSMA/CD access principles on its local connection to the switch. Provided that access using CSMA/CD rules permits the NIC to talk, the packet is sent to the switch. The switch sees the layer 2, media access control, destination address and puts the data out on the port where the host with this address is connected. The switch learns the addresses of all the devices connected to the LAN configuration, using a broadcasting technique when it doesn't know the proposed destination address, so all NICs on connected devices hear the broadcast. The switch is then able to build up a picture of the location of each MAC address by listening for the responses to such broadcasts. This is similar in approach to the way bridges learn addresses, covered in more detail in Chapter 11. If an NIC remains dormant for a period of time, then the switch 'forgets' the address in a process known as aging. This allows a device to be moved in the network and the new location to be automatically 're-learnt'. The aging parameter can be locally set, frequently at about 300 seconds.

In a second example, let us assume that station D now wishes to talk to G whilst the earlier data transfer is still ongoing. It is able to do this on exactly the same basis, and a second data transmission stream is established. We can, in principle, establish as many concurrent links as there are available pairs of connections on the switch. Each switch port is designated to operate at a specific speed, e.g., 10 Mbit/s or 100 Mbit/s. Switches may support different speeds on different ports. The switch is able to perform auto-negotiation with the NIC, so if the NIC supports both 10 Mbit/s and 100 Mbit/s but the switch's port is able to support only 10 Mbit/s, then auto-negotiation configures the connection at 10 Mbit/s.

The switch clearly plays an important role, and various types of switch are currently available in the marketplace. Some switches are able to establish the link between the two parts as soon as the Ethernet frame header containing the destination address has arrived from the source station. These are known as cut-through switches, and data is streamed through to the switch's destination port, which can send the Ethernet frame out on that connection, but still observing the CSMA/CD rules on that connection. Hence, it may have to buffer the traffic in memory on occasions. Other switches do not operate as quickly, and complete packets have to be sent to the switch before the outgoing link is identified and established. These switches are operating as store-and-forward devices. A cut-through switch often has the capability of falling back to a store and forward mode under operating conditions where high error rates are being experienced. There is a third mode of operation, sometimes referred to as fragment free, but it is currently not a dominant mode of operation.

Different internal architecture of the switch, including its processing speeds and bus structures support these different approaches. These architectures include matrix arrangements, shared memory or a high-speed bus approach.

Question 8.20 What is the main benefit of a fast switch over the standard 10baseT hub approach?

For stations wishing to pass data frequently between themselves (e.g., graphic workstations or image processing devices), switching removes many of the restrictions encountered in the 10baseT or 100baseT approach. Details of the 10baseT or 100baseT approach are given in Chapter 9. The release of Gigabit Ethernet products has already led to the development of switches which support 1 Gbit/s, and the proposed new standard of 10 Gbit/s Ethernet in 2002 may well see future developments in the switch area.

Inherently, Ethernet is a half-duplex operation, since we have a single channel to send data in either direction. We use CSMA/CD to control the circuit to ensure that there is only one transmission on this circuit at any one time. Given that category 5, twisted pair cable has 'spare' pairs, some devices requiring higher transmission speeds or greater bandwidth could be given a second pair of wires in the cable to create a full-duplex arrangement. Effectively, traffic will be sent in one direction on one pair and in the other direction on a second pair. A second Ethernet card will typically be required in the device to support the second channel (see Fig. 8.41).

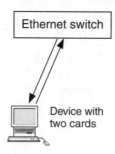

Fig. 8.41 Full-duplex Ethernet

Such a configuration may be ideal for a busy file server on a network because it can receive data at higher speeds such as 100 Mbit/s and send at 100 Mbit/s simultaneously. Because we are using dedicated pairs in the switch, there can be no collisions on the circuit and collision detection is therefore redundant in full-duplex operation of the switch. All of the available bandwidth can be utilized in each direction. Early upgrades from 10baseT networks to switches were frequently based on 2 ports operating at 100Mbit/s to support servers, with the remaining ports operating at 10Mbit/s supporting 10baseT hubs or direct connections.

Further questions

(There are answers to the questions marked with an asterisk at the end of the book.)

1. *Explain why an encoding technique is used in most LANs.
2. *Is baseband transmission likely to be more expensive than broadband transmission to implement?
3. *Is it possible to put a headend device in the middle of a cable run? What would be the impact on the maximum cable lengths?
4. *How many adjacent 6 MHz broadband channels are we likely to jointly use to transmit a 10 Mbit/s signal?
5. *Is the collision detection enhancement to CSMA worthwhile?
6. *Why should we bother with the extra cost of a structured cabling approach?
7. The token ring has an inherent automatic acknowledgement built into the access control/data transfer mechanism. Does CSMA/CD have such an inherent automatic acknowledgement mechanism?
8. Why did the manufacturing organizations with real-time applications, such as General Motors, prefer token bus networks to 802.3 access techniques?
9. How does a station 'join the ring' in a token bus LAN?
10. A slotted ring LAN such as a Cambridge Ring has 2 bytes of data carried in a minipacket. If a station wishes to send 256 bytes of data, how will it achieve this in such a network?
11. Why do we need monitors in ring networks?

Answer 8.1   The answer depends on whether the receiving clock is running 10 per cent faster or slower than that of the sender. If it is slower then it will sample the transmitted signal 90 times, and if it is faster it will sample the transmitted signal 110 times. In either case, the wrong number of bits is going to be read.

Answer 8.2   In baseband techniques the transmitted signal occupies the whole of the bandwidth and hence it is a single channel communication. It is normal to create multiple channels for broadband signalling where frequency channels are created from the wide bandwidth supported by the transmission medium. We will see more details of broadband transmission later in the chapter.

Answer 8.3   The encoded signal is shown in Fig. 8.42.

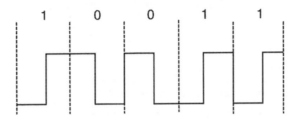

Fig. 8.42 Signal encoded using Manchester encoding

Answer 8.4   No. Indeed the whole idea of having a preamble is to give the receiving station time to synchronize with the transmission. OK, so several bits are missed, and the number missed will be unknown. But once synchronization has been achieved, the receiver determines that the end of the preamble has occurred when two consecutive 1s arrive. The following bits are then part of the data structure.

Answer 8.5   The encoded signal is shown in Fig. 8.43.

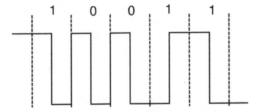

Fig. 8.43 Signal encoded using differential Manchester encoding

Answer 8.6   No. Neither J nor K are valid signals, and therefore they cannot represent any data signal. They are exclusively used in a particular sequence to represent the start and the end of the token or data transfer.

Answer 8.7   The encoded signal is shown in Fig. 8.44.

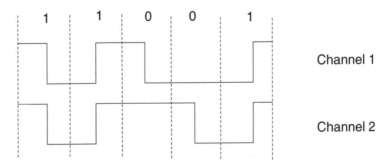

Fig. 8.44 Signal encoded using phase modulation

Answer 8.8   This is quite a hard question, and it requires you to put a few concepts together. Both broadband transmission and carrierband transmission use analogue signals. In order to regenerate these analogue signals at an appropriate point along the transmission medium we will need to use an amplifier. Amplifiers only amplify in one direction, and they offer a high impedance in the other direction. Hence, if a system operates with amplifiers in the circuit, it is a unidirectional communications channel. This restriction does not apply to baseband signals, which are digital in construction. It should be noted, however, that a token ring, which is a baseband environment, implements a unidirectional approach.

Answer 8.9   There are two major drawbacks. Firstly, there is twice as much cable to buy and install, and secondly each station needs two taps to be attached, one for each of the cables. It is this second point that is the expensive issue. The trade-off is therefore the extra cost against the extra bandwidth. If the network is a large, multi-purpose system, the extra costs may be justified.

Answer 8.10   The result would be a corruption of the data and all the transmission attempts would have been useless. It would then be up to the protocols that had been implemented to determine how we were going to recover from this situation, i.e., how retransmission was going to be implemented.

Answer 8.11   The larger the size of the data elements being normally transmitted is, the longer it will take for that transmission to complete. It is therefore more likely that other stations will be queuing up for an opportunity to transmit if a long transfer has been under way. This will result in a greater probability of a collision occurring when the long transmission has ended. A short transmission is less likely to have held the communications channel long enough for more than one other station to be waiting for access. This makes CSMA/CD particularly good for short, bursty traffic.

Answer 8.12   When a collision occurs, the station will back off from retransmitting for either zero or one time slot, i.e., a 2^1 interval range. If a further collision now occurs, then the back-off becomes zero, one, two or three slot times, i.e., a 2^2 interval range. If collisions continue, then the back-off range will grow to 2^n interval choices. If 16 consecutive collisions occur the transmission is aborted. Hence the maximum value for n is 16.

Answer 8.13   In this case, either the previous condition or the situation where the stations are at opposite ends of the cable will be the worst case or take the longest time to detect a collision occurrence.

Answer 8.14   Because of obstacles, etc., not all stations can hear every other station when they are transmitting. Hence, one station could be transmitting to a base station whilst a third station is unaware of any transmissions. As a result, the third station may start transmitting, and be unaware that a data collision has occurred.

Answer 8.15   Simply because, when a fault develops (as it surely will), then it is easier to isolate the problem when there are central points such as MSAUs in the cable structure. The more intelligence that is built into the MSAU, the easier fault-finding becomes. In an unstructured system you could spend some time just locating where the fault was.

Answer 8.16   If you remember from earlier in the chapter, we can use the encode violation conditions of J and K to uniquely identify the start and end of the token data structure.

Answer 8.17   If the data construct had set aside a single bit so that the monitor could invert it when it went by, this could (and should) be reset by the original sending station. If this sending station has developed a fault, then the data construct passes the monitor for a second time. The monitor recognizes this by the continuing inverted state of this monitor bit. The station acting as the monitor then proceeds to clean up the ring and release a new token, etc.

Answer 8.18   Typically two bits. One to say whether the address was recognized by the intended destination station and the other indicating whether the data was copied by the destination station or ignored because it was busy. They are known as the A and C bits, i.e., 'address recognized' and 'data copied', respectively.

Answer 8.19   Every network has a maximum bit throughput rate. We have seen that, to ensure that a delivery is successful, the data we wish to deliver is wrapped up in a protocol (including checksums, etc.). The greater the number of additional bits of protocol that are transmitted to enable the data to be transferred, the lower is the percentage use of the transmission rate for sending the original data bits.

Answer 8.20   Each switched connection has a typical data rate of 10 Mbit/s or 100 Mbit/s. Since multiple connections can be established, multiple 10 Mbit/s or 100 Mbit/s circuits can be operated simultaneously. Hence the hub, which remains part of a single collision domain, cannot have increasing traffic levels without performance problems arising if you continue to add to the configuration. A switch, on the other hand, has multiple collision domains, one for each NIC to switch port.

9 Popular LAN standards

1. Introduction

The work of the IEEE 802 committee was introduced in Chapter 8 when we examined the issues relating to signalling and access. In this chapter, the various LAN standards are examined in some detail. These standards, together with the signalling and access elements, complete most of the bottom two layers in the OSI model. Fig. 7.6 showed the media access 802.*x* positional equivalence in the OSI model. It should be noted that there have been a number of products within each of the standards (see Fig. 9.1). This is not meant to be an exhaustive list and it is under constant development.

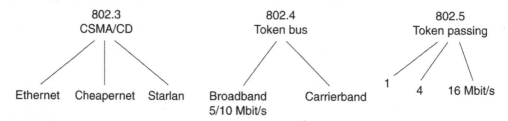

Fig. 9.1 Early 802.*x* standards

Additionally, there are networks that fall outside the earlier definitions of local area networks because of the geographical distances involved or their very high speed capabilities. The IEEE 802.*x* committees originally specified 20 Mbit/s as the upper boundary point of their remit but current products are operating at 100 Mbit/s, 155 Mbit/s and above.

It is worth considering those developments here. One of the most important, although it was originally outside the IEEE 802 committee's remit, was the ANSI Fibre Distributed Data Interface (FDDI) and FDDI II standards. This was a particularly interesting development and it has frequently been used to provide backbone network capabilities. Secondly, the IEEE 802.6 committee has, eventually, agreed on a standard for metropolitan area networks (MANs), and there were early developments and implementations of this in Australia, the USA and Germany. The UK has seen implementations of MANs, which are becoming particularly popular in the university sector where groups of institutions are connected together via a MAN which in turn offers interconnection onto SuperJanet. A copper wire medium version of FDDI has been developed that is called the Copper Distributed Data Interface (CDDI). The IEEE 802.12 committee has also established a range of 100 Mbit/s LAN standards based on Ethernet, and Gigagit Ethernet is also now available.

There has also been significant developments in a standard called Asynchronous Transfer Mode (ATM), which is separately covered in Chapter 10.

Question 9.1   Why might CDDI be preferable to FDDI?

---

2. IEEE 802.3 standard

The original supporters of the IEEE 802.3 approach were Xerox, Intel and DEC (sometimes referred to as DIX), with Xerox playing a major role. The approach was directed at the automated office environment to provide connectivity for engineering workstations or general computer-to-computer linkage. Originally, a range of speeds were supported between 1 Mbit/s and 10 Mbit/s, all utilizing the CSMA/CD access control technique. It is upon this standard that many early local area network products were based, such as DECnet.

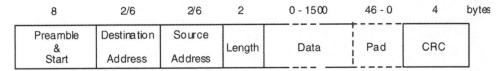

Fig. 9.2 802.3 Ethernet frame structure

The 802.3 standard allows for a variable length of data transfer up to a maximum of 1500 bytes in any individual frame. If we examine the frame structure shown in Fig. 9.2, it can be seen that there is always a minimum data and pad length of 46 bytes, i.e., if the data length field is 0 bytes, the pad has 46 bytes. The pad field reduces to 0 bytes when the data field increases to 46 or more bytes. This ensures that there is a minimum size frame of 64 bytes, including header bytes, which is required to ensure that collision detection works effectively. The data element carried in the Ethernet frame structure is the Logical Link Control (LLC) frame, i.e., the data payload is the protocol resident in the top of layer 2, which is immediately above the Media Access Control (MAC) structure and is normally the IEEE 802.2 LLC.

The preamble field, which is a series of 0s and 1s, allows the receiving stations to synchronize exactly with the signalling speed of the transmitting station. The final byte in this zone is the start delimiter which concludes with two consecutive 1s to indicate the end of this synchronizing activity.

The two address fields of destination and source give rise to a number of interesting discussion points. Firstly, the address lengths may either be 16 bit or 48 bit fields, this being a local implementation choice. Once the option has been selected, it must be consistent for all stations on that particular LAN. The addresses are the hardware addresses of the individual network interface cards which connect devices to the network. They are always used on the LAN to identify the exact station IDs between which any packet transfers take place. The address is often referred to as a device's Ethernet address or MAC address.

If 48 bit fields are implemented, then the address is predetermined and will be unique worldwide. The standards committee allocates blocks of addresses to the network manufacturers, who use the allocation to provide unique addresses for each Ethernet card. These are permanently set during the process of manufacturing the Ethernet card. Hence the local installer does not have to be involved in allocating numbers, but clearly, if an Ethernet card is changed at a station because of a fault, that station gets a new Ethernet hardware address! This is an important point, which we need to examine later, but if we connect the LAN to a wide area network to allow access to users on remote

119

LANs, then there needs to be a mechanism in place which removes the requirement of needing to know that remote users' Ethernet addresses. You couldn't possibly keep an up-to-date record of every hardware address of all the stations you might want to contact around the world, especially if these hardware addresses were to change if a card is replaced. It will be seen in Chapter 12 that unique Internet addresses (a different addressing mechanism operating at higher levels of the OSI model) can be globally allocated. These global addresses are associated with the Ethernet hardware addresses within the local network using an address mapping process.

If the 16 bit addressing field approach is specially selected by an installation, then unique addresses can be locally assigned to each connected station which can then remain the same at each station, even when NIC changes are necessitated. These addresses will be unique on any given network, but may be duplicated on separate, independent networks. In most networks the 48 bit addressing mechanism is used, which requires no action by the network administration. It is this addressing mechanism that is implemented by default. As each Ethernet frame is sent onto the shared medium, all the interfaces look at the first 48 bits. Each NIC checks to see if this address compares with its own. If it does, then the card reads the rest of the frame and passes it to the software running on the station which it is connecting to the network. If the interface doesn't recognize the address, it ignores the frame and does not pass it to its host station.

A broadcast (all stations hear) or multi-cast (a selected group of stations hear) facility is also provided through the use of the first two (high-order) bits of the address field. This facility will be required when the network protocols attempt to map the local Ethernet addresses with the global Internet or Internet Protocol (IP) address.

The length field can be interpreted in two different ways depending on the detail behind the standard being implemented (802.3 or Ethernet are variations of the same standard). Since the length of the data/pad combination can be anything between 46 bytes and 1500 bytes, then a length field is required to provide a pointer to the boundary point between the end of the data and where the beginning of the 32 bit cyclic redundancy check field occurs. If a fixed length LLC data component occurs, as in the case of fixed format LLC protocol management commands, the length field can alternatively be used to indicate the type of structure contained in the data field. Also, the length field can be used to interpret the types of higher level protocol being carried, e.g., to indicate that this is TCP/IP data. This can be useful, particularly where several services coexist on the same cabling structure. For example, Novell and TCP/IP protocols can coexist on the same LANs. 'Coexist' doesn't mean each protocol is understood by all stations. An analogy here is a number of people in a room speaking a range of foreign languages. The spoken word will be heard by 'all', but not necessarily understood.

A number of variations are allowed within the 802.3 standard which dictate the maximum length of a segment, the type of cable, the type of tap or connection and the connection spacing. Each of these variations is now considered, since they play an important role in the design of the cable installation or network topology. Although almost all new installation work is based on twisted pair cable or fibre, there is a legacy of a few remaining networks based on coaxial cable. The approach taken in this text is to cover them all in their historical order of development.

10base5 standard

The 10base5 standard within the IEEE 802.3 standard is the 10 Mbit/s, baseband, 500 m segment (10base5) version. It is often referred to as Ethernet, although Ethernet is frequently used (albeit technically incorrectly) as a generic term applicable to the whole 802.3 set of derivatives. 10base5 allows a maximum of two repeaters between any two points on the network. In some installations this may be interpreted or specified slightly differently. The important thing is that we must ensure that between any two network devices there can only be a maximum of three segments which have connected devices. The difference between the interpretations relates to how a point-to-point link is defined. A point-to-point link is simply a segment with no active devices connected. In the strictest interpretation which we will consider there are two repeaters (see Fig. 9.3). This gives us a configuration of three segments joined together with two repeaters. Each segment can have devices connected to it. Each segment is up to 500 m long, so the length limit is 1500 m.

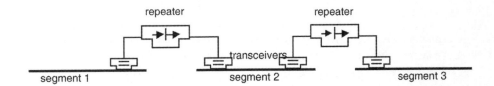

Fig. 9.3 1500 m Ethernet configuration

Of course this may present a difficulty in reaching the range of distances that need to be covered by a LAN. The standard allows for up to two point-to-point links (or segments with no active devices connected) to be added. This can extend the distances to reach some of the more distant locations on a proposed LAN site. The point-to-point segment(s) can be one link of up to 1000 m or two links of up to 500 m each.

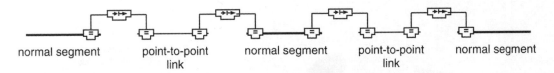

Fig. 9.4 2500 m Ethernet configuration

In the arrangement shown in Fig. 9.4 there are four repeaters and the maximum distance is extended to 2500 m. There remain, of course, only three active segments between any two connected devices.

The cable type is the special amber- or yellow-coloured Ethernet coaxial cable. This is 50 Ω cable and it is normally supplied with black ring markings every 2.5 m to indicate the points at which the transceiver connection taps may be placed. Each end of the coaxial cable segment needs to be terminated with a resistor to prevent signal reflections. When a signal reaches the end of the cable it just 'dies'. It is possible to use fibre optics for the point-to-point link.

To physically make a connection for a station onto the coaxial cable we need a transceiver with a tap capability. The taps and the transceiver units (sometimes referred to as MAUs) must not number more than 100 taps per 500 m segment. The tap and transceiver shown in Fig. 9.5 are normally one unit, as shown in Fig. 9.6.

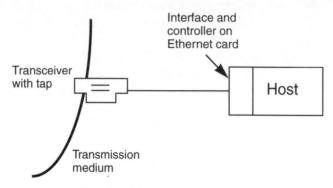

Fig. 9.5 10base5 components

The taps typically come in two styles. For a non-intrusive connector, a small hole needs to be made in the cable at the location of a black ring marking. The connector is frequently a 'bee-sting' arrangement with a spring loading connector pin which is placed in the hole to make contact with the coaxial cable's copper core. This is then clamped into place on the cable.

The alternative style is an intrusive connector, for which the coaxial cable needs to be cut and the ends connected to the MAU to re-form a continuous path.

Fig. 9.6 Transceivers and taps
(© Allied Telesyn, reprinted with permission)

Fig. 9.6 shows several transceivers. The taps shown on top of the transceivers are interchangeable, but in Fig. 9.6 a 10base5 tap is shown in the bottom left and 10base2 taps at the top. These taps are intrusive, so that the cable must be cut.

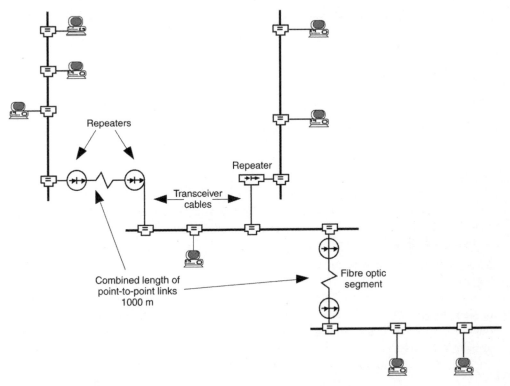

Fig. 9.7 Maximum 802.3 standard configuration

Question 9.2   Fig. 9.7 shows a LAN with four active segments. Does this conform to the requirement of there being no more than three segments between any two stations?

It is important to note here that the position of one of the segments becomes most important. Effectively, one of the segments forms a backbone and other segments become spurs off that segment (see Fig. 9.8). Hence the physical location of this backbone within a LAN layout is an important decision. Depending on where it is positioned, the ability to easily reach other locations is enabled or denied.

In total, no more than 1024 nodes may be attached to a maximum configuration. It should be remembered that in this set-up the maximum distance between any two points on the system is 2500 m (i.e., 2800 m between workstations on the system if each 50 m maximum transceiver cable run is included plus a point-to-point link). This limit has been set as a result of determining the maximum distance over which CSMA/CD

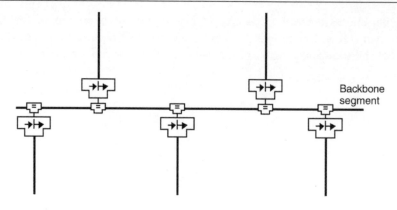

Fig. 9.8 Multiple segment Ethernet

can successfully be implemented with the minimum packet size of 64 bytes shown in Fig. 9.2. The delay in signalling from one end of the network to the furthest distance and back must be shorter than the length of the transmission time for the minimum frame size. In practice, this means that the delay must be limited to fewer than 512 slot times, which at 10 Mbit/s is a frame transfer time of 51.2 μs.

If we need to extend beyond these limits, then two (or more) networks may be joined together using a bridging device (see Fig. 9.9). This approach allows CSMA/CD to operate separately on both sides of the bridge, and the bridge acts as a store-and-forward device. Frequently, this is referred to as each side of the bridge having separate collision domains. Hence, we are operating what would function as two separate LANs, but they appear to the users and the administration as a single integrated LAN. Further details on the role and function of both repeaters and bridges are presented in Chapter 11.

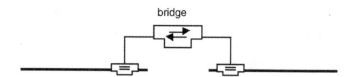

Fig. 9.9 Bridge connection to extend LAN length

Question 9.3   In Fig. 9.9, if CSMA/CD operates separately on both sides, how is a packet of data passed from one network to the other, i.e., how is access gained to the medium on the other side?

Now let us consider the issue of connecting devices onto the segment. The restriction imposed of a 2.5 m spacing between transceiver connections can be awkward where there are clusters of stations in a small area such as a laboratory. If the stations have simple or slow interfaces (e.g., dumb terminals), then the usual configuration is to connect these via a terminal server or Network Interface Unit (NIU) to the network. The NIU only requires a single transceiver connection. The NIU and transceiver jointly provide the necessary Ethernet framing and media access for the connected devices. The alternative would be expensive Ethernet connections for each of the relatively cheap devices plus coils of Ethernet cable looped between the devices to ensure 2.5 m spacing between the connections. Terminal servers or NIUs overcome this problem neatly, as shown in Fig. 9.10.

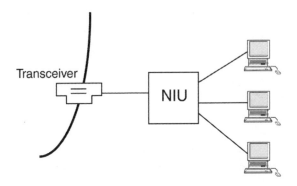

Fig. 9.10 Terminal connection to network

Question 9.4   Does an NIU or terminal server act as a concentrator?

Where a station requires its own Ethernet interface and connectivity, this is implemented via an Ethernet card in the PC or workstation. Fig. 9.11 shows the transceiver cable or drop cable connection to the Ethernet card's D connector. The other end is connected to a transceiver to complete the tap connection on the transmission medium. The transceiver cable is frequently known as an AUI cable and it may be up to 50 m in length. The transceiver cable also carries a power supply from the device to the transceiver, since the transceiver doesn't take its power from the medium. Indeed, the medium is called a passive medium because it carries only the data signals and no power supply.

If the clustering problem referred to earlier relates to intelligent stations such as PCs or Sparc workstations, then terminal servers are not normally used unless network access from these devices is restricted to terminal emulation. The individual transceiver cables can be used to connect each separate card and workstation to a fan-out box which typically supports up to eight connectors. A single transceiver is then required to connect that cluster to the network cable. This arrangement is helpful on two counts where a local cluster of PCs is configured. First, you don't have to coil large amounts of Ethernet cable to create a 2.5 m spacing between connections. Second, you only need to purchase one transceiver for all the clustered devices.

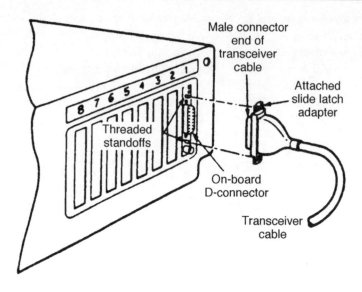

Fig. 9.11 Ethernet card attachment
(© **Learning Group International, reprinted with permission**)

Technically, if only one cluster needs to be networked with no connectivity required elsewhere, it is possible to run Ethernet within this box and have no transceiver connection. This is known as 'Ethernet-in-a-box' (see Fig. 9.12).

Question 9.5   If Ethernet was required only locally, instead of a fan-out box to achieve connectivity between workstations, couldn't we have a simple (and cheap) intelligent switch to pass data from one station to another?

The only time you are likely to encounter 10base5 networks will be on old installations. However, the principles explained in this standard underpin all of the more recent developments. Once these priciples are secure, the rationale for the way in which the more recent developments have occurred will be better appreciated.

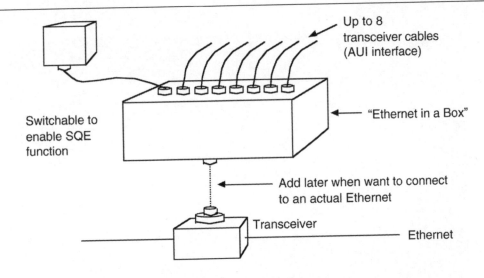

Up to 8
transceiver cables
(AUI interface)

"Ethernet in a Box"

Switchable to
enable SQE
function

Add later when want to connect
to an actual Ethernet

Transceiver

Ethernet

Fig. 9.12 Fan-out box (DELNI)
(© Learning Group International, reprinted with permission)

10base2 standard

The 10base2 standard is often referred to as Cheapernet or thin-wire Ethernet because the components are cheaper than the 10base5 equivalents. The specification uses thin (5 mm diameter) flexible RG-58 coaxial cable which is significantly easier to install than the rigid thick (10 mm diameter) wire coaxial cable used in 10base5 networks. In the 10base2 implementation the functionality of the transceiver is built into the Ethernet card. The nomenclature '10base2' for the standard is not strictly accurate as the maximum segment lengths are 185 m. However, a 10base2 network is still a 10 Mbit/s network using the baseband signalling of Manchester encoding. It allows up to 30 stations per segment with a minimum spacing of 0.5 m between connections. Some network vendors suggest that a slightly higher number of connections (such as 32) are permissible, but most good designers would keep the number of connections per segment well below this figure.

Question 9.6   Why might we choose to install 10base2 cabling rather than 10base5?

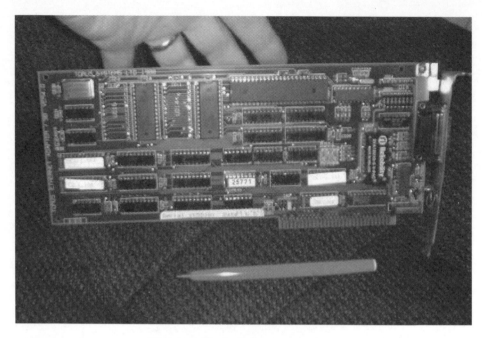

Fig. 9.13 Early Ethernet card

Fig. 9.14 Ethernet card with 10base2, 10base5 and 10baseT connectors
(© Allied Telesyn, reprinted with permission)

The majority of Ethernet cards which were manufactured during the late 1980s and the early 1990s provided both D connectors and BNC connectors. The card shown in Fig. 9.13 has a D connector, a BNC connector and a RJ45 correcter used for 10baseT described later. Fig. 9.15 shows how the thin wire connection is made to the Ethernet card using its BNC connector rather than its D connector.

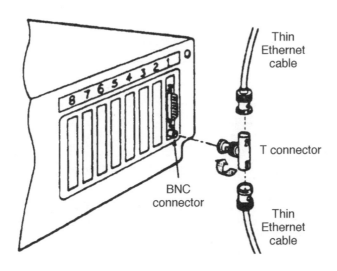

Thin Ethernet cable

T connector

BNC connector

Thin Ethernet cable

Fig. 9.15 Example connection for Cheapernet
(© Learning Group International, reprinted with permission)

Question 9.7   If 10base5 segments can cover 500 m and 10base2 segments cover only 185 m, what advantages can you see or suggest for opting for a 10base2 LAN?

Connection via the BNC connector will involve the use of the onboard transceiver. Connection via the D connector for 10base5 systems using a transceiver cable will bypass the onboard transceiver and requires an external transceiver connection. Installation of thin wire Ethernet with a series of T connectors effectively looks like a daisy chain of devices on the cable. However, it is only necessary for one fault to occur and potentially the whole segment will go down. For example, if the coaxial cable in the back of one of the workstations becomes loose or disconnected, then effectively the whole segment goes down. Installations rapidly moved to using wall connectors with a make/break feature to provide greater robustness. A make/break connector allows a connection to be plugged in with the automatic inclusion of this cable as part of the 'extended bus' without any significant disruption of the network. Perhaps the only impact during insertion will be the loss of one or two packets, which will be retransmitted when the higher level protocols time out and commence a recovery. On disconnection, the wall connector 'short circuits' the socket and makes a straight through connection. When we connect a station to the wall socket we must remember that this cable becomes part of the 185 m maximum segment length.

The wall socket approach (see Fig. 9.16) also makes future provision for user mobility by permitting the installation of a larger (perhaps significantly larger) number of wall connectors than the number of existing users. Users can then reconnect to a spare connector whenever they are moving within the office or network area without recabling being necessary.

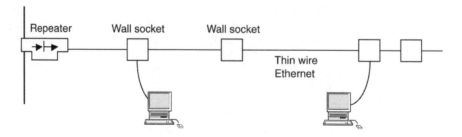

Fig. 9.16 Thin wire segment using wall sockets

Because the segment lengths are only 185 m, there tend to be more segments in a 10base2 network than in a 10base5 LAN. Multi-port repeaters are frequently used in this standard which allow configurations to look like the example shown in Fig. 9.17. This shows how the multiple segments can be linked together economically. Effectively, a multi-port repeater is a concentration of thin wire Ethernet segments (typically up to eight) into a single box. This will be considered in more detail in Chapter 11.

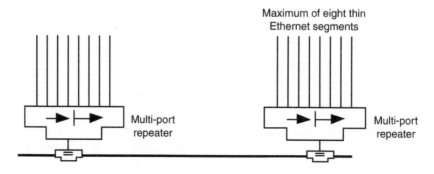

Fig. 9.17 Multi-port repeater

Question 9.8   In calculating cable length contributions in the 10base2 185 m segments, what distance should be added to the calculation for the cable run from any faceplate to the workstations?

All the other features and functionality of CSMA/CD operate as in the case of 10base5 implementations. Since one end of the RG-58 cable normally terminates at a repeater (or multi-port repeater), we only need to terminate the other end with a terminating resistor to prevent signal reflections. If no repeaters exist (i.e., there is a single segment 10base2 network) then both ends need to be terminated. Figure 9.18 shows a typical multi-port repeater.

Fig. 9.18 Multi-port repeaters
(© **Allied Telesyn, reprinted with permission**)

10baseT standard

CSMA/CD is also available at 10 Mbit/s over AWG24 twisted pair (TP) cable, which is normally unshielded twisted pair (UTP) cable. In many buildings, however, the twisted pair telephone wiring that may have previously been installed may not be of a suitable quality (e.g., not adequately twisted or of the wrong grade). If new wiring is required, serious consideration should be given to using Category 5 cable or a PDS (Premises Distribution Cabling System). Although Category 3 or Category 4 cable is adequate for the purpose of 10baseT cabling, Category 5 cable will conform to the requirements for higher performance networks and effectively future-proof the installation. Given the high costs of installing the cable in comparison with the relatively low cable costs, it is worth the investment to provide the higher specification cable now.

The Ethernet frame structure has previously been defined in Fig. 9.2 and it applies equally here. In 10baseT networks the approach taken provides 10 Mbit/s over distances of 100 m without repeaters.

Physically, the system looks like a central concentrator or hubs with local concentrators or hubs at the second level. An early example was the SynOptics' LattisNet shown in Fig.9.19. Effectively the hubs become the repeater as far as signal regeneration is concerned.

Question 9.9   What is the immediate disadvantage that may be perceived in the 10baseT implementation shown in Fig. 9.19 in comparison with 10base5 or 10base2 implementations?

Question 9.10 What advantages may the 10baseT cabling approach have?

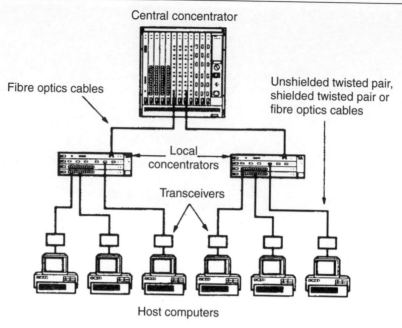

Fig. 9.19 10baseT configuration
(© Layer One, reprinted with permission)

10baseT Ethernet cards traditionally had twisted pair RJ-45 plug interfaces, and it was possible to buy the cards with just about any combination of the D connector, BNC connector and RJ-45 connector. Today's cards typically have a flat 15-pin connection, as shown in Fig 9.20, and need may need a small conversion cable to provide a RJ45 plug interface. It would be an acceptable arrangement for the twisted pair link to be taken directly from the local concentrator or hub to the host computer. Of course, to accommodate the issue of mobility of users, rather than have direct connections to each device it is more common to flood-wire the building and provide multiple cable runs to wall sockets. Whenever a user is located near a wall socket, the connection between his or her device and the wall socket is made. Equally, the hub is typically located in a wiring centre, with a patch panel normally being the termination point of the cable run. When the user is connecting to a previously unused wall socket, the network administration patches that line (physically connects that line) through to the hub. Hence we have many more cable runs to wall sockets than there are active lines, and they are only activated or patched through when there is a user requirement. This permits us to provide a hub only of the capacity required for the number of current users, and to keep the initial cost of installation as low as possible.

Fig. 9.20 Ethernet card and correction cable

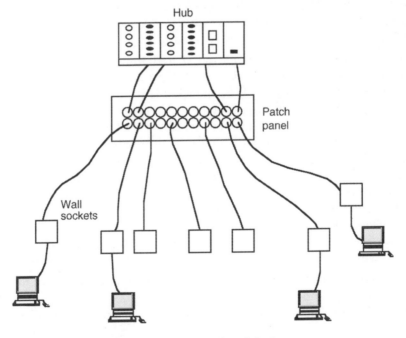

Fig. 9.21 Patch panel and hub

In the arrangement shown in Fig 9.21, we physically install n cable runs to provide n wall connectors. However, an n-port concentrator is expensive, so each cable is connected to the patch panel. In the example shown, we have only four devices. Only these four devices have a connection made from the patch panel to the hub. A four port hub is much cheaper then an n-port version. However, we are unlikely to have purchased a concentrator with only four ports since future expansion will almost certainly occur and new users are likely to want a connection in the future. This extra requirement is in addition to existing users relocating to different lines. Hence, we would normally plan some spare capacity at the concentrator level to accommodate this. These hubs are stackable devices and so, if we do run out of capacity, an extra hub can be stacked on top of the original hub.

This design is the basis of a structured wiring scheme. Modern hubs, in addition to being repeaters, are intelligent, manageable devices and they can isolate faulty links to individual users. Hence, they provide a more robust approach.

Question 9.11 CSMA/CD has been described in terms of a bus architecture. How does a hub or concentrator handle CSMA/CD?

Switched Ethernet standard

A recent addition to the Ethernet product range is the Ethernet switch. It builds upon the 10baseT infrastructure but replaces the hub with a switch. Hence the cost of the transition is limited and the hub may potentially be utilized elsewhere in the configuration.

As we noted in Chapter 8, switched Ethernet access allows multiple connections of ports through the switch, each pair-wise connection providing a separate circuit or bus. This provides a full 10 Mbit/s, 100 Mbit/s or 1 Gbit/s capability between the two switched stations. The switch learns the location of the MAC addresses on the network using the same technique as a bridge. This is covered fully in Chapter 11.

CSMA/CD as an access technique on shared transmission media has a significant performance problem under heavily loaded conditions, as we will see in Chapter 13. Switched Ethernet is designed to recognize this restriction and also recognize that the twisted pair cable infrastructure provides a largely dedicated cable structure, i.e., each station has its own cable to the hub which isn't shared with other devices. When CSMA/CD operates on cable structures with this dedicated medium, the probability of a collision occurring on the connection is considerably reduced. Hence the back-off features, which contribute to the reduced performance of Ethernet under heavy loads, are mainly avoided. The network is able to achieve performances close to full port speed on each switched link. The links however are still operating in half duplex mode. For those devices where performance is critical to the operation, such as servers, it is possible to run a port connection in full duplex mode. In this arrangement, separate pairs of wires in the cat 5 cable are used for the inbound and outbound traffic.

There has been rapid development of switches in the few years since their introduction. Early switches provided a number of 10 Mbit/s ports. A typical configuration is shown in Fig. 9.22, which accommodates existing cable arrangements in the new structure.

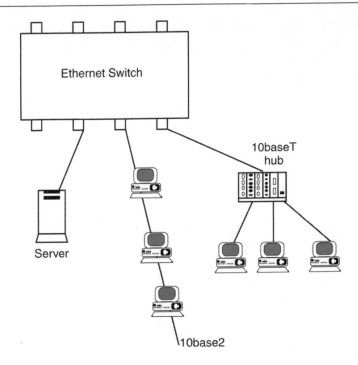

Fig. 9.22 Possible Ethernet switch configuration

As the demands for higher bandwidths have grown and the 100 Mbit/s Fast Ethernet standards have developed, switches became available which supported 100 Mbit/s and 1 Gbit/s port capability. In the evolution of switches this was initially provided on two of the ports, whilst the remaining ports provide 10 Mbit/s connections. In such an arrangement it was usual to see the network servers on the high speed ports running Fast Ethernet. The server simply needs a Fast Ethernet card running at 100 Mbit/s. The switch buffers the Ethernet frames between the 10 Mbit/s and 100 Mbit/s ports to maximize the throughput. The use of switches to support the higher speeds are shown in Figs. 9.26 and 9.27. As the cost of switches has fallen significantly over recent years, the provision of high speed links on all of the ports has become more prevalent.

Fast Ethernet standard

As the demand for higher bandwidth increases, so have vendors endeavoured to offer new products and develop the standards. This second generation Ethernet was designed to offer an improvement in performance that is an order of magnitude better than earlier standards. Thus Ethernet developments offering 100 Mbit/s were pursued, but these efforts went along two separate paths. On the one hand, Hewlett-Packard led the developments which removed CSMA/CD as the media access technique but kept the Ethernet and token ring frame structures. This has been adopted by the IEEE 802.12 committee and is covered in section 7 of this chapter. The other group kept within the IEEE 802.3 specification, still using CSMA/CD, and released a high speed version known as 100baseT. These ideas were proposed in 1992, and, from the first draft in 1994, it only took 13 months for the standard to be approved in mid-1995. Of course, Manchester encoding needs too high a signalling rate at these high speeds and 5B/6B encoding techniques adopted from the ANSI FDDI standards were used instead.

The 100baseT standard uses either two pairs of Category 5 UTP or four pairs of Category 3 UTP. The result is a set of standards which are based around a 100baseT hub. Fig. 9.23 shows the range of distances covered by the various cable types supported. In the category 5 arrangement one pair of wires is used for transmission and the another pair used to signal collision detection. In the category 3 cable approach three pairs of wires are used to carry the data (33 Mbit/s each), and the fourth pair is used for collision detection.

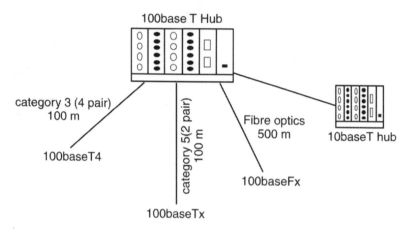

Fig. 9.23 100baseT configuration

The maximum number of hubs in a single network is limited to two, and so a maximum configuration is as shown in Fig. 9.24. This shows the maximum end-to-end distance of 205 m using Category 5 cable throughout. The 5m run between the hubs can theoretically be extended to 10 m provided that all the hub to station cable lengths are reduced to 95 m. In practice, this isn't sensible, and so it is better to keep to a 5 m run between hubs. This limit results from the requirement discussed earlier that the minimum size Ethernet frame mustn't take a minimum of 512 bit times. At 10 Mbit/s this is 51.2 μs, but at 100 Mbit/s it is 5.12 μs, and hence the limitation on network size. This is a direct consequence of maintaining the criteria for CSMA/CD. Remember that in this original design, we had a trade-off between minimum frame size, speed of transmission and twice the end-to-end propagation time. If we change the transmission speed element by a factor of 10, then we have to change one of the other parameters, in this case the transmission time.

In the configuration shown in Fig. 9.24, the whole of the configuration is a single collision domain. Hence, if we increase the level of traffic with more host machines or applications requiring greater network bandwidth, then the incident rate of collisions will increase. The network performance is clearly affected when recovery from collisions occur, and so the implementation is not scalable and any growth after the initial design may require further configuration to keep within operational guidelines. These performance concerns are considered in greater detail in Chapter 13.

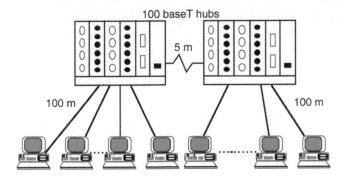

Fig. 9.24 Two-hub Fast Ethernet

The price of a 100 Mbit/s Ethernet card can be as low as £25 in 2002, and normally has the capability of fall back to 10 Mbit/s operation whenever necessary. It achieves this dual speed capability with auto-negotiation, picking up the highest speed the network port is able to support. To support an architecture which is based on a number of physical layer options, the data link layer is often represented as two sections as shown in Fig. 9.25.

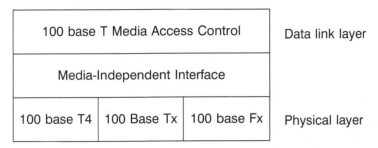

Fig 9.25 Architecture showing media-independent interface in the MAC Layer

Gigabit Ethernet standard

Network bandwidth is under continuing pressure. When Ethernet was first introduced, it was difficult to imagine why we would ever need 10 Mbit/s. With the demand for higher transfer speeds coming from applications that have embraced high-resolution graphics, video, etc., the existing bandwidth continues to be under pressure. Other application areas that are making demands on the networks include desktop video-conferencing, distributed databases, interactive whiteboarding, data warehousing, the Internet and intranets, network backups, modelling, and medical imaging and informatics. Hence, there is a requirement for a generation of Ethernet development, with another order of magnitude of improvement in speed. This standard typically provides backbone services because of the design issues relating to distances, rather than providing end-user services.

The IEEE 802.3z standard created a 1000 Mbit/s or 1 Gbit/s (gigabit per second) network and continues to use the Ethernet frame structure. This was an important decision because it maintains the ability to move Ethernet frames across the whole LAN, without any reformatting. Hence the upward compatibility of the Ethernet architecture is achieved. The access control to the medium is still CSMA/CD, although the collision domain will be limited to one repeater. This is simply because the original design tradeoffs of speed, minimum packet size and round trip time which were designed to enable CSMA/CD to operate successfully still need to be secured. Compared to Fast Ethernet, if we increase the speed tenfold, and keep the minimum packet size the same, then the maximum size network needs to be decreased tenfold to keep the round trip time back in balance. However, that would produce a network which could be as short as 20 m. Clearly, that would have been a major limitation. Instead, there was a solution in which a longer slot time of 512 bytes on the network is guaranteed. This technique is known as carrier extension, i.e., we ensure a carrier presence equivalent to a minimum of 512 bytes slot time on every transmission, even though the minimum Ethernet frame may still be as short as 64 bytes. Early implementations have been based on Fibre Channel's short wavelength fibre optics (780 hm) running at 1250 Gbit/s, since the standard uses 8B/10B encoding techniques. This encoding approach is based on the same principles we discussed earlier with 5B/6B encoding. The result is multi-mode fibre supporting distances of 200 m and single mode fibre supporting typical distances of 2 km. Progress in introducing a cat 5 and cat 5-e (enhanced) twisted pair cable, operating at shorter distances of up to 100 m continues to be made, using PAM-5 coding and pulse shaping techniques to condition the transmitted spectrum. Because the standard will use the same frame format, then all the benefits of relatively easy migration to this next generation of Ethernet will be realized. Hence, switches in the system can be upgraded or directly replaced to accommodate the new standard. Indeed, switches have become a major part of the migration strategy. With the limitation of overall distances, the resulting configurations have placed the high speed Gigabit Ethernet as the back end systems, whilst retaining Ethernet or Fast Ethernet as the user end standard. The result is Gigabit Ethernet used to support server farms or provide links between switches. With the use of switch technology, the standard also supports full duplex mode. Typical configurations are shown in Figs. 9.26 and 9.27.

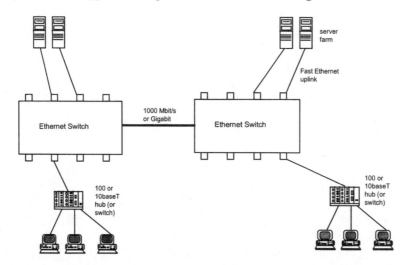

Fig 9.26 Gigabit Ethernet link between switches

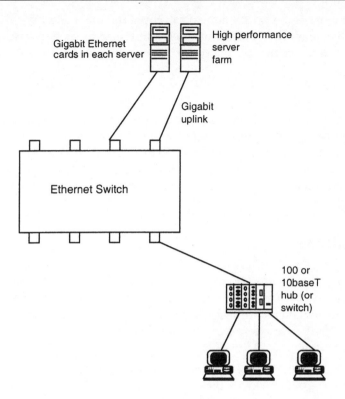

Fig. 9.27 Gigabit Ethernet supporting server farm

In the same way that we saw a refinement in the data link layer for Fast Ethernet, the model can be further refined as we combine part of the underlying ANSI X3T11 standard into the Gigabit Ethernet protocol specification. The resulting model is shown in Fig. 9.28.

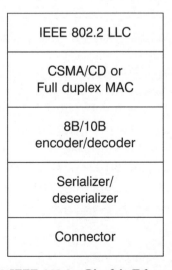

Fig 9.28 IEEE 802.3z Gigabit Ethernet Model

Existing management tools and techniques will provide the continuing expertise needed to maintain the network with the same network reliability as has been achieved with the structured cabling approaches that were introduced with the 10baseT standard back in 1986.

10 Gigabit Ethernet

The 10 Gigabit Ethernet Alliance are already working on this higher speed standard. In most respects, it will retain the upwards compatability concept. However, it will be based on full-duplex-only arrangements, so that CSMA/CD will not be required. It will also be a fibre-only standard. The concept of designing a range of physical-media-dependent interfaces into the mode is retained. The standard is also based on 64B/66B signalling.

3. IEEE 802.4 standard

The original supporters of the IEEE 802.4 standard were General Motors, along with others including Motorola and Allen-Bradley. The standard was aimed at providing a deterministic access to the transmission medium using token passing for media access control. Normal implementations are based on broadband or carrierband technology, although commercial derivatives were available such as Arcnet. Typically the range of speeds supported is 1 Mbit/s to 10 Mbit/s.

With General Motors support, this standard has been implemented largely in the industrial scene where guaranteed response times are required. The higher level Manufacturing Automation Protocol (MAP) specifies 802.4 as the supporting network and it was really the MAP protocols that were the driving force behind the General Motors support.

>1	1	1	2/6	2/6	< 8182	4	1
Preamble	Start delimiter	Frame control	Destination address	Source address	Data	CRC	End delimiter

Fig. 9.29 IEEE 802.4 packet structure

In this standard, the start and end delimiters use non-data symbols that cannot legally occur elsewhere, and the packet structure thus controls the variable length by means of these delimiters (see Fig. 9.29). The frame control field has three functions:

a) *MAC control function*: This is largely used for determining and controlling access techniques with the following primitives:

    i) claim token (during ring initialization);

    ii) two variations of solicit successor (to join the ring);

    iii) who follows? (to recover from lost tokens);

    iv) resolve contentions;

    v) token (passing);

    vi) set successor (to leave the ring).

b) *Logical link control function*: This is essentially used to handle data frames using priority setting and possible flow control, with acknowledgement provisions for future implementations.

c) *Station management*: This relates to issues such as error state logging, diagnostics, etc.

It is the MAC control function that is probably the most interesting element since it controls the important aspects of initializing, joining or leaving the 'ring'. Note that this is a logical ring, even if it is physically a bus. The token is passed from station to station on the basis of a predetermined order (address size), with each station knowing its position in terms of its upstream and downstream neighbours' addresses.

To initialize the ring at start-up, a station is able to send a claim token frame, followed by a variable length field with a duration of zero, two, four or six response windows. The intention is to establish which station has the highest address, and this station then becomes the head of the queue. Then the next highest address is sought, and so on until the logical ring is established.

A similar activity takes place to regenerate a token when timer events indicate that a token is lost because a station, for whatever reason, has not successfully forwarded it to the next station in the logical ring.

Question 9.12 Under what sort of circumstances could a token become lost?

Solicit successor and resolve contention primitives or commands are used to continue the initializing process or periodically, when a station holds the token, to allow others to join the 'ring'.

Question 9.13 Once a logical ring has been established and is operational, why would we want to allow other stations to join?

To leave the ring correctly, a station waits until it holds the token and then a set successor frame is sent to its predecessor (including the address of its successor) to reset the logical ring. Should a station develop a fault and not leave the ring cleanly, an upstream station that has forwarded the token to the faulty station will recognize that no further frames have been generated. If a second attempt to pass the token fails, then a 'who follows?' frame is generated so that the downstream station from the failed unit responds. Pointers to the faulty station are now removed from both the upstream and downstream stations and the faulty station is out of the logical ring.

When a station is holding the token, it is able to do so on the basis of a token holding time. This is a complex value, which takes account of any congestion on the LAN and reduces the token holding time by any individual station when the LAN gets busy. This approach does allow for quite large single transfers to take place, e.g., over 8 kbytes.

4. IEEE 802.5 standard

The token ring proposals were actively promoted by IBM and resulted in significant interest from many parties. The original specifications were for 1 Mbit/s and 4 Mbit/s versions, but 16 Mbit/s became the main standard. Some token ring interface cards are able to support dual speed operations, but it should be noted that, in any ring, the speed will fall back to that of the slowest interface card. We will see later that where a structured implementation occurs, intelligent devices can switch 'slow' stations out of the ring to ensure that the higher speed capability is preserved. Higher speeds are planned to cope with the growing demands for additional speed and bandwidth.

The original intention of the token ring standard was to provide a means of transporting data between workstations (such as PCs) and servers (such as file servers). This was supported by the additions to the PC operating systems to allow controlled access to server facilities to be employed. Further work in developing network operating systems (NOSs) by companies such as Novell created additional facilities and functionality. The Novell approach was also designed to be LAN-independent. Indeed, the initial popularity of such network operating systems is due to the wide range of underlying networks which will support the operating systems.

Token structure

To ensure that the start and end points of the token are unquestionably recognized, use is made of the two encode violations J and K in the differential Manchester encoding signalling technique. Both the start and end delimiters contain the J and K symbols (see Fig. 9.30).

Fig. 9.30 Token structure

Before a station can transmit, it must hold the token. It waits for a free token to pass through its interface and is able to claim it. When the token is claimed, a single bit in the access control field is flipped over from a 0 to a 1 to indicate that the token is busy and the data is inserted at the end of the field. Hence the circulating packet structure is of the form shown in Fig. 9.31.

Fig. 9.31 Circulating packet structure

Media Access Control (MAC)

The data that is passed to the interface for placing on the network results in a packet structure that is similar to that in the IEEE 802.3 and 802.4 standards (see Fig. 9.32). The LLC data carried is the same as we identified in section 2 of this chapter.

Fig. 9.32 IEEE 802.5 MAC packet

The operation of the network lies in the detail behind the access control byte (see Fig. 9.33).

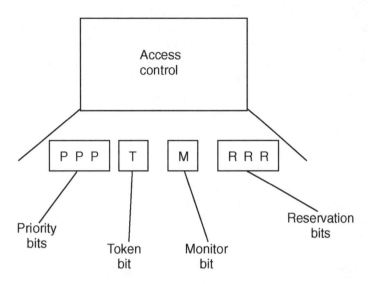

Fig. 9.33 IEEE 802.5 access control field

The free token state is simply represented by the T bit set to 0. For a station to claim the token this bit is set to 1 as it passes through the station and the data is inserted behind the access control byte, as shown in Fig. 9.31. The station that generated the data is also responsible for removing the data and replacing the free token onto the ring.

Question 9.14 If the station that generated the data is also responsible for removing it, instead of the destination station doing this, what feature can be built into the data structure?

Under error conditions, it is possible for a situation to develop where a station 'dies' before it removes the data it has previously placed on the network. To prevent a 'dead' packet from circulating constantly, the monitor station in the ring plays a role. It sets the M field to 1 whenever the token passes through the monitor station. This is reset to 0 when the station holding the token puts a free token back onto the ring. Should a packet pass by the monitor with the M field already set, then clearly the packet has not been removed and an error condition is flagged. The monitor now plays an active role in 'cleaning up' the ring and releasing a new token.

Each station has the capability of being the monitor station, but only one station can be an active monitor at any given time. When the network is powered up, each station makes a bid to become the active monitor. Within the protocol to handle network management issues one of the stations gains control, with the other stations going on standby. The standby stations will periodically enquire whether they can become the monitor and so the network will always carry some traffic, even when there is no data to send. Within this management protocol, stations are also aware of the address of their upstream neighbours.

The miscellaneous or frame control field shown in Fig. 9.32 indicates whether the packet is a data packet or whether this field is the token ring MAC management protocol.

The token ring standard allows a priority system to be used. To use its priority mechanism, a station wishing to talk waits for the next token rotation. If it is not free, then it places its allocated priority value in the reservations zone of the access control field. When the station currently holding the token releases a free token on the ring, it moves the reservation field to the priority field. Only the bidding station or one with a higher priority is then able to claim that priority token. This allows stations with priority traffic (e.g., a real-time application with synchronous data flows or slow scan video) to be supported.

It should be noted that, if a reservation at a particular priority value is made, another station with a higher priority could overwrite the lower value reservation.

There is a significant point here, as you will note that it is possible, using this implementation technique, to stack the priorities. The station setting the priority into the PPP zone of the access field is also responsible for resetting it to its previous level, and not the bidding station!

Question 9.15 Why should the station which upped the priority be the one responsible for resetting it, rather than the station which used it at the raised priority level?

The destination and source addresses are each 16-bit or 48-bit fields. The IEEE 802.5 committee designed the token ring to implement an addressing scheme based on source routing, i.e., the source station defines the route to be taken to reach a destination station. Hence each LAN has an ID number and each station has an ID number or hardware address on the LAN. An address format using 16 bits can be implemented if locally-assigned addresses are in use; otherwise the default token ring card address of 46/48 bits is utilized. Locally-assigned addresses are not frequently used, but where they are it is often to take advantage of easy mapping between local and global IP addressing schemes. Hence it is possible for the hardware address of the station to remain static even when the interface card is changed.

Question 9.16 What benefits may accrue from having the hardware address and the IP address as the same value?

In a small token ring, all the stations will be connected in the arrangements that we saw in Figs 6.10 and 8.27. If a larger network is to be implemented, then we can join two or more rings together using a bridge. The principle is the same as that shown for Ethernet in Fig. 9.9, and a typical ring configuration is shown in Fig. 9.33. If a bridge is present in the ring then the originating station must provide routing information for the packet to reach the destination. This routing information is included in the frame format and Fig. 9.32 is enhanced to include this routing data as shown in Fig. 9.34.

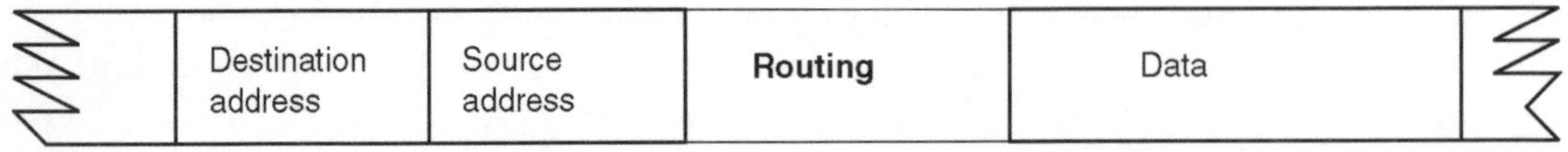

Destination address	Source address	**Routing**	Data

Fig. 9.34 Packet structure with routing

The routing information is in multiples of 16 bits, each specifying the bridge number (4 bits) and the LAN number (12 bits) to reach the destination. Hence a station may specify a route such as that shown in Fig. 9.35 to reach station Z from station A in the configuration shown in Fig. 9.36.

| Bridge A | LAN 2 | Bridge B | LAN 4 |

Fig. 9.35 Example routing address

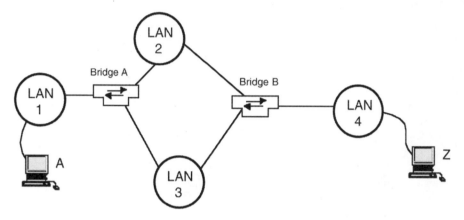

Fig. 9.36 Source routing in a token ring

The trick here is how each station knows how to route to any destination. To enable any station to determine the location of another station, it is able to broadcast a discovery frame to request possible routing information. As broadcast frames, these are sent through all bridges and the routes taken by the broadcast are recorded in the frames. A station recognizing its address in the discovery frame responds to the sender, returning all the information recorded in the frame. Where multiple routes to the destination have generated more than one broadcast message reaching the destination, each one is answered and the source selects the route with the best performance (determined by some algorithm such as the least number of hops or bridges to traverse) and keeps the alternative routes responses as standby routes.

It should be noted at this point that a bridge will have two (or more) hardware addresses, one for each network interface connection (NIC).

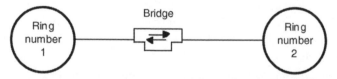

Fig. 9.37 Interconnected rings showing the ring number

Question 9.17 Why does a bridge have two (or more) addresses (see Fig. 9.37)?

The status field at the end of the packet structure contains two significant bits known as A and C bits which, if marked, indicate that the destination has recognized the address (the A bit) and copied the data (the C bit). Note that the change is outside the fields covered by the CRC, so as not to upset the checksum. The result of this combination of AC bits means the following:

a) AC = 0 0: packet not recognized by any station;

b) AC = 1 0: station active but busy;

c) AC = 1 1: data received and copied.

Physical structure

The installation of a token ring, as we have previously seen, may not appear as a physical ring. Hence we saw in Fig. 8.27 that an MSAU provides a means of device concentration looking like a star. A single device connection may look like that in Fig. 9.38.

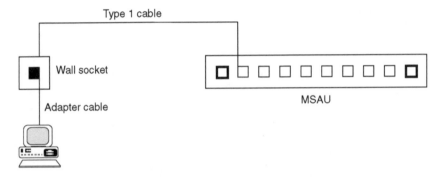

Fig. 9.38 Station to MSAU connection

Question 9.18 Why do we bother to use an MSAU instead of simply coupling adjacent stations together, which must be cheaper?

A number of interconnected MSAUs may logically look like a ring, as shown in Fig. 6.10. However, physically, these interconnected MSAUs are frequently housed in a wiring rack and may look like the arrangement in Fig. 9.39.

Maximum configurations are a little more complex than in other IEEE designs and the rules are quite diverse. One influence on the design of the ring is the types of MSAU being used. The use of Type 1, 3 or 6 cable, the number of wiring closets, the number of MSAUs, the speed of the network, and the possible use of line drivers to extend the range will all influence the calculations.

The maximum length of the cable in the ring, or at least the lobe length from the MSAU to the connected device, is based on which of the cable types is used. If a number of MSAUs are present, as we have seen in Fig. 9.39, they are rack mounted and interconnected using Type 6 patch cables, each of which has a maximum length of 2.5 m.

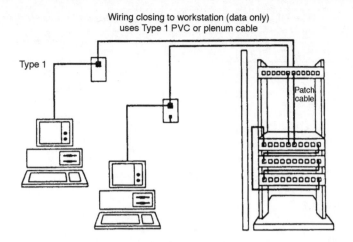

Wiring closing to workstation (data only)
uses Type 1 PVC or plenum cable

Fig. 9.39 MSAUs in rack
(© Learning Group International, reprinted with permission)

If more than one rack is present, then Type 6 cable is used to interconnect the racks with a maximum patch length of 10 m. An example is shown in Fig. 9.40.

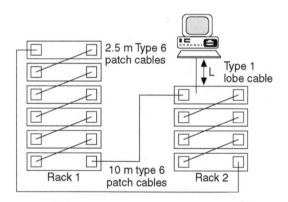

Fig. 9.40 Multiple racks in a single wiring closet
(© Layer One, reprinted with permission)

Additionally, a number of wiring closets or centres may be needed, normally interconnected using Type 1 cable with a maximum distance of 200 m. (Note that a maximum of 12 wiring closets is specified in the standard.)

Of course, when cable runs are introduced between wiring closets, it may appear that some of the robustness of the ring is more exposed than might be ideal. What would happen if one of the wiring closet connections were rendered inoperable? Fortunately, if one of the MSAU connector cables is removed, the ring remains intact (see Fig. 9.41).

Dual twisted pair cable, i.e. each line represents a cable pair

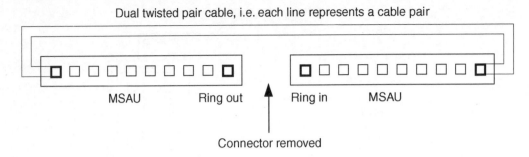

MSAU   Ring out   Ring in   MSAU

Connector removed

Fig. 9.41 Ring with a cable removed

The connection between MSAUs, racks and wiring closets is a dual twisted pair construct and in normal operation only one pair is in use. Should a fault occur in one cable connection, the MSAUs at each end are able to wrap around and automatically configure the ring to use the redundant pair in the remaining cables to form a complete ring again. As an example, in Fig. 9.41, the single cable connecting the two MSAUs will have one pair of the twisted pair carrying the signal from the left-hand MSAU to the right-hand MSAU and the standby twisted pair carrying the signal back once it has passed through all the devices connected to the MSAUs. Fig. 9.42 shows how the two MSAUs have overcome the absence of a good connection between the ring out and ring in ports.

Dual twisted pair cable, i.e. each line represents a cable pair

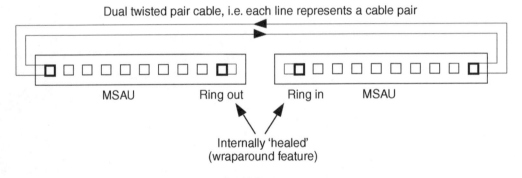

MSAU   Ring out   Ring in   MSAU

Internally 'healed'
(wraparound feature)

Fig. 9.42 'Healed' ring

The critical figure to be calculated is the maximum distance without signal regeneration that may be cabled. This is called the maximum transmission distance. As a norm, each station is also a repeater and the signal is regenerated in the token ring card and passed through the lobe cable runs to the next station. This station could be in the next MSAU, rack or wiring closet. We need to calculate the cable lengths to ensure that the distance between two stations is within the maximum limits before signal regeneration is required.

The worst scenario is the situation when only one station is attached (maybe the rest are inoperable or simply not connected) and the shortest cable link connecting the MSAUs is removed from the ring. The station must drive the signal around the whole ring, including twice the distance of the active inter-MSAU cable connections in place. Since the maximum distance for sending a signal is critical, all configurations will have a figure for the maximum length of lobe cable permitted, given that the worst scenario outlined above could happen. Of course this is a pretty useless network with only one station talking to itself, but the network should be designed to keep its integrity under all conditions.

Question 9.19 Why is it necessary to have a maximum transmission distance?

Question 9.20 Why is the lobe cable length dependent upon the number of patch cables in place?

Each MSAU vendor provides a technical specification which includes the factor to be used in the calculation of lobe length using their product. This factor represents the signal delay and quality reduction introduced into the ring by the insertion of the MSAU. If a mixture of Type 1 STP and Type 3 UTP cabling is used, the entire ring must be engineered to Type 3 rules.

For networks operating at 4 Mbit/s, IBM recommend a maximum lobe cable length of 45 m for a two closet situation, but up to 100 m is permissible for a single closet operation. The maximum transmission distance is set at 145 min total between two stations.

If an upgrade to 16 Mbit/s is planned, the design intention is to be able to use the existing 4 Mbit/s cabling where possible. The maximum transmission distance for 16 Mbit/s is set at 173 m for Type 1 cable and 65 m for Type 3 cable. To accommodate the new limits and to use existing cabling from 4 Mbit/s implementation, it is common to simply use a purpose built repeater between closets. Indeed this approach overcomes distance difficulties that might have been observed. Most implementations are operating at 16 Mbit/s.

Question 9.21 What technical reasons might IBM have had for delaying support for 16 Mbit/s on Type 3 unshielded cable, and preferring Type 1 shielded cable?

As a rough rule of thumb, Table 9.1 may be helpful.

Design feature	4 Mbit/s		16 Mbit/s	
	Type 1	Type 3	Type 1	Type 3
Maximum number of stations	260	72	260	72
Maximum transmission distance (m)	385	145	173	65
Maximum number of MSAUs	33	9	33	9
Typical maximum length of lobe cable (m)	100	45	50	25
Maximum distance between wiring closets (m)	200	120	200	120

Table 9.1 Typical token ring cable limits

Normally, the connections between stations and the MSAU are not taken directly to the station. A punch-down block is used to provide the configurability of the network. Such an arrangement is shown in Fig. 9.43. The use of punch-down blocks or patch panels is the preferred approach in a structured cabling environment. This is because extra cable runs can be laid to the patch panel provide flexibility of configuration and they future-proof the installation's potential growth and future connection requirements. As previously noted, it is certainly cheaper to lay extra cable at the initial installation time than to get the cable installers to return and lay extra cable lengths one cable run at a time.

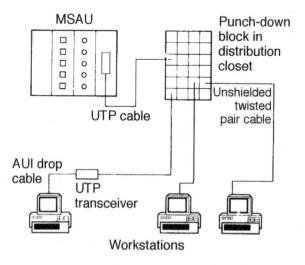

Fig. 9.43 Use of punch-down block
(© **Layer One, reprinted with permission**)

Question 9.22 What benefits can be gained from including a punch-down block in the cable structure?

---

5. IEEE 802.6 standard

Although not strictly a LAN standard, the IEEE 802.6 metropolitan area network (MAN) standard is covered here because of its ability to integrate individual LANs by providing the interconnecting backbone structure. Hence, larger networks can be formed which can extend to the physical limits of a MAN. Where available, the MANs are operated by the PTTs or other network providers such as cable companies, and they probably offer shared facilities between large numbers of users from different organizations.

It has taken a long time to define this standard and a number of different technical approaches have been attempted based on satellite communications, cable television networks and the slotted ring architecture. Eventually, a standard has been agreed using the Distributed Queue Dual Bus (DQDB). Much of the work was undertaken in Australia and sponsored by Telecom Australia, and an offshoot company QPSX has been the leading design authority.

The architecture consists of a slotted system using a dual-unidirectional user system operating at 155 Mbit/s. The head station (network controller) at one end generates the frame synchronization which is transmitted on one bus and the controlling station at the other end generates a frame pattern with the same synchronization on the other bus (see Fig. 9.45). The slot format of DQDB is shown in Fig. 9.44.

1 byte	52 bytes
Access control field	Protocol data unit (PDU)

Fig. 9.44 DQDB slot format

The access control field contains three bits used for request purposes. Each station is able to queue a request to talk on a bus by putting a reservation on the other bus. Every station has two count registers, one for each bus. A count register is incremented by 1 every time an upstream station's reservation is seen in a passing slot. This register is decremented by 1 for every empty slot that flows in the opposite direction on the other bus. These slots can then be used by the upstream stations that made the reservations.

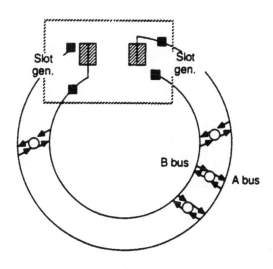

Fig. 9.45 MAN dual bus
(© Learning Group International, reprinted with permission)

151

A station waiting to 'talk' on a bus therefore makes a reservation on the other bus in the first free reservation field. A copy of the request count register is made, and this is decremented for each empty slot passing by on the alternative bus until this copied register equals 0. The next empty slot space is then used. Meanwhile, the request count register continues as normal in case further requests are made.

The whole operation is mirror-imaged for transmission on the other bus to 'talk' in the opposite direction. Priority operations can be achieved by having separate distributed queues for each level of priority with separate reservation bit setting, etc.

At low data levels, the performance is good, and indeed it is superior to that of a token ring, but at high loads the protocol is not fair (particularly to end stations).

6. IEEE 802.11 standard

Between the IEEE 802.6 and 802.11 committees are a number of committees which are primarily technical advisory groups on broadband, fibre optics and security issues that are not LAN standards. The IEEE 802.11 group is a relatively new group that addressed the wireless (WLANs), cordless or cableless LANs (CLANs), and has looked at the various alternatives. These options include infrared line of sight transmission, power line transmission, spread spectrum transmission, and microwave transmission. The IEEE 802.11 standards have defined the media access and physical layers for wireless LANs as shown in Fig. 9.46.

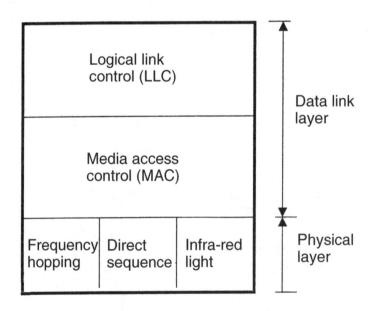

Fig 9.46 Architectural model of IEEE 802.11

Since the three access techniques shown in Fig. 9.46 tend to be higher priced products than the traditional wired LAN components, then they were initially targeted at niche areas such as:

a) situations where stations frequently move;

b) situations where cabling may be problematic (e.g., point-of-sale terminals);

c) terminals in listed buildings or buildings with marble surfaces (e.g., in financial institutions);

d) areas of hazardous installation for cabling (e.g., asbestos lined areas).

Recent years have seen the development of many devices which are more mobile, such as laptops, palm-held devices, PDAs, and hand-held devices such as data-collection devices. As each of these become part of our daily routines and need to be integrated into the existing IT systems, then the volume sales of cableless connections is impacting directly on the price. Of course, the current higher prices seen for the cableless connection can be offset by the non-requirement to install and maintain any transmission media. This is clearly a major saving and with the release of robust products, currently operating at up to 11 Mbit/s, then the developments in this area look likely to be a 'lively' part of the future approach with large scale adoption and operation. Another significant development has been the evolution of personal area networks, which are based on wireless LANs. Bluetooth as a standard is a subset of the 802.11 wireless networks, and has created a new range of applications for LANs, e.g., it is worth noting that significant developments in the car industry are taking place using Bluetooth, particularly at the luxury end of the car market, where the support of hands-free telephony, automatic emergency calls and roadside assistance built into safety and security aspects are already available. Future developments in this sector are likely to embrace navigation and traffic capabilities and entertainment systems enabling the easy integration of portable DVDs and laptops, etc., Additionally the in-built diagnostic capabilities offer enormous potential, both during manufacture and lifetime maintenance. The mass market of the car industry and the use of Bluetooth as the personal network standard to connect all of these devices should result in major developments and open up other opportunities such as cableless networks in home entertainment systems etc.

The introduction of the IEEE 802.11 standard, and the range of devices typically found in wireless networks, has led to the evolution of two styles of configurations. Peer-to-peer networks have evolved in which each wireless station is able to 'talk' to any other device in the vicinity. Typical configurations look like Fig. 9.47. It is not unusual for one of these devices to be a server, providing a service to any other devices that are able to communicate. It is also possible in such an *ad hoc* network, for the stations to simply be devices that have found themselves in proximity with each other, e.g., laptops in a conference room.

Fig. 9.47 Peer-to peer configuration

Of course in many cases the network applications will require access to wider resources than those normally associated with such freestanding configurations as Fig. 9.47. In these more formal structures, one or more wireless stations communicate with a base station known as an access point. This arrangement provides the normal building block of a wireless network, each area providing a cell as part of the basic service set. A wireless network may then comprise a number of overlapping cells to provide coverage across a designated area. Fig. 9.48 is indicative of a basic service set or cell.

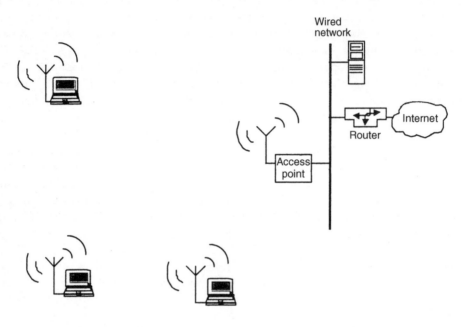

Fig. 9.48 Basic Service Set in a wireless network

The wireless approach has partly grown from cellular radio technology, and is based on Spread Spectrum Transmission (SST) technology. The bandwidth of the transmitted signal is 'spread' by modulating it with a random code sequence. The SST approach was developed in the Second World War. Instead of signalling with all the power in a narrow frequency band, the signal power is spread over a wider frequency bandwidth. Hence, much lower signal strengths or densities can be used than in conventional radio signalling.

This SST signal is restricted in terms of the distance it can travel and it cannot penetrate major obstacles. At the destination, the signal is captured and interpreted to recover the transmitted data.

SST contributes to the security of wireless networks, but clearly on its own is not sufficient. It is normal that additional privacy measures such as encryption of data are also implemented, which is adequate for most purposes. The Wired Equivalent Privacy (WEP) option in the IEEE 802.11 standard provides the mechanism to implement either a 40- or 128-bit RC4 encryption key. The secret key is used to encrypt packets before they are transmitted, and an integrity check is used to ensure that packets are not

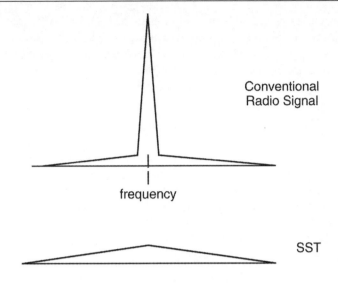

Conventional
Radio Signal

frequency

SST

Fig. 9.49 SST signalling

modified in transit. In practice, most installations that implement encryption use a single key that is shared between all stations.

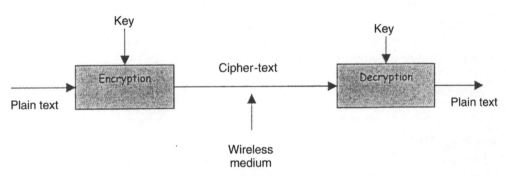

Fig. 9.50 WEP algorithm producing cipher-text

To avoid encrypting two cipher-texts with the same key stream, an Initialization Vector (IV) is used to augment the shared secret key and produce a different RC4 key for each packet. The IV is also included as part of the packet. However recent concerns in security continue to identify the ease with which signals can be received and potentially interpreted. Indeed the BBC SCI/TECH News' report on 6 November 2001 noted that two-thirds of an identified sample group of ten sites in one of London's streets were 'wide open', with little effective security evidenced.

The original operating frequency allocated to wireless networks has been problematic. In the USA, early developments took place in the 902 to 928 MHz range. However, this clashed with the UK cellular operation of Cellnet and Vodafone, etc., Hence an alternative frequency range was necessary to achieve worldwide acceptance. The 2.4 GHz frequency area has been deregulated and the UK, in common with most other countries, has assigned the unlicensed Industrial Scientific Medical band (ISM), 2.4GHz to 2.483GHz, as a band in which wireless LANs may operate. It is in this frequency band that we now see worldwide implementations occurring.

The IEEE 802.11 standard was introduced in 1997 and implements CSMA/CA as the media access technique. The standard defined two forms of spread spectrum operating at data rates of 1 or 2 Mbit/s, namely Frequency Hopping Spread Spectrum (802.11 FHSS) and Direct Sequence (802.11 DSSS). In 1999 the standard was updated and the DSSS was redefined as 802.11b, providing data rates of 11 Mbit/s, but new developments are actively considering a 22 Mbit/s enhancement within the existing standard. This is the area where current product development is being focused at the time of writing. The IEEE 802.11 and 802.11b standards operates in the 2.4 GHz ISM band. An IEEE 802.11a standard was also defined in 1999, operating in the 5 GHz range, and providing speeds of up to 54 Mbit/s.

Future developments up to 100 Mbit/s are exploring the use of higher frequency bands, looking at the feasibility of 60 GHz. With the power limits imposed for health and safety reasons (and battery conservation for hand-held devices), the operational range at 60 GHz would be about 10 m.

The range for current 2.4 GHz implementations is typically 50 m to 100 m. Example approaches are:

a) 3COM's Airconnect which implements DSS to achieve speeds of 11 Mbit/s;

b) Cisco's Aironet which also implements DSS at 11 Mbit/s.

Generally, if a high carrier frequency is allocated, then a higher bandwidth network can typically be supported. The result is a range of wireless networks, which can behave like a token ring or Ethernet, without the inconvenience of cabling.

Question 9.23 If wireless LANs can avoid the cost of cabling and accommodate frequent device relocation without cost, will all future LANs be wireless?

Frequency hopping

With the ISM band available, it was divided into 79 individual radio frequency channels spaced 1 MHz apart. Frequency hopping transmits in one channel for a maximum period of time or dwell time, typically 400 µs. It then hops to another channel in a pseudo-random manner, using a technique known as the spreading code, to send the next part of the transmission. Both the transmitter and the receiver use the same code to lock into the channel hop sequence. Implementing 1600 hops/s on average, there is a small gap between the transmission on each channel to allow the hop to take place. Fig. 9.51 shows a typical transmission sequence using frequency hopping.

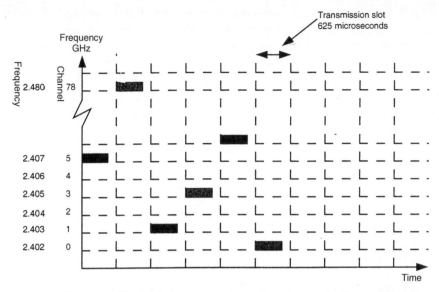

Fig. 9.51 Typical frequency hopping transmission sequence

The transmission during each of these slots is based on a specific modulation type depending on which data rate is being implemented. GFSK (Gaussian Frequency Shift Keying) is typical of the modulation approach used, where the frequency of the channel in use is modulated by a fixed amount in either direction from the central frequency of the channel. This frequency modulation is used to represent a 0 or a 1 bit.

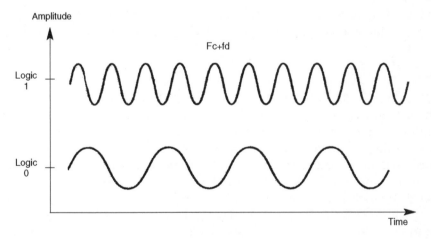

Fig. 9.52 GFSK

Direct Sequence Spread Spectrum (DSSS)

This approach takes each individual data bit to be transmitted, and represents the 0 or 1 value as a multiple bit sequence. The number of bits used to represent the 0 or 1 value is dictated by the chipping code used. Hence, if a chipping code of 11 is set, then one of two different 11-bit sequences will represent each of the two possible data bits. A sequence of 11 bits, based on the standard known as the Barker sequence is normally implemented. The code uses a wider frequency band to achieve transmission. In the IEEE 802.11b standard, the DSSS may have up to thirteen transmission channels available, each channel with a 5 MHz bandwidth.

The IEEE 802.11 encoding scheme used for signalling the transmission is DBPSK (Differential Binary Phase Shift Keying) for 1 Mbit/s rates and DQPSK (Differential Quadrature Phase Shift Keying) for the 2 Mbit/s rate. Fig. 9.53 shows how the four levels are used to signal two bits at a time.

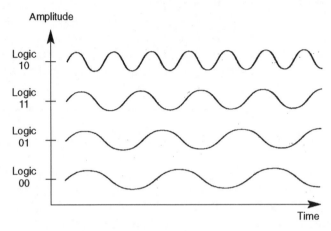

Fig. 9.53 DQPSK

To achieve data rates of 11 Mbit/s defined in the IEEE 802.11b standard, a more complex modulation scheme known as CCK (Complementary Code Keying) is employed.

MAC layer

The MAC layer in the IEEE 802.11 standard is defined as providing station services (which include authentication, deauthentication, privacy and packet delivery) and distribution system services (which include association, disassociation, etc.). Authentication is needed to provide control of who is able to gain access to the network and involves exchanging management frames or use of shared key WEP algorithm. Association is the process of a station linking into an access station. It can only be associated with one access point. If a station roams into another cell area, it needs to re-associate with another access point. To deliver these services a MAC frame structure is shown in Fig. 9.54. A number of address fields may be necessary for those occasions when a transmission between two stations is via an intermediate station such as the access point.

7. IEEE 802.12 standard

The IEEE 802.12 standard has been promoted by companies such as Hewlett-Packard and IBM. It recognizes that the existing investment made by organizations needs to be protected as far as possible. At the same time, the requirement for higher bandwidth to

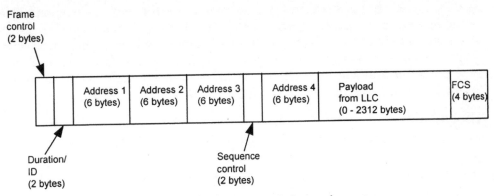

Fig. 9.54 IEEE 802.11 MAC frame format

accommodate the new and developing applications such as multimedia are overtaking the capacity of currently installed LANs.

Perhaps the most significant change in LAN installations since the early 1990s has been the rapid move towards installing structured wiring schemes. Hence the topologies are similar, regardless of whether the intention is to install 10baseT or token ring (see Fig. 9.55). It was on this platform that the new proposal for 100VG-AnyLAN was launched. 100VG-AnyLAN is one of the early implementations of the 802.12 standard.

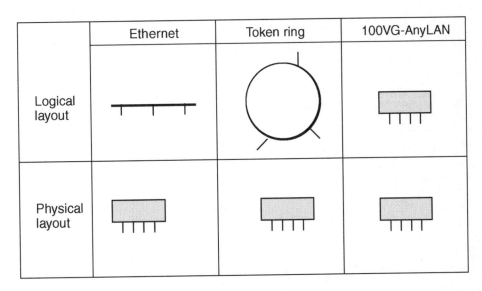

Fig. 9.55 Network topology of 802.12 standard

100VG-AnyLAN has also attempted to accommodate the two earlier approaches by providing a standard that can operate with both Ethernet and token ring frames, albeit that a hub is only configured to handle either one or the other of the frame formats. Given that there an estimated 80 million existing Ethernet and token ring users, it was an important design consideration to provide an upgrade path for this existing user base rather than implement a completely new design.

Physical layout

The proposal provides 100 Mbit/s on four-pair Category 3, Category 4 or Category 5 rated UTP. The intention is to also offer this on two-pair UTP Category 5 cable, on two-pair STP cable (such as IBM Type 1 cable), and on fibre optics cable, although this may not be supported in the first products that are released.

The standard implements a demand priority access approach, and consists of hubs which provide node connections to other devices. To make provision for a number of device attachments, normally up to 784, the hubs may be cascaded down to level 3. Using a four-port hub for simplicity, this would look like the configuration in Fig. 9.56. In practice, hubs have 12, 24 or 48 ports.

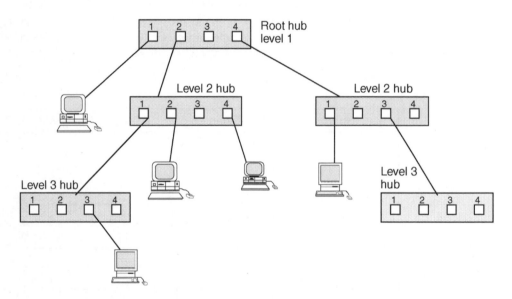

Fig. 9.56 Cascaded hub arrangement

Existing 10baseT or 802.5 networks can move to 100VG-AnyLAN by two methods. The interim approach is simply to bridge the existing LAN into the new network (see Fig. 9.57).

Question 9.24 Why do we need a bridge between the 10baseT and 802.12 LANs rather than a repeater?

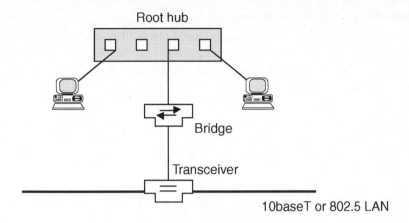

Fig. 9.57 Bridge configuration

If the 802.12 network needs a connection to services discussed later, such as FDDI, ATM or WANs, then a router is attached to one of the root hub's ports. Provision can also be made for an Ethernet switch to be connected to the 802.12 hub. This approach allows the continuing use of existing facilities as the 802.12 network is developed and expanded.

To fully migrate to a 802.12 network, the existing cable structure of the 10baseT and 802.5 networks can be used, including the same modular RJ-45 connector. If the 802.12 hub is placed in the wiring rack, it is simply a case of unplugging the connector from the existing arrangement and plugging it into the new hub. At the device end, the existing network card needs to be replaced with an 802.12 card. This provides the different speed and media access capability. It is the cost of a new card that makes the conversion quite expensive and hence the interim approach is likely to be used in those centres wishing to make the transition.

Because existing cable structures can be utilized, we have said little about the cable lengths. However, for completeness, the data in Table 9.2 provides a good guideline. However, it is better to keep all TP cable to 100 m, which fits in with all structured wiring schemes.

Cable	Length of cable from hub port to device
Category 3 and 4 UTP	100 m
Category 5 UTP & STP	150 m
Fibre optic (single & multimode supported)	2000 m

Table 9.2 802.12 cable lengths

Data encoding and transmission

100VG-AnyLAN uses 5B/6B encoding to transmit the data. Depending on the transmission medium, different arrangements are in place to achieve the 100 Mbit/s transmission rate whilst keeping within the frequency emission regulations. For UTP cable, all four pairs are used in parallel with an approach called quartet coding (see Fig. 9.58). Each pair carries 30 Mbit/s, and hence the four pairs can carry 120 Mbit/s. Given the 5B/6B encoding, this means that there is a data rate of 100 Mbit/s for the attached device. Although each pair is carrying 30 Mbit/s, because NRZ is implemented, the maximum frequency on any pair is 15 MHz, and hence this is well within the frequency emission limits.

Question 9.25 Why would we want to use 5B/6B encoding rather than Manchester encoding in an 802.12 LAN?

The MAC level data is partitioned into 4×5 bit units, and the first 20 bits are sent in parallel across the four-pair UTP cable, followed by the next 20 bits. This allows 5 bytes of data to be sent in two stages.

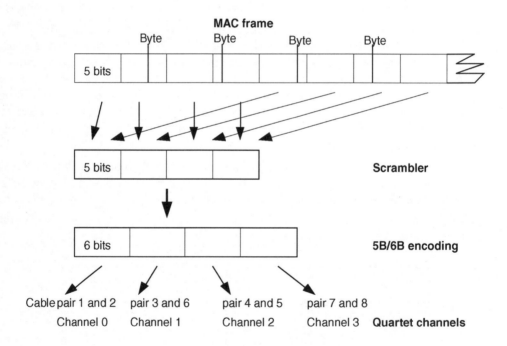

Fig. 9.58 Quartet coding

In the cases of STP cable and fibre optics cable, four parallel circuits are not physically available. Hence the quartet requirement is achieved by multiplexing the sextets into either two channels for STP cable or one channel for fibre optics cable. Both of these require higher transmission frequencies as a result, but are still within the established guidelines for that particular type of medium. Hence, for a two-pair STP approach, the arrangement would have one pair supporting channels 0 and 2, whilst the other pair supported channels 1 and 3.

Question 9.26 Why does the UTP approach need to use four channels to sustain a data rate of 100 Mbit/s?

8. Fibre Distributed Data Interface (FDDI)

The Fibre Distributed Data Interface (FDDI) is a dual-ring network (shown in Fig. 9.59). The standard was initiated by the ANSI 3T9.5 committee and has been adopted as the ISO 9314 standard.

FDDI provides a backbone network capability to move data at 100 Mbit/s in a private network. The distance can be 2 km between active nodes, with a maximum of 500 attached nodes and a maximum of 100 km overall length. Hence, much of the fibre optics cable is 'rented' from the PTT.

FDDI uses many of the previously defined features of the 802.4 and 802.5 standards. The address/copied flags and token capture/release mechanisms of the 802.5 standard are implemented, and the timed token with priorities of structure of the 802.4 standard are used. It uses step-index fibres with a core diameter of 62.5 µm and a cladding of 125 µm.

Two types of node are available, with class A devices being connected to both primary and secondary rings whilst class B devices are connected to the primary ring only. Hence, with a dual ring, some resilience to cable faults is available via self healing within the dual attachment nodes. Class B stations could be isolated in a fault situation.

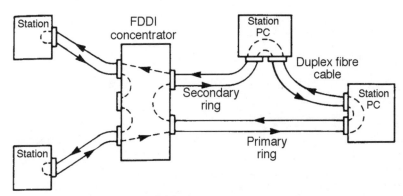

Fig. 9.59 FDDI component structure
(© Learning Group International, reprinted with permission)

FDDI uses the Station Management Protocol (SMT) which is equivalent to the physical layer and MAC layer (see Fig. 9.60). With the addition of the LLC functionality, this is equivalent to the bottom two OSI layers as shown in Fig. 7.6.

Because the connections are brought out to locations in the user locality, laser light is not used (it could damage the retina of a curious user if the power of the signal were stronger!), and so LED/PIN arrangements are used instead. Manchester encoding and differential

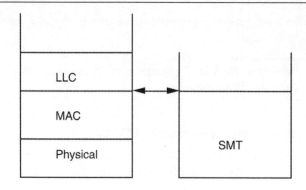

Fig. 9.60 FDDI/OSI relationship

Manchester encoding techniques require high signalling rates to accommodate the embedded clocking singles. If one of these standards were adopted, then the high signalling rates would require very expensive transmitter/receiver pairs.

Instead, a 4B/5B encoding is implemented where each 4-bit pattern is transmitted as a 5-bit pattern, which ensures that a reasonable number of signal changes are accommodated and no long runs of 0s or 1s are permitted. Hence, there is a requirement to transmit 125 Mbit/s to carry 100 Mbit/s of data. The reduction to 125 Mbit/s instead of 200 Mbit/s reduces the transmitter/receiver price by up to 80 per cent.

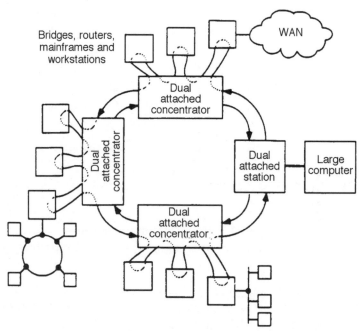

Fig. 9.61 FDDI concentrators
(© Learning Group International, reprinted with permission)

Frequently, the attachment to the network is via concentrators which can attach a variety of hosts, workstations, routers or bridges with up to eight devices on a single concentrator (see Fig. 9.61).

Hence, the primary use of FDDI is either to carry data from one LAN to another by playing the role of a fast backbone or to handle the large data volumes generated by powerful workstations or host machines which are directly connected.

FDDI II has the ability to carry voice, so stations may book a slot in synchronous packets. These circulate every 125 μs with 96 slots to carry the traffic (i.e., three megastream links and four links). As a result, each synchronous packet can carry 96 voice links and occupies 6 Mbit/s of the 100 Mbit/s bandwidth.

Question 9.27 Why do we need both MANs and FDDI as standards?

A large FDDI backbone may connect a number of free-standing LANs together. Fig. 9.62 shows an example using Ungermann-Bass component connections.

Further questions

(There are answers to the questions marked with an asterisk at the end of the book.)

1. *Why should we be concerned that the IEEE 802.3 packet needs to be a minimum of 64 bytes long?

2. *Why is it important to have unique hardware addresses for each station on a given LAN?

3. *An office 25 m long has four PCs to be attached to a LAN. This LAN has connections in a second office 700 m away, where another fifteen PCs and a server are located. This second office is approximately 40 m long. Suggest a possible IEEE 802.3 configuration, or state any assumptions you might need to make.

4. Would a switch help in the scenario in Question 3?

5. If the two offices in Question 3 had to be connected across open space (i.e., they were in separate buildings), but the space was on a privately owned industrial estate, what type of link between buildings might be appropriate?

6. The 100baseT standard is a popular IEEE 802.3 standard implementation. Outline the reasons for this popularity.

7. An office measuring 200 m by 200 m has 200 devices evenly spread out over the floor space. Suggest an IEEE 802.3 layout that is suitable to achieve connectivity of these devices.

8. Why has twisted-pair cable become the normal transmission medium in LANs?

9. Suggest why the IEEE 802.4 standard is not as widely implemented in an office environment as the 802.3 and 802.5 standards.

10. Why do we need to have an address scheme such as the IP address?

11. Since up to 30 per cent of users physically move each year, why might a punch-down block approach be helpful to accommodate such mobility?

12. Could FDDI be used as a backbone network to connect large central processors and their controllers together?

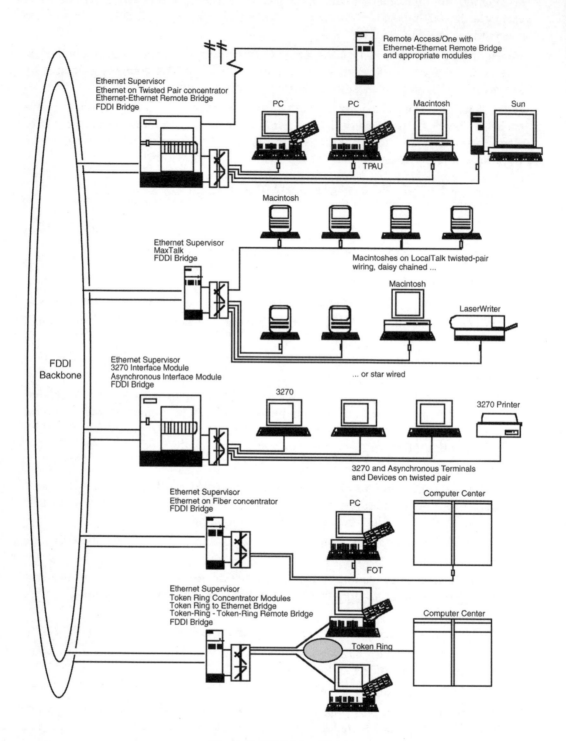

Fig. 9.62 FDDI backbone
(© Ungemann-Bass, reprinted with permission)

13. Why do we need high speed networks such as Gigabit Ethernet networks?

14. Why do we often connect servers directly to ports on an Ethernet switch?

Answer 9.1	The Copper Distributed Data Interface (CDDI) has been developed at 100 Mbit/s, which is the same speed as that for FDDI. There are many installations where suitable copper wire has already been installed for use at lower speeds, but Fast Ethernet is also used now. Thus the user can avoid the necessity for an expensive installation using a fibre optics backbone cable, provided that we are only considering a local installation covering the distances involved in a single building or campus. If greater distances are involved and cable is being rented from the PTT, then FDDI (or a MAN) or ATM are the high speed backbone options.
Answer 9.2	Yes. Although four segments are shown, between any two attached nodes the maximum distance to be travelled is still only three active segments. Hence, one of the segments effectively acts as a backbone cabling system. It is possible to have many more active segments in a maximum configuration than those shown in Fig. 9.7, providing there are never more than three active segments between any two connected devices.
Answer 9.3	This is simpler than the question sounds. The bridge acts like any attached node on the networks. A message can be generated on one side and heard by all the stations on that side including the bridge. If the destination is on the other side of the bridge this is recognized by the bridge which is now buffering the whole data packet that has been transmitted. The bridge will now compete with all stations on the destination side for access to the transmission medium and will relay the message at the earliest opportunity.
Answer 9.4	Yes, in as much as there is a single connection to the transmission medium because of the single transceiver connection.
Answer 9.5	Theoretically, yes, but in doing this you are probably setting up a system which will allow a single pairwise connection at any given time. The biggest problem is that only a few networks remain small. They inevitably grow and frequently require external access. If this is to be successfully managed, it is better to keep to a standard which will support this growth than to limit yourself to the size that the proposed switch might support.
Answer 9.6	10base2 cabling is more flexible and easier to install than the more rigid 10base5 version. This detail is important when considering bend radii and shorter distances between connect points with Cheapernet (10base2) products. Perhaps even more importantly, the cost per connection for 10base2 cabling is significantly less than for 10base5 cabling because the latter needs an external transceiver and transceiver cable which add to the cost (see Fig. 9.14).
Answer 9.7	The 10base2 standard allows us to install cheaper connections than the 10base5 option. Hence we can use the simple BNC connector to get directly onto the card's onboard transceiver, with the daisy chain option. Of course, we can also introduce the more flexible make-and-break wall sockets.
Answer 9.8	For each attached workstation we should include twice the cable length from the faceplate to the interface card. This is because the signal has to travel to and from the interface card, so this is all part of the 185 m maximum length for that segment.
Answer 9.9	Before we operate even the smallest 10baseT network, we need to have a hub. The price of these has been decreasing, and they start at approximately £20 per port. Thus there is a start-up cost, even for a small LAN, but that is not a significant barrier to entry.
Answer 9.10	10baseT cabling offers the opportunity to implement a more resilient cabling structure, with some structured management capability.

Answer 9.11   We can consider each hub as being a repeater, with a collision domain operating over the whole configuration. CSMA/CD then operates as though it were a single 'bus'.

Answer 9.12   There may be a number of reasons, but the most likely reason would be that a faulty station did not pass the token onwards or that it developed a fault as the token arrived and then crashed.

Answer 9.13   A logical ring may need to be extended when, for example, a station that was previously offline becomes active and wants to join a live network. We would not want to close down the operational network to allow this to happen, and so procedures to periodically allow stations to join the logical ring at the correct point by soliciting successors is the technique that is employed in this standard.

Answer 9.14   Because the station that generated the data is also the station responsible for removing it, it is a simple extension to attach a few bits to the end of the data unit such that the destination station can indicate whether the data has been received. The sending station can then perform a quick check to see if this acknowledgement (ACK) is present, and it will immediately recognize whether a resend is required.

Answer 9.15   There are a number of reasons why this arrangement is used. Firstly, it is just possible that the station that requests the high priority fails before a free token reaches it. However, much more relevant is the engineering principle behind the arrangement, which has close analogies with a stack. Whichever station makes a change upwards is also responsible for making the change downwards. (The analogy being that whoever pushed the data onto a stack is responsible for popping it off.)

Answer 9.16   If the least significant end of the IP address is identical to the hardware address, then the translation from this level 3 address to the hardware address is a simple job of masking out the most significant bits of the IP address, which leaves the hardware address (which has been assigned to the board locally).

Answer 9.17   Each bridge is connected to two (or more) LANs, with each connection being via an interface card with its own hardware address.

Answer 9.18   An MSAU provides us with a level of protection that is not afforded by a simple coupler. For example, if we wished to extend the degree of terminal concentration in that area, an additional MSAU can simply extend the ring or a mini MSAU can be plugged into an MSAU node to provide a sublevel. If a station fails, the MSAU can easily allow reconfiguration without the offending station.

Answer 9.19   We determined in Chapter 2 that a signal degenerates in quality as it is propagated along a cable. The maximum transmission distance is simply the furthest that we expect a signal to travel before it has to be regenerated. If it is allowed to propagate further without regeneration then the quality of the signal can deteriorate to the extent that the signal is misinterpreted.

Answer 9.20   The maximum lobe cable length permitted in any configuration depends on how many MSAUs and how many racks are used. Consider the worst scenario laid out in the text. Only two lobe cables are connected, one to an MSAU in one rack (with three MSAUs) and the other to an MSAU in another rack (with two MSAUs). If this is the current connectivity, the signal has to be propagated through all the MSAU patch cables, the inter-rack cabling and the second lobe cable before being regenerated. Since the limit of the total cable length is set, the maximum lobe cable lengths are therefore dependent on the number of patch cables used in the configuration.

Answer 9.21   Type 3 cable is not shielded, whereas Type 1 cable and Type 2 cable are shielded. The higher the operational speeds are, the greater is the technical difficulty in sampling the signal at receiving stations. Shielded cable reduces any interference on the cable which could cause misinterpretation of data. Hence IBM have favoured a cautious approach.

Answer 9.22   In most LAN environments, users do not physically remain at fixed locations, but move their desks (and workstations), perhaps quite often. Since we would not wish to re-cable with every move, flood-wiring the area by providing many spare network outlets may be worthwhile. Not all these outlets need connecting to the LAN simultaneously, but only those where the users are located.

Punch-down blocks provide a convenient means of patching outlet sockets into the LAN whenever such a move has occurred and a user is wishing to be reconnected.

Answer 9.23   The volume of sales is beginning to increase as confidence in the security of wireless LANs becomes proven (recognizing that there are still concerns that unless active security is employed, wireless networks are more vulnerable). Where applications are content that shared speeds of 11 Mbit/s will be adequate for their needs, then wireless LANs are becoming attractive. The simplicity of installation and the flexibility offered to user mobility are powerful concepts that appear to outweigh the concerns. I believe this will be a serious technology in the coming years.

Answer 9.24   The access techniques of the two networks are different and so we need a bridge to resolve the differences.

Answer 9.25   5B/6B encoding results in 120 Mbit/s being transmitted down the transmission medium. Manchester encoding, if it were used, would result in 200 Mbit/s being sent with all the disadvantages of trying to transmit at higher speeds.

Answer 9.26   Each channel supports 30 Mbit/s. The four channels permit 120 Mbit/s to be carried, which maps back to 100 Mbit/s of data when we implement 5B/6B encoding.

Answer 9.27   A MAN is owned and operated by a PTT, and hence a user would be sharing the capacity with PTT customers from other organizations. It might be felt that this is too great a security risk. An FDDI network, on the other hand, is completely owned and operated by a single organization, and hence has none of the security risks.

10 ATM

1. Introduction

Asynchronous transfer mode (ATM) developments came in a changing climate of communications needs. Early wide area networks to support data transfers were established when end computers were slow and expensive and interconnection services were typically unreliable. At that stage, the protocols to support any communication interchange provided the mechanisms for error detection and correction to ensure a secure delivery. In reviewing these arrangements, it was recognized that the end computers were now powerful and cheap and able to carry out the error handling themselves. Meanwhile, the digital communications channels now available are more reliable by several orders of magnitude. Hence, it may be better to undertake the error handling at the end points and concentrate on the communications channels providing fast, efficient and lightweight services. Such a premise was certainly recognized in developing frame relay and ATM.

ATM is a rapidly developing technology that embraces the aspects of both wide area networks and local area networks. It is discussed as a separate chapter because of the seamless interconnection that it provides between WANs and LANs using the same technology. It is likely to be a key technology of the future and is worthy of separate treatment.

A number of companies have invested heavily in creating an ATM product range. This development recognizes the increasing processing power of workstations, and the fact that applications have moved from alphanumeric interfaces through to graphical client–server models, and potentially into video client–client interfaces. The result of these application developments is an enormous increase in bandwidth requirements, frequently on a pairwise basis. Hence a topology supporting 100 Mbit/s or higher with a scaleable bandwidth and distributed routing is viewed as the market direction. This is the basis of ATM with a 155 Mbit/s interface as the main port support, although other options are available. For example, four ports may be combined to provide 622 Mbit/s as a basic channel capacity. Scaleable bandwidth maintains a predictable and constant level of service, regardless of the number of simultaneous users (see Fig. 10.1).

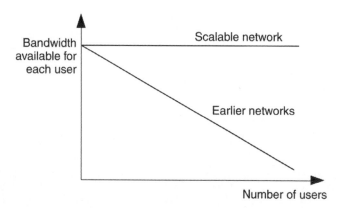

Fig. 10.1 Scaleable bandwidth

The intention of the vendors is to provide ATM technology in the form of both LAN and WAN services. Data would leave the ATM NIC in one workstation and be delivered without the structure being changed to any other ATM workstation. Ideally, the whole of the transfer would be across ATM networks. The data may travel at different speeds across various parts of the ATM networks, but this can easily be managed by the network, and would be transparent to the two end devices.

2. Background to ATM development

The early digital services provided by WANs were based on ISDN and built around 64 kbit/s channels. The basis of this decision is well recognized, 64 kbit/s being viewed at that time as the bandwidth needed to support a digital voice channel. In an era when 100 Mbit/s LAN networks are commonplace and Gigabit LANs are available, ISDN appears to have limitations as an interconnection service, especially between LANs. The high speed LANs have been developed to meet the demands of the new applications such as imaging, video and data warehousing, and it is important that the interconnection is able to support services which span across a number of LANs. The ITU-T standards body (formerly the CCITT) has been active in developing the next generation of WAN services known as broadband ISDN (B-ISDN). Whereas ISDN is a circuit switching technology, the decision was taken to build B-ISDN on what is fundamentally a packet switching network. Packet switching has been covered briefly in Chapter 2. B-ISDN packet switching is based on small size packets called cells, and it is essentially the ATM technology. To establish ATM was a significant decision because the existing WAN copper cable and switches that are in place will become redundant. Only the fibre optics cable will be useful. Given the size of the existing worldwide investment and the cost of implementation of ATM, the process of migration to ATM as the WAN is a long term strategy.

Question 10.1 If we break data down into small packets or cells for transmission, how does each cell know its route to the destination?

The basis of using cell switching is simply to move the data as quickly as possible across the network, through high speed switches. The cell size was optimized to handle the new generation of data. The high speed switching and circuits ensure that all data transfers reach the destinations in a timely manner. Hence, it is particularly useful in handling bursty traffic.

Question 10.2 If the cell size had been significantly bigger, given that the applications generate large amounts of data, wouldn't that have been more efficient from the viewpoint of protocol overheads?

The cell size that was agreed is based on a 53-byte structure, comprising 48 bytes of data and a 5-byte header, as shown in Fig. 10.2. A virtual circuit approach to transferring cells has been adopted. This means that, before we transfer any data, we must first establish the route between the source and the destination. This approach to routing data enables the data to flow along the virtual circuit route that has been established, using only small header components in the cell structure to identify the virtual circuit or route.

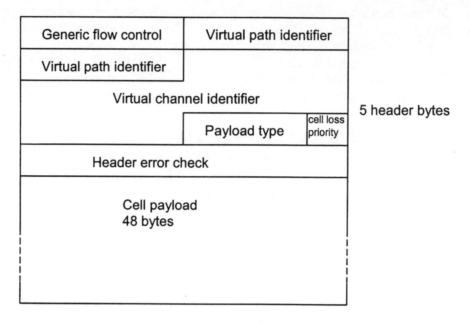

Fig 10.2 ATM Cell

The requirement to establish a virtual circuit across the network before sending data raises several interesting technical design points. The ATM Forum, which was influential in establishing the ATM standard, designed the Private Network-to-Network Interface (PNNI), which supports dynamic routing (switched virtual circuits known as SVCs). Dynamic routing protocols adapt to changing network conditions such as traffic levels and topology changes. In comparison, static routing requires reconfiguration whenever a network change occurs and implements permanent virtual circuits (PVCs). PNNI is a dynamic routing protocol. ATM supports both static and dynamic routing, but encourages SVCs because they are established dynamically which reduces any reconfiguration complexity.

The routing algorithm allows the connection stage to request a particular quality of service (QOS) metric. These metrics include the following:

a)   the maximum cell delay;

b)   the maximum cell delay variation;

c)   the maximum cell loss ratio;

d)   the administration weight;

e)   the available cell rate.

Hence, the basic connection is a virtual circuit (or virtual channel connection), carrying a single stream of cells between two end points. A number of virtual circuits between two end points can be grouped together as a virtual path connection, and routing or any necessary failure recovery can be managed on this higher level path identification. Between two ATM switches the routing of a virtual path connection is likely to comprise a number of different user virtual circuits.

3. ATM LAN configuration and migration strategy

A typical configuration of a LAN ATM hub is currently ten ports, with 100 port switches also available. It is believed by the vendors that a switch with 10,000 ports can be produced! Given the existing installations that are in place, the likely configurations at the outset are shown in Fig. 10.3. This takes advantage of existing hardware and provides an evolutionary or migration approach.

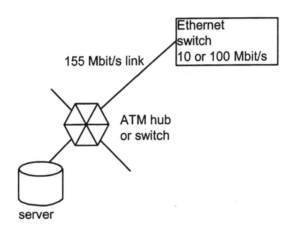

Fig. 10.3 ATM switch

Provision to allow a gradual migration from existing LAN networks is needed if a significant take-up of ATM is to be achieved. Essentially, a mechanism is needed to allow LANs such as Ethernet, primarily, but also token rings and FDDI, to connect to ATM switches, whilst some real improvement in both short term performance and long term strategy is offered. To take advantage of the high speeds in a network, it is possible to place the servers as a direct connection to the ATM switch (Fig. 10.3). This allows a high speed link to service multiple clients with a rapid response capability. The current developments provide connectivity between the ATM switch and shared media LANs. Fig. 10.4 shows how shared media LANs can be interconnected. The market will be difficult to move in the ATM direction at the moment, given the rapid take-up of Ethernet switches, the 100baseT and Gigabit Ethernet standard and the arrival of the 10 Gigabit Ethernet standard.

Typically, switches are available in two basic ranges. One range is a small workgroup switch or edge switch, typically operating at 1.6 Gbit/s with multiple multi-fibre (OC-3) 155 Mbit/s ports and a three priority level operation. The other range is a backbone switch operating at 12.8 Gbit/s and with connections to seven workgroup switches. This allows very large networks to be designed.

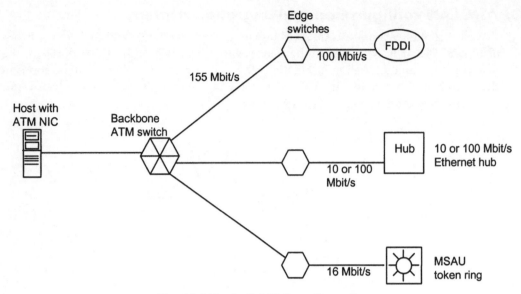

Fig. 10.4 Typical ATM configuration

4. ATM switches

The ATM switches designed for LAN operation have a primary requirement to meet the needs of a backbone communications system. Normally, a connection is allocated to a single port on a switch. The principle is to switch the incoming cell to an outbound port as quickly as possible. The switch architecture to achieve this is frequently based on shared memory. For those switches that are non-blocking, input cells are connected to output ports immediately and not buffered. Only when two or more input ports have cells to be switched to the same output port simultaneously do we need to buffer cells. The selection of which port's cell is allowed to go first must be random and not prioritized, or else there is unfair treatment of some cells.

Switches typically offer traffic management and congestion control features. The traffic management aspects include the support of policies which flexibly handle the bandwidth allocation. Congestion control will typically have the targets of avoiding congestion, minimizing congestion whenever it happens, and preventing the spread of congestion when it occurs. During the call set-up stage, which is sometimes referred to as the call level, the congestion control can exercise connection admission control, resource reservation, virtual path connection routing and load balancing. Connection admission control covers both resource related and policy related issues. Resource related issues include bandwidth availability and end-to-end QOS metrics. The policy related issues cover aspects such as access lists, time and date and the maximum number of connections. During a data phase cell transfer, which is sometimes called the cell level, the congestion control is concerned with buffer management, scheduling and delay priority control and loss priority control.

Question 10.3 Why is cell loss an acceptable mechanism? Wouldn't it be better to deliver the cell a little late rather than not at all?

---

5. ATM and the reference model

The ATM developments have not mapped directly across to the OSI model. Instead, they followed a similar approach to the other high-speed network designs and introduced a number of sublayers. Fig. 10.5 shows how the ATM layers map onto the OSI model. These sublayers are designed to provide interface points such that a number of alternatives can be supported, e.g., a number of different types of transmission media offering a standard upwards interface.

ATM Reference model   OSI

ATM adaptation layer	3/4
ATM	2/3
Physical layer PMD and TC	1/2

Fig. 10.5 ATM reference model

The physical layer consists of a Physical Medium Dependent Sublayer (PMD) and Transmission Convergence (TC) sublayer. ATM has been designed to be as independent as possible from the transmission medium, and it does not require a specific set of rules to be followed. Indeed the ATM cell could be carried as a payload in another network, provided that it conformed with the QOS requirements. The TC sublayer ensures that the bit stream delivered to and from the PMD is structured in cells, and it is responsible for the error handling routine using checksum generation and verification.

The ATM layer is where flow control and virtual circuit management takes place, and the ATM Adaptation Layer (AAL) provides the necessary segmentation and reassembly for the cell structures.

Further questions

(There are answers to the questions marked with an asterisk at the end of the book.)

1. *Why are modern communications systems more suited to switching small cells of data quickly to the destination than assembling large packets of data and routing them?

2. Given that the OSI model already existed, why didn't the ATM developments keep more closely to the OSI model in their design?

3. Why is dynamic routing preferable to static routing in an ATM network?

4. *In the QOS metrics, what features is the administrative weight likely to address?

5. *Given the development of Fast Ethernet and Gigabit Ethernet, is there a marketplace for ATM as a LAN?

6. Why has the ATM standard allowed any layer 1 service to carry the traffic, rather than being precise about the network structure?

Answer 10.1   A small 5-byte header at the front of each cell contains sufficient information for the packet to be sent along a predetermined route which is a virtual circuit. The virtual circuit is set up as the first phase of a data transfer, before the data cells flow. Hence, the header is a route identifier.

Answer 10.2   Of course the fact that the lower the percentage of header bits is in relation to the data bits, the higher is the efficiency of the protocol is a basic calculation. There are other important issues to consider here also. If the size of the data cell were larger, then the delay in assembling the cell could make the speed of transfer useless for the application. It is the changing user applications and the way that they are using the networks that is really dictating the design. If we were to take a voice transfer as a digital communication, at the receiving end it is better to get a steady flow of data than it is to get data arriving in larger units but more intermittently. Hence, efficiency measured in terms of 'does this small cell size meet the needs of the service requirements?' would support the approach being taken here.

Answer 10.3   If the data transfer is video or voice, there is no point in delivering a cell too late. Given the redundancy of information content in these applications, the user receiving such data wouldn't be aware of the loss. For those applications which need to capture all cells, then the error recovery end-to-end protocols can come into action and handle the situation.

---

11 Interconnection

1. Introduction

The distances which can be covered by a single LAN are limited and frequently there is a requirement to extend the range. Existing sections may be joined together using one of a range of interconnecting devices (see Fig. 11.1). Each of the interconnecting device types meets a specific need and will be appropriate for a particular requirement. Deciding what is appropriate is the subject of this chapter.

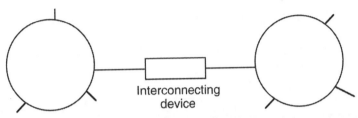

Interconnecting
device

Fig. 11.1 Extending the network range

It may be that an existing network needs to be partitioned into two (or more) separate entities. The rationale for this may be to provide additional security for a particular area, so that shared traffic within a 'secure group' is not seen by everybody. There may also be a requirement to partition a network because the existing network is reaching its maximum throughput capability and further growth without a split would result in performance degradation. By partitioning a network into two or more joined networks we can create smaller networks with only a fraction of the combined traffic on each. This gives us a performance benefit for each of the newly created smaller networks because of the lower traffic levels.

Another consideration may be that there is a desire to couple together existing freestanding arrangements, since the network manager is frequently not starting from scratch because there are already installed facilities. In this case there may well be a wish to integrate these existing facilities to create a new coherence. The origins of the existing arrangements may be many and varied, but typically there will have been individual initiatives. Some systems may have been purchased because a particular vendor offered a unique solution to a given problem.

A good example might be a site which has a number of Apple Macintosh machines linked together via an Ethernet network alongside a token ring linking together a number of PCs, with a second Ethernet provision because there are a number of SUNs on site. These systems may have been installed as separate initiatives aimed at resolving unique requirements such as those in publishing, engineering design, etc., Equally, a merger between two organizations that previously had separate types of LAN will require some coherent interconnection.

At some stage, however, the requirements may well change, and we will need to look at integrating some of the disparate entities to form a new cohesive structure. The approach taken may vary, but the process can typically be viewed as multi-vendor integration.

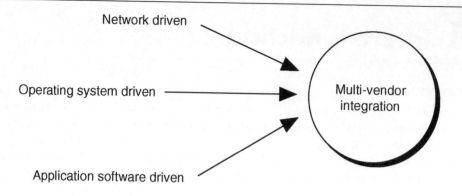

Fig. 11.2 Approaches to multi-vendor integration

However, it must be recognized that achieving this level of multi-vendor integration is a non-trivial exercise. It can be viewed as a two stage operation, as shown in Fig. 11.3.

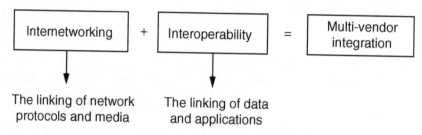

Fig. 11.3 Components of multi-vendor integration

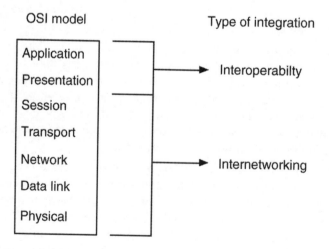

Fig. 11.4 OSI and multi-vendor integration

We can see in Fig. 11.2 that there are several approaches to achieving multi-vendor integration. This is not an exhaustive list of inputs, and there are other approaches than the three shown. To achieve the integration sought, one or more of these ideas will be implemented. Fig. 11.4 indicates where a particular approach fits in the OSI model. Standards at the bottom of the model have existed and been relatively stable for some years, and contribute to the internetworking element. More recently, we have seen serious attempts to integrate at the higher levels to achieve interoperability. At this level the existing platforms are much more diverse.

Question 11.1 Is the internetworking problem likely to be easier or more difficult to resolve than the interoperability problem?

In any particular situation the amount of effort involved in achieving the interconnection will depend on the similarities of the two networks being connected. This chapter will explain the four major types of relaying or interconnecting device. Often in the past these were all referred to as gateway devices, but this is simply a generic name. Perhaps a more useful generic term (which prevents there being any confusion) is relay device. In the interests of describing the connecting devices more accurately, the OSI model provides a useful reference point as a basis for discussion. We will initially examine the relay device operating at the lowest level in the model, and later move up through the OSI model.

Question 11.2 Why might it better to achieve the connection at a low level in the OSI model rather than within the higher levels?

---

2. Repeaters

At the simplest level of interconnection, we can operate at the bottom layer of the OSI model. If both 'sides' are identical and the requirement is simply to repeat and boost the digital signal transmission across similar media, then a repeater is required, as shown in Fig. 11.5. This assumes that the same signalling processes exist on both sides, e.g., that we are coupling Ethernet segment to Ethernet segment and *not* Ethernet segment to token ring. Retiming capabilities are also provided on some repeaters. Various vendor's repeaters are also capable of reconstructing the preamble if this has become partially lost or destroyed. Auto-partitioning, to isolate faulty segments from the rest of the network with automatic reconnection once normal data transfer has been achieved, is available as a repeater feature in some models. For example, a fault may be declared after 30 successive collisions in a CSMA/CD LAN. If the network is a broadband facility, then the regeneration of the analogue signal is via an amplifier, which is contained either in the headend or provided as an in-line device powered from the cable.

Question 11.3 How can we provide power (to the amplifier) via the same cable that is transmitting analogue data on a broadband system?

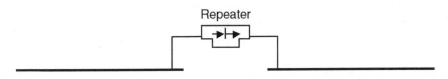

Fig. 11.5 Repeater

We can now see where the devices shown in Fig. 6.3 fits in the OSI architecture model. Typically, we are extending the transmission range of a network such as an IEEE 802.3 LAN. In the case of an Ethernet network, we have already seen three active segments connecting any two devices on the LAN, and so the model may look like that shown in Fig. 11.6.

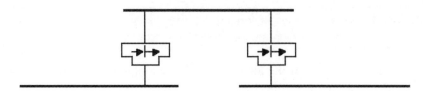

Fig. 11.6 Extended bus network

We also noted in Chapter 9 that, in the original Ethernet 10base5 standard, it is also permissible to include a single occurrence of a 1000m point-to-point link with repeaters, which are often called half repeaters at each end of the link, giving the configuration shown in Fig. 11.7. Alternatively, two separate point-to-point links making a total of 1000 m are also allowable.

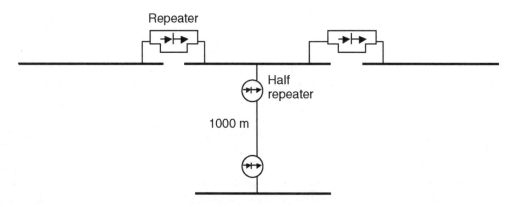

Fig. 11.7 Maximum configuration

In the format shown in Figs 11.6 and 11.7, there are only two repeaters between any two end devices. Devices may be attached to any of the active segments, but not the point-to-point link.

The definition has been redefined to specify five connected segments, using four repeaters, to exist between any attached devices. However, only three of the segments are allowed to support attached devices and are considered to be active segments. The maximum distance remains 2500 m and all other characteristics stay the same. In this case, the two segments which have no attachments are point-to-point links, and they have a half repeater at both ends. Frequently, the point-to-point links are fibre optic cable runs.

In Fig. 11.7 the top centre horizontal segment has become a backbone segment off which all other segments are spurs, whether connected directly or via a point-to-point link.

This is a significant feature, since the location of the backbone segment becomes an important element of the LAN design. Depending on the physical location, other spur segments may or may not be able to easily reach all the devices requiring connection.

The performance of a repeater does not have an impact on the network access techniques. It typically introduces a delay of a few bits whilst the signal is boosted, i.e., it works at bit level. Hence, if the network is operating at 10 Mbit/s, so does the repeater.

Since the repeater works at bit level to extend the network, and it places the incoming data on the outgoing side, typically with a delay of only a few bits, the media access technique is now operating as a single entity across the extended network. For example, in the Ethernet case, CSMA/CD operates over all the joined segments as though they were a single cable. The repeater does *not* separate CSMA/CD access techniques on either side of the repeater. The total zone over which CSMA/CD operates is known as a single collision domain.

In the case of a token ring network, each interface has a repeater function because each node plays an 'active' role. Clearly, we cannot have too many inactive nodes in a token ring, or else the signal may travel extended distances without being regenerated and possibly become unrecognizable. The case for a structured wiring scheme is therefore strengthened.

Question 11.4 Why is the case for a structured wiring scheme strengthened by the possibility of having many inactive token ring interfaces in an unstructured system?

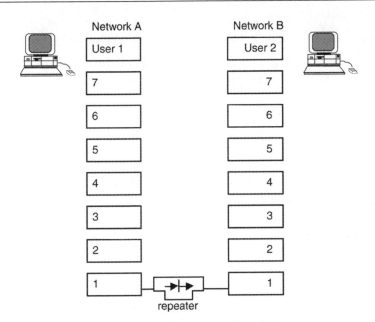

Fig. 11.8 Physical layer repeater

Repeaters may be defined as local repeaters, fibre optics repeaters, multi-port repeaters or mixed media repeaters (see Figs 11.9 and 11.10). Fig. 11.5 shows a local repeater situation where two adjacent segments are joined together. Fig. 11.7 shows an example with two segments joined by a fibre optics point-to-point link with a fibre optics repeater, or half repeater, at both ends.

Fig. 11.9 10baseT repeater module
(© **Allied Telesyn, reprinted with permission**)

Repeaters for IEEE 802.3 networks can be used to mix most combinations of media attachments. Additionally, multi-port repeaters are available which can be configured to give an extended range. An example of this is shown in Fig. 9.17. The original work was undertaken for thin wire multi-port repeaters, where a number of 185 m thin wire segments could be connected to a thick wire segment at a single location (typically eight segment configurations). The use of multi-port repeaters allows us to access a high number of users within a fairly limited area (perhaps a department within an organization), and make a single connection to the backbone segment.

Multiport repeaters or hubs are available to connect a number of users, as shown in Fig. 11.10.

Hence, a network could grow to become a large network just through the use of repeaters. An example of such a network is shown in Fig. 9.7. As networks have evolved, whilst the functional requirements of a repeater have not changed radically, the devices which deliver that repeater functionality have changed.

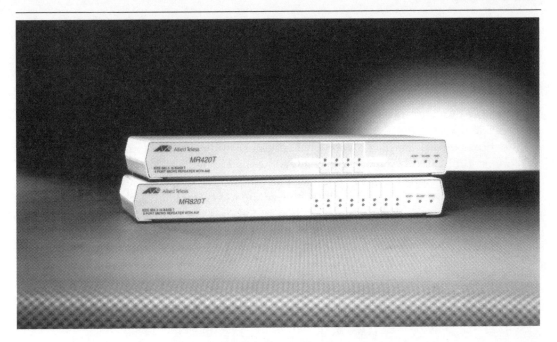

Fig. 11.10 Multiple-media concentrator
(© **Allied Telesyn, reprinted with permission**)

Typical of the new networks are 10baseT and 100baseT, which use a hub as part of the architectural model. In principle, this functions as a multi-port repeater. Each transmission from a device, when received at the hub, is propagated onto all other ports. More recent technology implements switching. However, an Ethernet switch works on MAC addresses and as a result has higher level functionality than a repeater. Hence, we can see there are devices offering interconnection at higher layers in the OSI model, which will include repeater functions. It is important to remember that a repeater is strictly a layer 1 device and operates at bit level. It does not normally interpret the significance of any of the bits, but simply regenerates each bit to a good signal strength and forwards it on the outbound path(s). Equally importantly, it is transparent to other devices and the available bandwidth is spread over the extended network, with collision detection also operating over the extended network as though it was a single entity. Thus we have an extended collision domain.

With the current developments, the bandwidth demands of individual connected devices have increased. Thus, large networks created by multiple repeaters which share the available bandwidth are not now the preferred approach. Instead, it is 'better' to create multiple collision domains or sections of networks which are not sharing fixed bandwidth. Such networks approach the scaleable network definitions we saw in ATM networks. As indicated above, switches provide such facilities and are consequently 'favoured' above the older repeater scenario.

Question 11.5 Suggest why fibre optics cable is preferred for the point-to-point connection between two segments when the segments are in different buildings.

---

3. Bridges

A bridge provides a facility which is closer to the concept of multi-vendor integration provision. Each side of a bridge need not be an identical network or even an almost identical network as in the case of a repeater. Bridges were nominally designed to connect IEEE 802.x LAN technologies together and provide a relay service at the Media Access Control (MAC) layer. Because they operate at the MAC level, bridges act as store-and-forward devices, i.e., the whole of the MAC frame is received, error checked for integrity, and then selectively forwarded on the connection supporting the destination address. Technically, each side of the bridge operates as a free-standing LAN, each with their own collision domain in the case of an Ethernet network. The data which is being forwarded also needs to compete for access on the destination LAN.

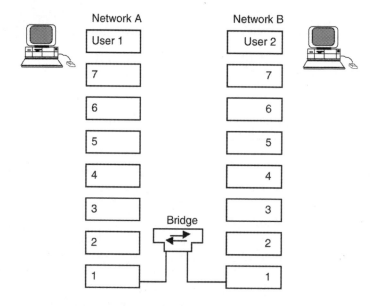

Fig. 11.11 Bridge functionality within the OSI model

Fig. 11.11 is indicative of the position in the reference model, but is not a strictly accurate model since the MAC layer doesn't map directly to the OSI data link layer. The model in Fig. 11.12, where the functions of the data link layer are split, is more correct.

The straightforward use of a bridge is simply to extend the distance or the range that a workplace LAN is able to cover (see Fig. 11.13). As an example, if an Ethernet LAN is to extend beyond 2500 m or thereabouts, then a bridge could be used as an extension relay.

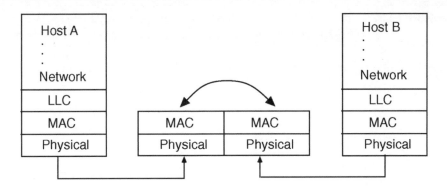

Fig. 11.12 Bridge functioning

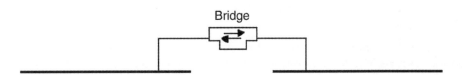

Fig. 11.13 IEEE 802.3 bridged network

The LANs on either side of the bridge function independently of each other, and only traffic with a destination that is known to be on the other side of the bridge, or is of unknown location, will be passed through the bridge. The bridge functions as a filter, separating the traffic that can be isolated on either side, and essentially only allows data to pass through which ought to be seen on the other side. For a bridge to pass the data onto the other side, it has to compete with all the other devices for media access on that LAN. In the case of Ethernet LANs, each side of the bridge will be a separate CSMA/CD area, i.e., they are separate collision domains. The bridge will have a separate hardware address on both sides. Indeed it is possible to have a multi-port bridge, in which case each port will have a separate MAC hardware address.

The rationale behind using a bridge could be described as providing a little robustness in a LAN. With a bridged LAN, either side can function without the other in the event of a catastrophic failure. Also, heavy traffic being generated in any one area or segment may be contained within that area because the bridge filters out the bulk of the data, provided that the destination of this heavy traffic is also on the same segment. Another feature of this traffic filtering is that the integrated network will have enhanced security with the traffic only appearing on those areas necessary for the destination to be reached. Hence, in a LAN with multiple bridges, small workgroups can be set up where traffic between the workgroup members is not seen outside the workgroup. The performance of the separate entities will also be improved.

Question 11.6 Why would it not be appropriate to place a file server on the other side of a bridge from a number of diskless workstations which it services?

Bridges can also be used to link between IEEE 802 media and standards, as shown in Fig. 11.14, where two 802.x LANs are interconnected.

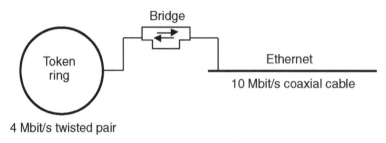

Fig. 11.14 Bridge between IEEE 802.x LANs

The IEEE 802 committees could not agree on the basis of the addressing mechanisms, and so a bridge can be required to operate in two modes. The 802.3 committee felt that the bridge should be transparent in the system, whereas the 802.5 committee decided that source routing was preferable. Hence, devices need to be aware both that a bridge is present and that it is an addressable device. There are some complex issues to be resolved in bridging two dissimilar LANs. It is more common to see higher level resolutions to such interconnection requirements, given the complexity and cost of mixed-standard bridges. Indeed, bridges are normally found in old configurations.

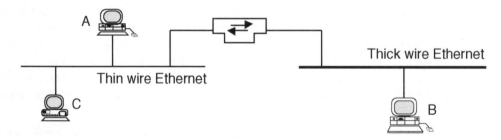

Fig. 11.15 IEEE 802.3 interconnection

Let us consider a situation where the configuration shown in Fig. 11.15 has just been established and the bridge currently does not know the location or address of any attached devices. The normal arrangement is for bridges to be self-learning. Hence, if station A starts to talk to station B, at this point the bridge does not know where station B is located. It receives the packet, acts as a store-and-forward device and passes the data onto the second segment. Since the source address was included as part of this data exchange, the bridge has now learned the location of station A. For convenience, Fig. 11.16 shows the address in the simple form of identification that we are using in the text. Of course, in reality, the contents would be the full hardware address of station A.

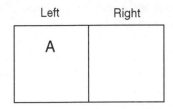

Fig. 11.16 Bridge's internal address table

When station B responds to station A, the bridge examines the table, recognizes that station A is on the other side, and passes the packet onwards. It also now records the location B, the address of which was in the source address of the reply (see Fig. 11.17).

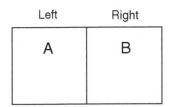

Fig. 11.17 Bridge's internal address table

Further exchanges between station A and station B will be passed through the bridge. If station A then talks to station C, when the first packet reaches the bridge the attempt to locate station C in its address table will not be successful. The bridge therefore passes the packet through to the right-hand segment. On this segment no station recognizes the address of station C and the packet dies. Hopefully, on the originating segment, station C recognizes its address and responds to station A. On hearing this response, the bridge recognizes that the destination is on the same segment as the originating station and does not pass the data through. It has also now located the whereabouts of station C, with the result shown in Fig. 11.18.

<table>
<tr><td>Left</td><td>Right</td></tr>
<tr><td>A
C</td><td>B</td></tr>
</table>

Fig. 11.18 Bridge's internal address table

Further exchanges between station A and station C will be contained within the single segment and will not pass through the bridge, which is actively filtering the traffic. The bridge also has a purge mechanism to remove entries that haven't been used for a while. It is important to understand this 'self-learning' process, given that it forms the basis of the approach taken in Ethernet switches.

Question 11.7 Why might it be helpful for the bridges to forget addresses that are not actively being used?

Although in an 802.3 network a loop is not allowed, implementation of the IEEE 802.1D Spanning Tree Algorithm (STA) permits redundant or backup paths to be established. This provides better network resilience. Bridges conforming to the STA can detect possible loop situations and block redundant paths (see Fig. 11.19).

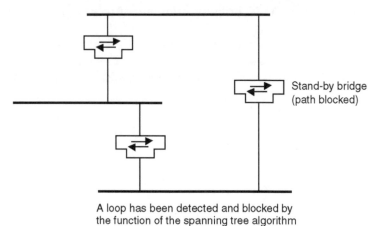

A loop has been detected and blocked by
the function of the spanning tree algorithm

Fig. 11.19 Spanning tree algorithm operation

Should a failure occur, the bridges can activate an alternative path, should one exist (see Fig. 11.20).

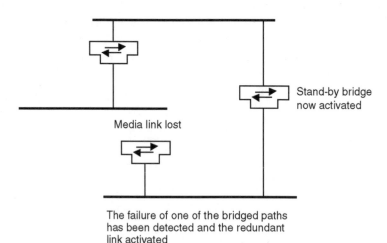

The failure of one of the bridged paths
has been detected and the redundant
link activated

Fig. 11.20 Detection of network failure with STA

STA bridges and non-spanning tree bridges may be mixed freely on a network.

This type of bridge is typically used in IEEE 802.3 and 802.4 LANs, and it is easy to install and use. However, the token ring fraternity prefer source routing as an approach, which assumes that the sender knows the destination location. If the destination is not on the local ring then the packet header has to contain the route to be taken. Each bridge on a given network must be uniquely numbered (using 4 bits). Additionally, each LAN has a 12 bit ID. The header then contains a series of bridge, LAN, bridge, LAN, etc., routing IDs. The bridge needs the high-order bit of the destination address field to be set to implement the routing. This was previously covered in Section 4 of Chapter 9.

Clearly, to implement source routing, the main issue is that of knowing which routes are available. These are determined by sending broadcast packets or discovery frames. These discovery frames are returned to the originator with the outbound path recorded within the returned frame. The negative aspect is that these broadcast messages introduce more traffic to the LAN which may be a considerable volume of data.

Because of the risk of flooding networks with broadcast messages, bridges can be configured to pass or not pass broadcast messages.

The IEEE 802.1 committee has specified that all bridges ought to be able to operate the spanning tree approach but may optionally implement source routing.

Question 11.8   Consider a LAN based on the IEEE 802.3 standard which has a number of bridges. Is it important to ensure that each address in the system is unique?

Question 11.9   Does the answer to Question 11.8 mean that a bridged LAN should be treated as a single entity for administrative purposes?

Question 11.10 Does the bridge shown in Fig. 11.14 have to be 'cleverer' than the bridge shown in Fig. 11.13?

The bridge acts as a store-and-forward switch and hence provides buffering facilities between the LANs. It will also perform the relevant access control on both sides. There is obviously more work to do in a bridge than in a repeater. A bridge collects complete packets before onwards transmission, with the requirement to convert between IEEE 802 frame structures if necessary. Hence, performance-wise, there is a delay in using a bridge, but typically bridges can filter up to 15,000 packet/s and copy about one-half of the filter rate, although higher speeds are available at a price. Bridges usually support management protocols such as SNMP and provide all of the resilience features of repeaters. SNMP is covered in more detail in Chapter 14.

A remote bridge allows us to connect together LANs that are distant from each other and for which a leased line is required for interconnection (see Fig. 11.21).

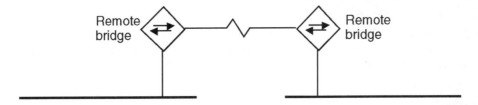

Fig. 11.21 Remote bridge

It is worth examining the mapping effort of converting the various IEEE 802 MAC protocols (see Fig. 11.22). Clearly the protocols have much in common, but the various committees could not agree on a common standard, hence the reformatting. There is no overwhelming technical reason why commonality could not have been achieved given a little compromise. The activity of the reformatting requirements results in the removal of some fields (such as priority settings) and the recalculation of checksums.

Field / Standard	Preamble	Start delimiter	Access control	Frame control	Addresses	Length	Data	Pad	Checksum	End delimiter	Status
802.3	✓	✓			✓	✓	✓	✓	✓		
802.4	✓	✓		✓	✓		✓		✓	✓	
802.5		✓	✓	✓	✓		✓		✓	✓	✓

Fig. 11.22 IEEE 802 packet format comparison

Question 11.11 What happens to any priority status of a MAC packet on a token ring when it is bridged through to an 802.3 environment?

Within enterprises, it is not unusual to see the development of LANs being organized by the information technology division, but with local departmental needs being recognized. Hence the strategy can be one of placing the best local LAN solution in each department or work area and integrating them into a backbone LAN for inter-departmental and external communication. However, keeping a consistent approach to your LAN design is preferrable, especially in terms of future maintenance. The backbone architecture needs to be carefully chosen on the basis of the volume of inter-departmental or external traffic, and it may well be that an Ethernet or token ring will service the need, with the choice reflecting the interconnected departmental LANs. The possibility of FDDI and ATM backbones exist, but for many Ethernet sites it is usual for high speed Ethernet standards to be implemented. Bridges can then used to link with such a backbone arrangement (see Fig. 11.24). Increasingly, however routers are being used to provide the connection to a high speed backbone network, and bridges are rarely installed today.

4. Routers

The interconnection devices considered here work at the network layer of the OSI model and are used to interconnect two or more separate networks (see Fig. 11.24). By separate, we mean that the networks can be administratively separate. Each one can be set up without knowledge of the other(s) and maintained and operated as separate entities.

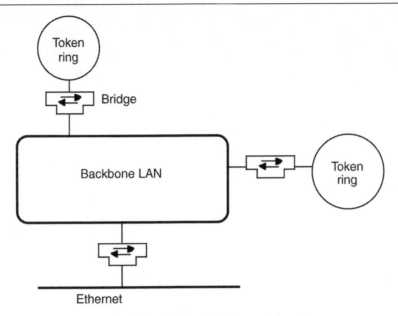

Fig. 11.23 Backbone LAN configuration

Hence each LAN may be in the same building or geographically distant from the other(s), and owned by completely different organisations.

Routing devices operate at the network layer and are concerned with layer 3 addressing. Routers are seen at both the source and destination networks and the layer 3 packets are addressed to the routing device and are thus not transparent to the source. Be careful to note here that the address upon which we route data is contained in layer 3, and it is a different address from the hardware address that was used to pass frames between NICs and hence devices on a LAN.

The layer 3 addressing concept is simple, and covered in more detail in Chapter 12. Each device is assigned a layer 3 address which remains with that device whilst it is live on that network. A static address assignment is carried out by the network administrators, but dynamically assigned addressing is permissible and the address will be valid for the duration of the device's connection to the network. The address is made up of two components: the LAN address element and the individual device's address element on that LAN. The details behind the address structure are covered in Chapter 12.

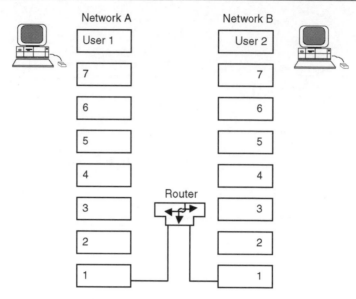

Fig. 11.24 Network layer relay

Question 11.12 Why would a device's layer 3 address need to be changed if the device were relocated on another network?

To maintain an up-to-date record on a network of the current hardware addresses, some routers periodically broadcast a message asking for the LAN station which recognizes a given layer 3 address to respond. This approach is known as the Address Resolution Protocol (ARP) and it is used by TCP/IP networks, for example. Occasionally in networks, an attempt is made to ensure that the 16 bit hardware address is the same as the least significant 16 bits of the layer 3 address, and then mapping between the two addressing schemes becomes trivial (a case of masking). This latter approach is not often used.

Question 11.13 Can you suggest why both types of mapping between hardware addresses and Internet addresses are in use? Why doesn't everybody use the simpler version?

Once again, the old adage that the nice thing about standards is that there are so many to choose from applies to layer 3 addressing schemes: there are a number of standards. Whilst some routers work only on a single Internet protocol, others are able to handle multiple protocols correctly.

A router may be used when the two end networks that are being interconnected have the same transport layer or recognize each other's transport and Internet formats. For example, if in Fig. 11.25 both token rings are using TCP/IP or both using SNA, then we can route the packet from one to the other. The end-to-end protocols between the two devices A and B will ensure that the data delivery is secure.

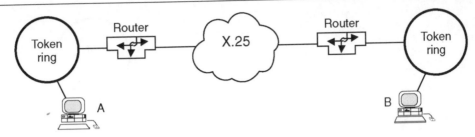

Fig. 11.25 Example of router

Question 11.14 In Fig. 11.25, could a device connected to the left-hand token ring be allowed to have the same hardware address as a device connected to the right-hand token ring?

Consider device A on the left-hand token ring in Fig. 11.25 which wishes to talk to station B on the right-hand network. The two LANs are linked via an X.25 WAN, and they could be, to all intents and purposes, on the other side of the world from each other. Clearly it is unreasonable for the current hardware address of the remote station to be known, but the Internet address is a reasonable compromise. We must at least be able to determine the Internet address through some form of "directory service".

Hence, device A will send a LAN-formatted packet containing data holding the destination of B's Internet address to the local router's hardware address. The router will unwrap the packet until it reaches the Internet address level, determines which onwards route is appropriate to reach device B, and rewraps the packet in an X.25 frame for onwards transmission. On delivery, the router connected to the right-hand token ring recognizes that the Internet address refers to this LAN, and maps the remaining part of the identifier across into device B's hardware address. The LAN packet will then be placed on the right-hand token ring containing the original data from the left-hand token ring.

Question 11.15 Why should the two end networks be running with the same transport services for this interconnection to work?

Typically, routing devices can handle up to 5000 packet/s, although vendors do have routers that are capable of working at much higher speeds than this.

In Fig. 11.23, we have considered how an organization can interconnect a number of LANs using the concept of a backbone LAN. Alternatively, where the sites are further apart, WANs such as X.25 can provide the integration backbone, and the organizational network then becomes an enterprise network (see Fig. 11.26). No geographical limits are placed on such a network which uses routers to provide the interconnection.

Question 11.16 Why might an organization opt to use a router rather than a bridge for interconnection to a backbone LAN?

Routers are intelligent devices; they can be programmed to allow data from particular users or data of a particular nature (e.g., broadcasts) to pass or not pass through. They

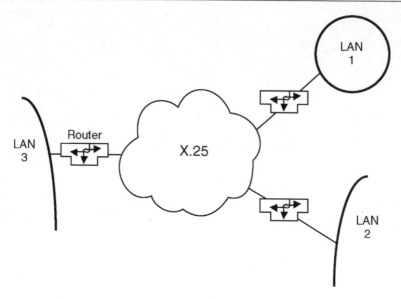

Fig. 11.26 X.25 backbone configuration

act as an effective firewall around a LAN installation, providing as much or as little isolation as is deemed necessary by the network administration. Most routers also provide extensive network management information, supporting a minimum of the Simple Network Management Protocol (SNMP). This will be addressed in Chapter 14.

If user demands for multi-vendor connectivity and better performance are to be met, issues of how routing is achieved will be critical. The use of dynamic routing, as opposed to static hand-loaded tables, is imperative. The Routing Information Protocol (RIP) is typically associated with Berkeley Unix and TCP/IP, and it is based on distance vectors derived from Xerox's sorting protocol. Recent advances support link state algorithms such as the Open Shortest Path First (OSPF) algorithm, and only update routing tables to reflect changes. Distance vector algorithms such as RIP regularly broadcast the entire table (somewhere between every 30 s and 120 s). A table entry is typically 20 bytes, so large networks could generate a lot of data just to keep up to date. It is possible for an individual router to be able to handle a range of different layer 3 addressing protocols, known as multi-protocol routers. However, there is no translation between the protocols, and each set of protocols remain within their own, freestanding systems.

5. Gateways

To operate at the network layer or above, a gateway is used to interconnect two dissimilar networks or different protocols (see Fig. 11.27).

In this case, significantly more translation between the two networks takes place, making the gateway a slower and more expensive device than the other interconnecting relay devices. Much of the original work achieved in the gateway area provided

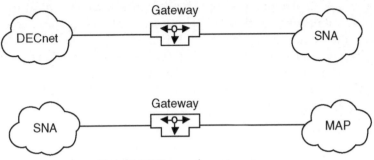

Fig. 11.27 Example gateways

pairwise solutions to the big problems, such as connecting DECnet to SNA. This was a good example of commercial pressures being sufficiently strong for a solution to be provided for the connection between two important networking approaches.

This is the most sophisticated level of exchange of all the relay devices. The lowest point of commonality between the two original networks may be the application program, and consequently we may have to work at this level to exchange information between the two systems (see Fig. 11.28).

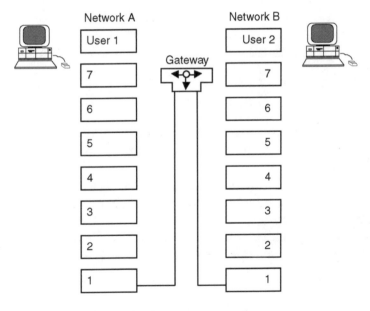

Fig. 11.28 Gateway operation

Other approaches have been to provide a protocol stack within a host machine to handle the different networking strategies. For example, if a Novell network (running IPX/SPX protocols) is connected to a host with the VMS operating system, the Novell data to be exchanged needs to be interpreted. This interpretation is typically undertaken by running a Novell protocol stack within the host machine. Fig. 11.29 shows how the data generated in the Novell environment is mapped across to VMS formats. Within the VMS host, the drivers receive the Ethernet packets delivered to the host interface and pass them up to the right environment. This can easily be achieved because each Ethernet frame normally carries sufficient information to indicate the type of data payload that it is carrying, e.g., whether it is Novell IPX/SPX.

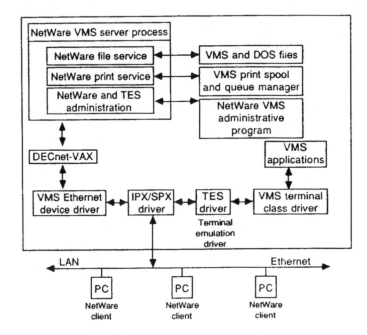

Fig. 11.29 Novell stack arrangement in a VMS host machine
© **Learning Group International, reprinted with permission)**

The provision of gateways also includes niche areas such as translating the email system of one side to that of the other side and vice versa. This is an interoperability issue, and it is treated as a full topic in the next chapter.

Question 11.17 Are we likely to see an increase or decrease in the number of gateway devices?

6. Brouters

There is a rather ill-defined device called a brouter (a term which has crept across the Atlantic). Brouters are capable of working as both routers and bridges. They examine the packet type (e.g., the Ethernet type field), and route those packets where they recognize the Internet protocol; otherwise, they act as bridges. This approach has been supported by a number of the leading vendors in this area. It is particularly useful for those multi-protocol sites which carry some non-routable traffic such as LAT protocols.

Hence, a brouter routes whenever it can and bridges whenever it can't.

7. Public networks

So far in this chapter we have concentrated primarily on the devices that are attached to a LAN to provide interconnection. Increasingly, it is apparent that the services of a PTT are required to provide interconnection over long distances. In the case of a remote bridge, a digital link is indicated in Fig. 11.21. With a router connection, the requirement for a public network such as X.25 is shown in Fig. 11.25.

A range of public networks are available, including X.25 services, although frame relay and ATM are alternatives. These networks could provide the basis of a full study programme in their own right. There are important design considerations in all of these public networks.

A simplistic view is taken in our approach in this text. Let us assume that the service is there and we are simply users of the service. The information required is an understanding of the interface and the various connection arrangements that can be made.

X.25

In its simplest form, an X.25 network can be viewed as the 'glue' between LANs, as shown in Fig. 11.30.

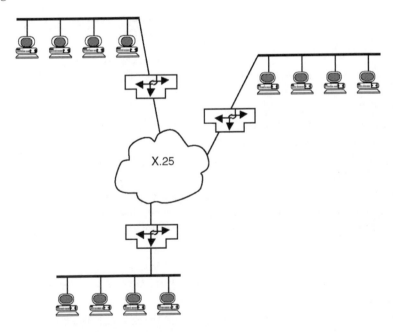

Fig. 11.30 Interconnection via X.25

Some devices have an X.25 interface built in, and hence assemble packets of information for transmission. Other, simpler, devices need an interface box to assemble the characters into a packet for them. A Packet Assembler/Disassembler (PAD) is such a device, and it takes data character by character from such devices, packaging them into

X.25 packets for transmission (see Fig. 11.31). They also disassemble an arriving packet for destination character devices. The X.3 standard covers the PAD parameters, which allow configuration of the PAD to the local situation. Parameters include the timeout period and local terminal speeds.

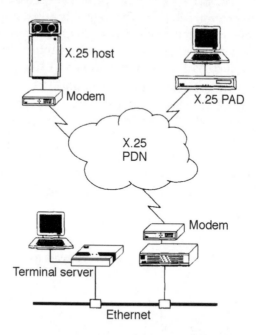

Fig. 11.31 PAD interface to X.25
(reproduced courtesy of Cray Communications)

The X.25 packet switching service is available worldwide, and so interconnection between LANs can be achieved on an international basis. The speed of the connection is nominally 64 kbit/s, but in practice lower speeds, such as 8 kbit/s, are achievable at busy times of the day. This makes the arrangement poor for the high speed bursts of data generated by some applications running on LANs.

Fortunately, most applications do not require sustained high speed limits, and so this is not too much of a disadvantage. In theory, higher line speeds than 64 kbit/s are available, and on Transpac (operated by France Telecom) speeds of 2 Mbit/s are available.

X.25 does provide good connectivity, good link resilience, interconnection to public data networks, and closed user groups. Switching delays may be minimized to 5 ms.

In reality, X.25 is a complete set of protocols. At layer 1 of the OSI model, X.21 defines the interface standard. Layer 2 ensures that there is reliable communication between the DTE and DCE, even though this may be a noisy telephone line. It uses a subset of the HDLC protocol called LAPB (Link Access Protocol Version B). Layer 3 manages connections between a part of DTEs which may either be virtual calls or permanent virtual circuits.

The three stages of call establishment, data transfer and disconnection are associated with this protocol, which is a connection-oriented service. To ensure that the data has been successfully delivered, end-to-end checking between the two hosts involved is carried out by the transport layer (see Fig. 11.32).

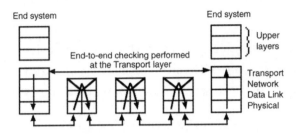

Fig. 11.32 X.25 network connection
(reproduced courtesy of Cray Communications)

Frame relay

Frame relay is a new networking technology, with a number of differences from X.25. X.25 implements addressing, routing and multiplexing at layer 3, but frame relay implements addressing and multiplexing at the data link level, or layer 2. Frame relay uses LAPF derived from the ISDN protocol LAPD.

Normally, frame relay networks operate with permanent virtual circuits. Frame relay implements statistical multiplexing of users' data streams called Data Link Connections (DLCs). Each DLC is given an identifier or call set-up (DLCI) associated with a particular link. A virtual circuit that requires a number of network links will have an associated number of DLCIs assigned. Frame relay services ranging from 64 kbit/s to 2.048 Mbit/s are becoming available. Also, the switching speeds are as low as 2 ms.

Frame relay has been developed because the digital circuits which carry the data have improved in quality to such an extent that they have low error rates. It is therefore possible to let the higher layer protocols provide error recovery, and remove the necessity to carry the overhead of checking from this level of functionality.

The frame relay works without network layer involvement, as shown in Fig. 11.33.

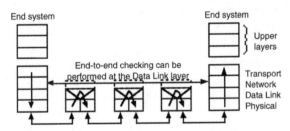

Fig. 11.33 Frame relay connect
(reproduced courtesy of Cray Communications)

Supporters of frame relay over X.25 point to the perceived limitations of the X.25 switch interface, the relatively simple software conversion of equipment from X.25 to frame relay, and the migration path to Asynchronous Transfer Mode (ATM) or cell relay. This technology is used in broadband ISDN (B-ISDN).

Frame relay can also be used to carry voice. The G.764 packet voice protocol makes it possible to lose part of the voice packet during periods of congestion and still maintain adequate quality.

Further questions

(There are answers to the questions marked with an asterisk at the end of the book.)

1. *What interconnection devices are available to link existing LANs together?

2. *Why might we choose to separate an existing LAN into two areas, relinked with a router?

3. *Why were multi-port repeaters used in large multi-storey office blocks?

4. *Routing within an individual LAN is not really an issue. However, if we link two bus structures with two bridges (one for redundancy/resilience), why does the internal address table become important?

5. *If an IEEE 802.5 network and an IEEE 802.3 network are to be 'joined', what is the likely approach?

6. When a network designer has to tackle the internetworking problems and differences in protocols, there are a number of critical points that have to be resolved. Identify as many of these differences as possible.

7. Outline the limitations on a single cable segment of a local area network conforming to the IEEE 802.3 (Ethernet) standard. Explain how these limitations are relaxed when multiple cable segments joined by non-filtering repeaters are used.

8. Explain the advantages of using routers rather than bridges.

9. A certain company plans to install 200 workstations with high speed data requirements on a site measuring 200 m by 200 m. All workstations require network access to shared resources; in particular, most workstations will make heavy use of files stored on other workstations on the site, using a proprietary remote file access protocol. To facilitate this, workstations will be grouped in clusters of about ten machines, with most remote file accesses being to other workstations in the cluster.

   With the aid of diagrams, suggest a suitable layout for a network conforming to the IEEE 802.3 standard. Justify your choice of layout. State explicitly any assumptions you make.

10. You are the network manager for the XYZ Company, and you are responsible for five networks. You have been asked to internetwork the five as soon as possible. What information should you have to achieve your goal of internetworking the five networks?

11. Fig. 11.34 shows a strategy in which the top bridge pair provides a backup bridge arrangement and the bottom bridge pair is a workgroup arrangement. If bridges were still to be used, discuss the relative merits of such a strategy.

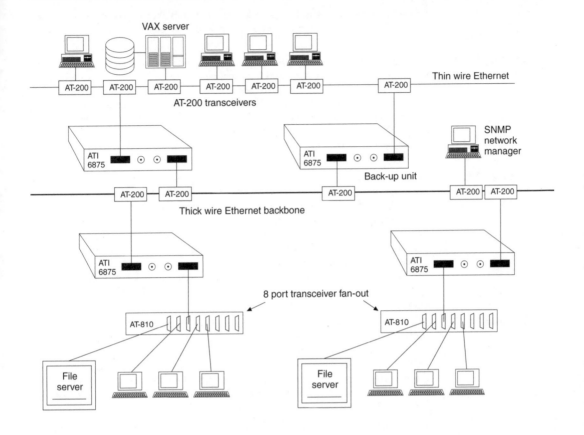

Fig. 11.34 Top bridge (ATI 6875) pair as a backup bridge; bottom bridge pair as a workgroup

Answer 11.1 The various standards that exist at the lower ends of the seven layer OSI model are well established. It is therefore reasonably easy to move data from one network to another along one or more well defined routes. However, making this data meaningful once it arrives at the destination network is an altogether different problem. An analogy here is the relative ease with which a letter written in French and posted in Paris may be delivered in London to an English speaker. The ability to make sense of the letter is then very much dependent on the ability of the receiver to translate or understand directly its contents.

It is much easier to internetwork (and exchange data) than it is to make the two networks interoperable.

Answer 11.2 The lower down in the OSI model that we are able to make the connection and map between the two (or more) networks, the more closely related the two networks are going to be. Hence, at the bottom layer, it may simply be a case of signal regeneration. At layer 2, a mapping of the MAC packet is required, and at layer 3 the issues of global addressing become relevant, and so on. If we are able to find the point of commonality between the two systems at the lowest level of the model, then we are faced with a simple problem which can be resolved with efficient (and cheap) connecting devices. The higher up the model we go, the more work is involved with the mapping, and consequently the more costly and greater is the required conversion effort. We will see later that there may be other sound technical reasons for using interconnection devices which are higher up in the model.

Answer 11.3   A broadband system may have a number of amplifiers in-line to regenerate the analogue signal. Remember that the technology has come from cable television, and these amplifiers could have been used in remote locations in the cable television environment. With broadband LANs, the frequency spectrum is split into discrete channels of operation, and these channels are well clear of the frequency range of 0 Hz to 50 Hz required for power transmission. It is in this range that power is carried to the amplifiers through the normal 75 Ω cable. In cable television, this is how power is delivered to remote amplifiers.

Answer 11.4   In an unstructured token ring installation, if a number of adjacent interfaces are powered down, then, since we normally regenerate the signal at each interface, it is possible that the signal strength will be weakened to a point where the signal will not be recognizable. There is little that the network administrator can do to correct this, other than to go to each of the stations and physically power them back up or provide line drivers at regular points in the network in case this happens. When a structured wiring approach is in use, each interface or group of interfaces is brought back to a central point (an MSAU). These multi-station access units are intelligent, and when an interface is powered down then that element (i.e., all the cabling) is effectively removed from the ring.

Answer 11.5   There are a number of reasons why this might be preferable. First, it is not unusual for two adjacent buildings to be at different earth potentials. By using fibre optics cable as the connecting transmission medium, we have electrically isolated the buildings as far as the network is concerned. Had we put a run of copper between the two buildings, then it would just be possible that we would experience those tricky earthing problems that are difficult to pinpoint and that can be responsible for a number of unaccountable 'incidents' on a LAN.

A second reason is the provision of security in the event of a lightning strike in the area outside the two buildings, where there is less protection for the transmission medium.

Answer 11.6   A bridge is designed as a filter device and is not normally capable of passing all data generated on one side through to the other side. Indeed, one of the useful features of a bridge is its ability to partition a network and keep as much traffic separated as possible. If a server is placed on the opposite side of a bridge from the diskless workstations which it is servicing, then all of this function of the bridge is nullified, and the bridge may not be capable of supporting the volume of traffic requested in server transactions. This would also introduce a level of delay into a major activity which may well be unacceptable. Hence, this is not a recommended practice.

Answer 11.7   Since it is possible to add new devices (and their associated new hardware addresses), move existing devices to new locations, or simply replace faulty interface cards, then it is also necessary to have a mechanism for forgetting addresses and relearning them whenever they are required again. It is not unusual for this time to be set in the tens of seconds range, and a bridge would remove addresses from its internal table that were not used within such a period.

Answer 11.8   Yes, a bridge creates a larger network under the same administrative control. Since transmitting a packet is meant to be transparent to the sender, it is implicit that there should be no duplicate addresses on the network, or else the wrong destination may receive the data.

Answer 11.9   Only by treating the network as a single entity can the network administrator ensure that no duplicate addresses have occurred. If they were separate entities then locally assigned addresses could produce a situation where duplication of the hardware addresses had occurred. This would only be acceptable in those situations where the LANs were separate entities, and interconnection would then be via a router.

Answer 11.10   The bridge in Fig. 11.13 is a simple self-learning device with a spanning tree algorithm to prevent looping where duplicate paths could exist through the provision of additional bridge devices in the network for resilience or in-built redundancy. The bridge in Fig. 11.15 has to be much cleverer because it is mapping between a system that wants to do source routing and a system that works on self-learning. Incidentally, a bridge that interconnects two token rings is the simplest of all the bridges, because all the routing has been predetermined. Indeed, an old PC with the appropriate software would almost certainly be adequate!

Answer 11.11   It simply is lost, as there is no field in which to map the priority value.

Answer 11.12   Part of a device's layer 3 address includes the LAN address itself. If a device were to be relocated to another LAN then it would need to be allocated a new layer 3 address which reflected that new LAN address.

Answer 11.13   For those networks which are using 16 bit hardware addresses (especially those that can be locally assigned) it is easy to make the least significant 16 bits of the Internet address the same as this hardware address. But not all networks use 16 bit addresses. Ethernet, for example, usually runs with 48 bit addresses. This is the reason why both systems are in operation.

Answer 11.14   It could, but we should really follow the rules about having separate addresses in any network entity under single administrative control. Of course, if we use the default card address, they will always be different. Also, the right-hand network may belong to a different organization and be under completely different administration or control.

Answer 11.15   Between the two routers of the source and destination network there may be a single reliable connection. Alternatively, this connection could be a whole series of networks, some of which do not feature highly in the reliability stakes. Each link across this connection may or may not be supporting error handling, etc., Since it is important to achieve the secure exchange of information (otherwise the exchange is almost pointless), there is a requirement for both ends of the network to ensure that this security of and confidence in a successful exchange has been achieved. Hence the transport or transmission control protocols at level 4 in our model put these features in place. This gives rise to the requirement for both ends to be running the same protocol to provide that secure exchange.

Answer 11.16   Remember that one of the benefits that a router provides is the administrative isolation of the LAN. Within that LAN we are able to allocate addresses, both Internet and hardware (where applicable), to local convenience and presumably within whatever organizational guidelines prevail. This will also isolate us from the discovery frames that parts of the enterprise network may be implementing in order to operate with source routing. Thus, although a router is slower and more expensive than a bridge, and there are additional administrative overheads, the addition of these benefits is probably worthwhile. The use of routers also allows easier expansion for connections to locations that have not yet been identified. Given that a router provides access to the Internet, this has become a key issue in most organizations. It also offers greater security levels.

Answer 11.17   The majority of vendors now offer TCP/IP alongside any proprietary approaches. With this approach, the need for gateway solutions at the lower level is disappearing. At the higher layers, e-mail gateways, etc., continue to provide translation between different application protocols.

12 Interoperability

1. Introduction

In Chapter 11 we examined the mechanisms for making connections between a variety of LANs. These connections may be between countries, across organizational or institutional boundaries, or at least inter-departmental. The intention behind the integration of separate and perhaps non-homogeneous networks is based on one of the early requirements, i.e., maximum flexibility in purchasing equipment from a variety of suppliers to achieve Internet capability. This takes the maximum advantage of existing equipment and offers the greatest achievable business flexibility. With this multi-vendor approach, computing zones can be equipped with the systems that are the most suitable for the local purpose, without undue attention being paid to the site's host machine suppliers. Growth in the range and volume of equipment can be incremental, and 'big bang' approaches to equipment changes could be a thing of the past, with carefully managed stepwise planning being achievable.

Whilst Chapter 11 showed how data could be transmitted between interconnected LANs, we now need to examine how two or more systems can be seamlessly and transparently connected to provide some form of functionality or usability which spans the interconnection. This area of interoperability can be more taxing than the aspects of interconnection already covered. It is in this area that changes continue to happen to support the integration of existing 'islands'.

Possible approaches to multi-vendor integration are outlined in Fig. 11.2. Hence identical or compatible operating systems could be provided across all platforms. For example, Unix could be the integrating mechanism. All the users on the integrated LAN would then see the same operating system environment.

Alternatively, the network itself could provide the integration using the same protocol suites, such as TCP/IP. This area has provided many organizations with the basis for creating enterprise wide networks, i.e., networks that span the whole of the company's or enterprise's LANs. Finally, one could consider using the same integrating application software across multi-vendor platforms. In this category, typical examples can be seen in the database area (e.g., Oracle on all platforms) or the same desktop environment (e.g., Microsoft Office on all platforms). This achieves a common user view of the system with minimum training and support.

Question 12.1 Can you suggest another area where a common application software approach would be a useful integrating vehicle?

---

2. Protocol suites

The area of integration using a protocol suite at the higher layers of the OSI model has been well utilized over recent years. Typical protocol suites are shown in Fig. 12.1.

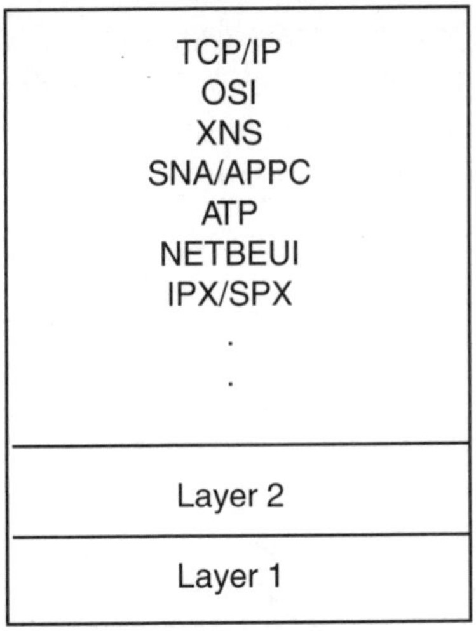

```
┌─────────────────────────────┐
│          TCP/IP             │
│           OSI               │
│           XNS               │
│         SNA/APPC            │
│           ATP               │
│         NETBEUI             │
│          IPX/SPX            │
│            .                │
│                             │
│            .                │
│                             │
├─────────────────────────────┤
│          Layer 2            │
├─────────────────────────────┤
│          Layer 1            │
└─────────────────────────────┘
```

Fig. 12.1 Protocol suites

Each of these protocols (plus others not specifically mentioned) has supporters within the computing and communications world. TCP/IP was developed in the USA during the ARPA DoD project. With its release in many Unix systems, its popularity and market penetration is unquestionable. OSI provides an alternative with TP, but this lacks the same depth of support. XNS, which was originally a Xerox offering and was initially taken up by Ungermann-Bass amongst others, might have disappeared. However, Novell indirectly supported this route with its proprietary version called SPX/IPX, which is based on XNS. This had the major benefit of being a lightweight protocol which is speedy and efficient, whereas TCP/IP is a heavyweight protocol designed to handle any underlying network, however unreliable and however low its quality of service. IBM introduced the SNA/APPC offering, which became a *de facto* standard. SNA/APPC has achieved some market penetration and embraced the token ring environment within the total IBM platform.

Other proprietary approaches come from organizations such as Apple, which is noted for doing things its own way, with ATP (the Apple Transport Protocol) as its product equivalent at layer 4. In most organizations attempting to interconnect networks, the probability is that a range of networks are already in place and that these networks may not use the same protocols throughout the company. The choice is, therefore, whether the move towards interoperability is achieved through gradual change to a common protocol such as TCP/IP, which major vendors offer (e.g., Novell offer a TCP/IP as an alternative to SPX/IPX), or whether the conversion of existing LAN implementations is achieved through the identification of a standard such as OSI, with the use of that standard for all intercommunication. In the later arrangement, all internetwork traffic is converted to this agreed standard. This has a parallel in the world of natural languages, where there was an initiative to use Esperanto as a common language!

Question 12.2 Why would we suggest the use of a lightweight protocol such as SPX/IPX on a LAN rather than a heavyweight, reliable protocol such as TCP/IP?

Question 12.3 The approach of converting all other protocols to OSI has its merits. What merits can be attributed to this approach?

Question 12.4 TCP/IP is seen by many as the way forward and a premiere integration tool. List the possible reasons why this view is held.

3. TCP/IP

If we consider the TCP/IP protocol suite which has been developed over many years in the USA defence sector, this will provide us with a background to understanding the functionality of the protocol suites that dominate in this area. Each protocol has its own approach, but the functionality must cover the ISO OSI layer 4 function plus the addressing requirements of layer 3, although it may take each element separately.

The work can be covered as two separate areas, i.e., that of the Internet Protocol (IP), which is layer 3, and that of the Transmission Control Protocol (TCP), which is the transport layer 4 protocol. Because TCP/IP is seen to be an integrating product, it has been developed to work across any network (local area or wide area). At concept, it was installed only across reliable networks, and the TCP/IP protocol did not have a large amount of in-built resilience. It simply provided end-to-end protocol support to ensure that the protocol data units (PDUs) were correctly exchanged, assuming that the underlying network carrying the traffic was reliable and error free. However, as the number of networks that were interconnected increased, the resilience of the end-to-end links became more 'suspect', and the requirement for greater in-built resilience within the protocol grew. The result is a protocol which offers a range of resilience levels or 'classes of service', including full error detection and correction, sequencing and flow control.

Question 12.5 Where in the overall system does the TCP/IP protocol physically reside?

Question 12.6 What is the difference between the terminology 'end-to-end' and 'point-to-point'?

IP

In the attempt to uniquely identify every node on every network on a worldwide basis with an ID number, a form of addressing included within the Internet Protocol was introduced as a standard. This IP addressing standard is equivalent to every telephone user having a worldwide unique number. Hence, to send data to any other user, we simply address the data to the destination's IP address. The use of IP as the mechanism for addressing is a fundamental part of using the Internet. The Internet protocol has the characteristic of being a datagram-oriented service. In many LANs that have no interconnection or outside links, the addressing provision has not been an issue. However, for any network with Internet connections, assigning IP addresses is a formal process for the network manager.

As we interconnect a number of LANs, the requirement to have unique addresses for every station becomes apparent. There needs to be an addressing scheme which has the capability of uniquely identifying each and every connected station. This unique address has been implemented at layer 3, e.g., in the IP protocol. When a data packet is delivered to a LAN from an external and possibly remote source, the unique IP host address is then mapped across to the local hardware address of the host's NIC. Once this conversion or mapping has been undertaken, the data packet is forwarded on the local network, encapsulated in a MAC packet structure.

Question 12.7 Why are routers used to handle IP addresses rather than bridges?

The worldwide uniqueness of each host's IP address is needed if communication outside the corporate enterprise network is required. The IP address is assigned to organizations by a central controlling authority, the Internet Assigned Numbers Authority. The allocation of IP version 4 addresses to organizations is now an issue, with the number unallocated addresses becoming exhausted on the next few years.

Version 4 of IP addressing, IPv4, set aside 32 bits for addressing, and originally defined a number of boundary points for interpreting the bits. These boundary points created what is known as classful addressing. Class A, B and C structures are shown in fig 12.2, and represent the addresses available for commercial organizations.

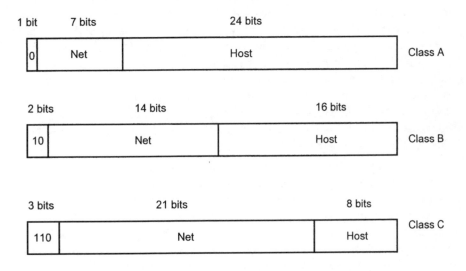

Fig. 12.2 Class A, B and C IP addressing scheme

The range of addresses available using 32 bits is proving to be a limitation, and Version 6 of IP addressing, using a 16-byte addressing structure, is needed to overcome the difficulty in getting an address allocated. Of course, a secondary problem is getting everyone to move to Version 6 of IP, given that this is a worldwide protocol with millions of users. Implementation options include having dual stacks to support both versions. We will consider IPv6 later in the chapter.

The IP addresses are normally recorded in 'dotted decimal' notation, with each byte of the 32-bit address in version 4 being written in decimal formal. Hence a typical class B address is shown in Fig. 12.3.

Since this address is used for routing traffic, each network interface is allocated an IP address. Routers that are connected to two (or more) networks will have two (or more) IP addresses. Fig. 12.2 shows that he Class A, B and C address ranges are as follows:

Class A: 1.0.0.0 to 127.255.255.255

Class B: 128.0.0.0 to 191.255.255.255

Class C: 192.0.0.0 to 223.255.255.255

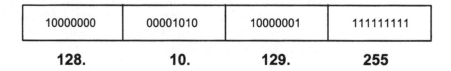

10000000	00001010	10000001	111111111
128.	**10.**	**129.**	**255**

Fig. 12.3 Class B address and its dotted decimal representation

Addresses in the range 224.0.0.0 to 239.255.255.255 are used for multicast purposes.

IP addresses are allocated in blocks of adjacent addresses, rather than lots of random or individual addresses. Initially this was done on the basis of allocating a network class which supported more hosts than was needed by the applying organization. For example, if an organization had 300 host devices, since a Class C network only supports $2^8 - 2 = 254$ hosts, it may have been allocated a Class B network. Note that two of the host addresses are used for special purposes (all 0s and all 1s), so two addresses are subtracted from the host range of addresses available. However, Class B networks support $2^{16} - 2 = 65534$ hosts. If applied to this scenario, a significant part of the unique addresses would be wasted by the organization and never allocated to hosts. In fact, in this scenario over 65,000 addresses would be wasted.

As a result, the address-controlling authorities changed the basis of address allocation. Instead of assigning classful addresses, they assigned classless addressing, using Classless Interdomain Routing. The network part of the address assigned by the authorities could be any length, rather than being fixed on byte boundaries, provided a sufficient number of bits were left for the hosts. In our example of 300 hosts, we would need at least 9 bits (i.e., 510 hosts). Based on this minimum requirement, that would leave 23 bits to identify the network. A classless network with 23 bits for the network address element is known as a '/23' network. The '/23' is often referred to as the network mask. Of course, it could be '/x', where x is the figure that is determined during the address allocation. For example, the Class B address in Fig. 12.3 could be reduced from offering 65534 to offering 510 host addresses by specifying an address

$$128.10.129.255/23$$

This means that the network prefix is

$$128.10.128.0$$

and the remaining 9 bits identify the hosts on this network. Normally, if we specify all the hosts' bits as zero, as in 128.10.128.0/23, then we are referring to the whole of the organization's network. Had we not used classless addressing, then 128.10.192.0 would belong to the same organization as 128.10.128.0. However, with classless addressing 128.10.192.0/23 can be allocated to a different organization than the one holding 128.10.128.0/23.

Subnet

In a large organization, it is possible that the allocated IP addresses are used by the organization to reflect its LAN layouts. Let us consider an organization with a Class B address with all 16 bits of the host addresses having been assigned. In principle, all of the organization's host machines could be physically anywhere in the organization, and each host could be randomly assigned an IP address out of this block of numbers. The routing table needed to locate all of these hosts would be large. These tables would be resident in all of the organization's routers.

It is possible to create a structured layout where a 'number' of the most significant bits within the IP host allocation are used to indicate a zone or LAN within that organization (see Fig. 12.4).

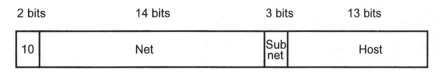

Fig. 12.4 Example of subnet

A number of routers can then be established within the organization to allow internal routing. Each local router then maintains a much smaller range of host machines within its individual table structure (see Fig. 12.5). Technically, of course, it is the host interface addresses, not the host, but this looser wording is commonly used.

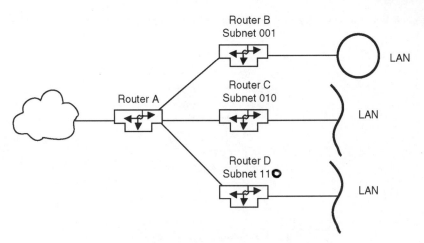

Fig. 12.5 Possible router subnet implementation

In this arrangement, router B only maintains table structures holding details of devices assigned IP addresses on the LAN directly attached to it plus details of the other routers and their range of IP addresses. When a packet arrives from the outside world, the router needs to split the host address component from the network address, (including the subnet). To achieve this, each router holds details the size of the subnet in the form of a mask. In the case of Fig. 12.4, we need to mask off the most significant 19 bits. Hence, the mask would be specified as 255.255.224.0.

To identify the appropriate router to which an incoming packet should be sent, the IP address and the mask have a Boolean AND performed on them, and the result is the base address of the individual router's IP address range. Hence, we know the router to which an individual data packet should be forwarded.

If we applied subnetting to our previous example, with 128.10.128.0/23 being the assigned block of IP addresses, we could use the 9 bits in a manner which best reflected the organization's structures. If we used 3 bits of the host address range to represent the subnet, then the remaining 6 bits can support individual hosts (i.e., $2^6 - 2 = 62$ hosts). The same principle described earlier of not using all 0s and all 1s applies to the subnet component. Hence, from the 3 bits, we can create six subnets as shown in Table 12.1.

Bit pattern	Subnet number
001	1
010	2
011	3
100	4
101	5
110	6

Table 12.1 Subnets

If we applied these six subnets to a typical configuration, then the structure could look like Fig. 12.6.

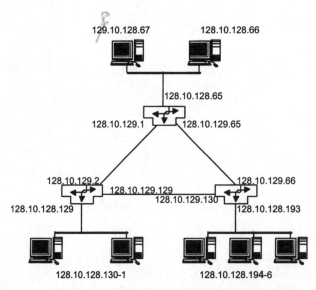

Fig. 12.6 Routers and assigned subnets

Question 12.8 Can you suggest a way in which the routing of broadcast or multicast messages may be implemented?

Question 12.9 Why does a router require more than one IP address?

Question 12.10 If the example in Fig 12.3 had chosen to use 4 bits for subnetting, what would be the required mask?

Question 12.11 What would be the dotted decimal network base address of subnet 5 in Table 12.1 when applied to 128.10.128.0/23?

Within an IP router device, the routing activity is undertaken using only IP addresses. The router receives packets and applies the mask to determine the network address. It then forwards the packet on the appropriate outbound connection. At the destination network the conversion between the IP address and the hardware address occurs. Since the network element of the address applies to the LAN, it is the remaining element, i.e., the host bits, which is mapped across to the hardware address. Normally, the mapping between IP and hardware addressing uses techniques such as look-up tables.

It is worth mentioning at this point that the 16 bit field type zone in an Ethernet frame can be used to identify the type of data being carried. Hence it is possible within the Ethernet frame to recognize the payload as TCP/IP frames and pass these directly to the correct operating system interface.

Question 12.12 What other protocols could be indicated in this 16 bit field of an Ethernet frame?

Traffic that is destined for stations outside the immediate network or workplace network will be sent to the routing station for forwarding elsewhere in the organization or onto the Internet based on the IP address contained in the packet. In fact, it is the network element of the address which determines the route on which to forward the packet. Remember that the router is an addressable device, and so it will have packets directed to it by any station on that LAN requiring delivery to remote destinations. When such a packet arrives at the local router it makes a routing decision about the method of forwarding the packet across the external networks or WANs available. Once the packet has been ultimately delivered to a router which resides on the destination station's LAN, then the mapping process described above takes place.

The various routing algorithms employed by routers have been identified in Chapter 11. So far we have only really considered the IP address structure. To deliver the TCP frame or segment in an IP datagram, this datagram needs a defined header structure, shown in Fig. 12.7.

Assigning addresses

We have so far considered that organizations have directly received their allocation of addresses from the Internet Assigned Numbers Authority. For many small organizations, this is not possible and the route then would be to go to an Internet Service Provider (ISP) to obtain an allocation. The ISP may allocate a block of addresses or may offer dynamically allocated addresses on a need to use now basis. If a block of addresses is held, from either source, these may be manually assigned to individual host

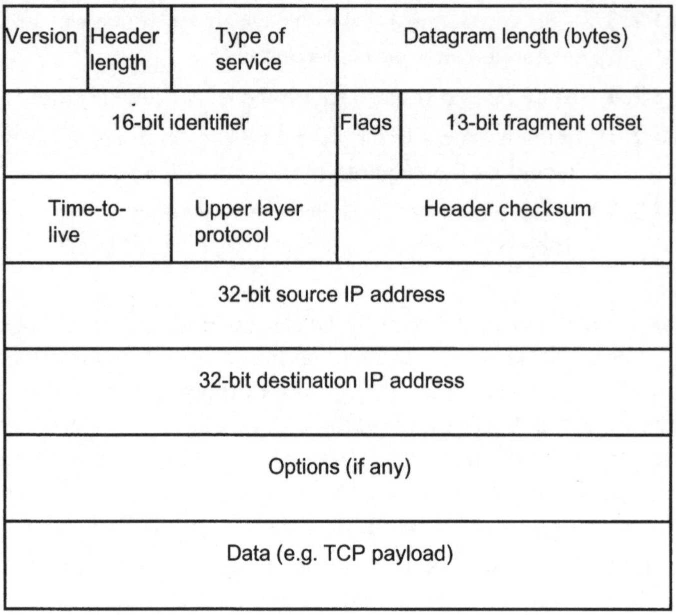

Version	Header length	Type of service	Datagram length (bytes)	
16-bit identifier			Flags	13-bit fragment offset
Time-to-live		Upper layer protocol	Header checksum	
32-bit source IP address				
32-bit destination IP address				
Options (if any)				
Data (e.g. TCP payload)				

Fig 12.7 IPv4 Header

machines, in a structured way. This task would be undertaken by the network administration. Alternatively, even if the organization has a block of addresses directly from the authorities, it may choose to operate with a dynamic allocation. In such cases a server is established, and dynamically assigns addresses based on client demand, using the Dynamic Host Configuration Protocol (DHCP). The server is known as the DHCP server.

IP Version 6

With the allocation of Version 4 IP addresses becoming exhausted, and with the real prospect of billions of users wanting an IP address allocation in this new millennium, a new mechanism was urgently needed. Indeed, it is possible that within the next few decades every home television, PC or one of a range of home electrical appliances could require its own IP address to take advantage of the new services being developed.

Version 6 of the IP protocol has been designed to meet the new needs. It has a 16-byte field to represent the address, which will clearly support an extended number of users. The result is that it is not compatible with Version 4 of IP. The IP Version 6 protocol header has also been simplified, even though it has large address fields, to speed up the routing stage. This was done by reducing the different number of fields that Version 4 supported, thus making the routing decisions less complex. An attempt has also been made in Version 6 to improve security concerns through the introduction of authentication fields.

One of the address areas, i.e., that beginning with the prefix 010, will support part of a registry service. Typical top-level registries, of which there are 32, are North America,

Asia and Europe. Within these registries, sublevels exist. It is these registries that will help in the location of addresses across the world.

To represent the IP address, the 'dotted decimal' notation has been abandoned and replaced with eight sets of four hexadecimal digits! Hence the address won't be quite as easy to recollect! The migration to IP Version 6 will be a slow process, and it could easily take decades to achieve, given the spread of users implementing Version 4.

TCP

Resident on top of the IP is the TCP, which provides sequenced delivery with flow control, error detection and recovery and port-level addressing (for service access). Hence the end-to-end reliable transfer of packets can be achieved between the source and destination hosts, both operating TCP. This end-to-end reliable transmission provision is required because the quality of each of the possible interconnected networks (including WANs and satellite connection) is unknown, with error detection and correction at lower levels not always being in place or available on the supporting network.

Since flow control, sequencing, error detection and correction are required in this layer 4 protocol, it is not surprising to see the protocol structure defined as shown in Fig. 12.8.

Mixed protocols on the same network can be supported, and routers are available that can manage a range of protocols. Hence TCP/IP, SNA and SPX/IPX can happily coexist on the same LAN, but not recognize each other unless translated somewhere.

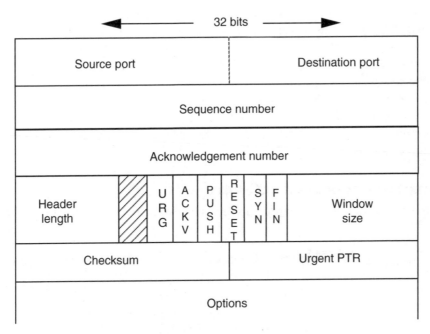

Fig. 12.8 TCP header

The basic features of a 'secure' protocol such as that offered by the IEEE 802.2 protocol are identifiable in this header format.

Clearly, it is important that the higher services that connect across TCP conform to a common standard, hence the File Transfer Protocol (FTP), Simple Mail Transfer Protocol (SMTP) and Telnet have been defined within the TCP/IP protocol suite (see Fig. 12.9). This is significant, because if we were to concentrate on TCP/IP as the major protocol (certainly it is the most commonly used), then there would automatically be a set of layer 7 services that would come with the protocol. Indeed TCP/IP is a protocol suite.

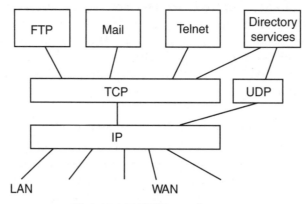

Fig. 12.9 TCP/IP services

TCP is a connection-based service which provides the reliability and other features needed for the higher-level services. However, some services do not need this heavyweight protocol. For small exchanges of data, where the overheads of establishing a connection and disconnection plus the overheads of sequencing, etc., are high, TCP is an over-provision.

The protocol suite which provides an alternative route using a connectionless protocol is called the User Datagram Protocol (UDP). This allows transfer of information where the data volumes are particularly low and the speed of response is better served by a datagram service.

4. Common application software

At the application level, interoperability has been achieved by a variety of means.

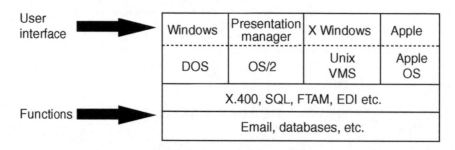

Fig. 12.10 Interoperable levels

If we take the top level, it may be the user interface that provides a consistent view of the range of services provided across the network (see Fig. 12.10). The user will always be presented with the same familiar interface regardless of the workstation or the application through which he or she is accessing the network.

Question 12.13 Why is a familiar interface considered to be useful?

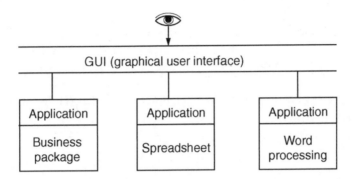

Fig. 12.11 GUI integrator

Access to each application, whether it be a Desktop Publishing (DTP) package or a spreadsheet, will be via a common Graphical User Interface (GUI) (see Fig. 12.11). A good example of this approach is that of Apple, where the layout and presentation of any application program to the user interface follows a standard. Hence users are able to move between products and applications with considerable ease.

At the file systems level, a range of techniques are available.

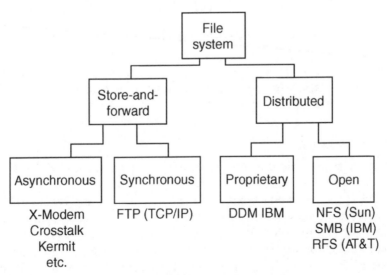

Fig. 12.12 File system integration

The extent to which your file will appear to be integrated will depend on where in the model of Fig. 12.12 the network is established. In a loosely connected arrangement, where little has been installed, old products such as Kermit, Crosstalk, etc., may be used to achieve file exchanges. In this case, a significant amount of user involvement is required to achieve the transfer and make remote files available for local use. At the other end of the spectrum, approaches such as the Sun distributed approach using the Network File System (NFS) and directory services can help to make the remote access transparent to the user.

Question 12.14 If products such as NFS are transparent, and products such as Kermit require considerable user intervention, why should it ever be necessary to use Kermit and why doesn't everybody use NFS?

Finally, at the application interface level, it may be particular application software that is the integrating feature.

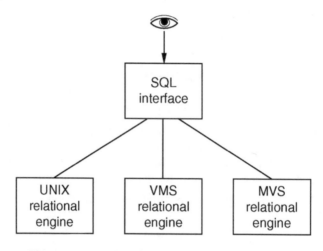

Fig. 12.13 Application interface integration

In the example shown in Fig. 12.13, the user tool is SQL, and this can be implemented as a standard across a variety of supporting platforms. Hence, all of the networked system provides the user with the same SQL interface.

5. Operating system

Each host on the system could run the same operating system environment and the user would see the same operating system interface at any station. Extensions to the stand-alone version of the operating system can enhance the system considerably such that resources that are remote from a particular workstation are seen as 'local'. The result is an extended virtual machine at each user's workstation. For example, in a Unix environment, the Unix file stores at each individual workstation may be viewed as a single entity by the user, with the path search for a particular directory/file taking place initially on the local workstation and then being extended through the searching of the other Unix file stores using remote procedure calls.

Another major benefit of having a common operating system is that the structure and access control to all the files is identical.

Question 12.15 Does the common operating system approach have any benefits in relation to system security?

Perhaps the biggest impact on operating system integration has been the developments in Network Operating Systems (NOSs). There are many very good NOS products available. On the basis of current popularity, Windows NT is considered here in a little more detail. An outline is provided of the types of facility that are readily available in such environments. Previously Novell Netware dominated this part of the market and so is also considered here.

Windows NT

The Microsoft network operating system is Windows NT, and, as you might expect, it offers a full range of client services such as file and print services. The client operating systems that can be supported as standard include DOS, Windows, Windows NT, Unix, OS/2 and the Macintosh operating systems. A particularly useful feature is the support that the operating system provides for file sharing where it supports NCS, X-Open, SMB and HTTP.

To manage the user interface, Windows NT has a few new features. The Start button/ Programs menu combination to find a program is equivalent to the old Windows Program Manager. Other options on the Programs menu include the following:

a) Windows Explorer;

b) MS-DOS Prompt.

Fig. 12.14 shows a typical range of options. Other options on the Start button/Settings menu are the Control Panel and Print Manager.

All the details about user accounts are kept securely in a database directory that has a directory service access. On the Windows NT server, a domain is established that holds a separate account for each user. This domain approach allows each user to have the following:

a) single log-on access to multiple servers;

b) centralized network administration;

c) access to all network resources.

A domain comprises all the network servers and stations that share the same security and access information. This is really helpful in a number of organizations. For example, in an academic environment, all the students in one department belong to a domain, so a log-on brings up the resources that exist across the whole of the department. Similarly, a group of staff working within a division of an organization see their division's servers, but not necessarily those of other divisions. This allows a single administration unit to look after a whole domain.

A user's account within a domain specifies which files, directories and printers are accessible to that user. The administration unit can simply look after one account for a user rather than having to look after multiple accounts across a range of servers.

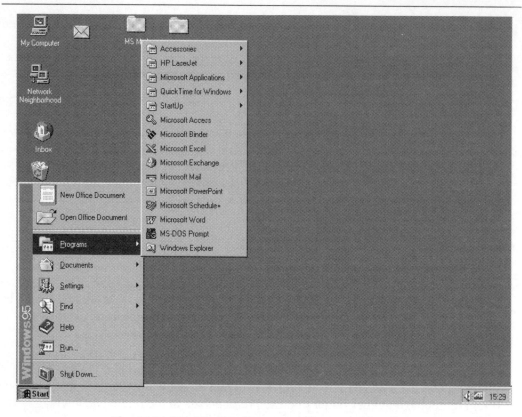

Fig. 12.14 Start button/Program menu combination

Novell NetWare

NetWare is aimed at the mass market, and used to be the most popular NOS. It is compatible with both IBM-compatible PCs and the Macintosh and onwards range of Apple systems. Originally, the product provided the end-to-end lightweight and efficient SPX/IPX protocol. One of the strategies behind NetWare is to make the NOS as open as possible to allow integration with other systems and other vendors' products. Hence, NetWare can now operate across IPX, TCP/IP, Appletalk and X.25 platforms.

The concept was to provide a server facility to multiple client workstations. Within this server is a common file system used by the clients, implemented through the NetWare Core Protocol (NCP). This protocol provides the following facilities:

a) file access (read, write, open, close);

b) file locking (one user can modify whilst others wait);

c) security (protection of access to owner);

d) tracking of resource allocation;

e) print server and queue management;

f) network management.

These facilities have been implemented using some of the robust features previously seen in the 'classic' mainframe operating systems of the past. Typical of this approach was the early introduction of fault resilience using separate spindles, multiple disk controllers or separate mirroring servers. File-caching and disk-seeking algorithms such as Shortest Seek Time First (SSTF) algorithm and background writing are all approaches introduced in the NetWare systems to support the services.

To keep the product as compact as possible, each system is built from a number of modules which may be loaded as necessary (NetWare Loadable Modules (NLMs)). Typical of such NLMs are the Unix NFS modules and multi-protocol router modules.

To help the network administrator manage the NetWare system, a set of administration tools called the monitor module can be run on the service to perform tasks such as the following.

a) set password;

b) establish server utilization;

c) examine file caching;

d) inspect user files and clear client connections;

e) view disk drive status;

f) check file locking.

Whilst the client–server approach of NetWare is the main approach, small scale implementations based on NetWare Lite use a peer-to-peer approach. Any computer with a hard disk can be a potential server. The 'server' is all of the computers that have made their applications, files or disk space available to others. Other workstations in this peer-to-peer arrangement can access the distributed server facilities. NetWare Lite offered the essential components of the following:

a) connectivity through its hardware and software;

b) network resource availability;

c) network commands and utilities.

The DOS Share utility is used to implement the environment for more than one user to access applications and utilities.

Further questions

(There are answers to the questions marked with an asterisk at the end of the book.)

1. *What is the difference between interconnection and interoperability?

2. *Outline the reasons why interoperability is more difficult to achieve than interconnection.

3. *Why is TCP/IP viewed as a major product in achieving interoperability?

4. An office department has developed two separate networks over a period of two years. A simple Appletalk network currently links Macintosh systems so that they share a laser printer. A 100baseT Ethernet system connects PCs and printers. This system uses Windows NT as its NOS. The department now seeks to integrate these networks to provide a range of departmental functions such as a mail service and diary system.

   Outline the issues that need to be addressed and suggest possible implementation options.

5. The department described in Question 4 is part of a larger organization with a SUN cluster as part of its central computing provision. The whole organization is now seeking to provide the same functionality across the corporate operation as this department has just implemented. Outline the issues that now have to be addressed.

6. Providing some of the higher level services shown in Fig. 12.9 requires efficient protocols to support the service. Does UDP have an active role to play here or not?

7. File system integration is seen as an important corporate goal by many organizations. Outline how such an objective may be achieved in terms of network technology.

Answer 12.1　You may well have a good answer to this question which is not listed below, but you may have identified one of the following areas:

a)　common e-mail;*

b)　common EDI (electronic data interchange);

c)　common spreadsheet software;*

d)　a common DTP (desktop publishing) system.

*these applications may be part of the common desktop environment.

Answer 12.2　TCP/IP is a really good transport protocol. It operates successfully across a wide range of underlying networks, no matter how poor the quality of those networks may be. To achieve this reliability, the product is a heavyweight piece of software, with rigorous checking and monitoring procedures. When Novell was designing its network system, it was envisaged as working across single LANs, such as workplace LANs, which have a reliability that is several orders of magnitude better than that of public networks. Therefore, a simpler approach that was much more efficient was selected. Hence the resulting SPX/IPX (Sequenced Package Exchange/Internetwork Packet Exchange) provides a lightweight and less cumbersome approach. It is worth noting, however, that much of the world is talking TCP/IP, and all of the network vendors, such as 3Com and Cisco, include TCP/IP as part of their product ranges. Also, the processing power and memory size of servers and workstations has changed so much in the last decade that the focus on 'lightweight' is not now relevant.

Answer 12.3　From the commercial viewpoint, there were a number of contracts which specified that OSI conformance was a requirement. Government procurement policies through the GOSIP (Government OSI Procurement) specification require vendors to tender on the basis of OSI conformance. Clearly, having a commercial strategy based on OSI is a significant aid. From the technical point of view, converting to a common standard of OSI reduces the number of pairwise conversions that could be required if multiple vendor approaches were being integrated on a single LAN. For example, if IBM's SNA and Apple's ATP were to be interconnected, the OSI approach would be ideal.

Answer 12.4　The spread of TCP/IP is now so great, and its availability in products so widespread, that it is impossible to ignore. The majority of interconnection 'boxes' provide TCP/IP services, and all computer manufacturers provide a TCP/IP alternative to their own operating system protocol. Network vendors such as 3Com provide TCP/IP paths within their products. Right now, if you had to select a protocol with interconnection and interoperability in mind and future-proof yourself for new products that might purchased at some later date, then TCP/IP is the automatic choice. There may, of course, be overwhelming reasons why an alternative approach may be chosen.

Answer 12.5   This is a simpler question than it may appear. TCP resides in layer 4 of the OSI model. If you revisit Fig. 7.9 you can see that it is a software implementation. It resides in the host machine interface to the network as a communications channel or socket. When a TCP/IP PDU (protocol data unit) arrives at the communications interface it will be passed to the TCP/IP stream. (Note that it is possible that multiple protocols are operating in the host system).

Answer 12.6   End-to-end protocols control the exchange of PDUs between the two host machines. What sits between the two host machines is not a consideration, and it could be a straight-through connection or a series of interconnected LANs and WANs.

Hence, the end-to-end protocol works on the basis that there is a transparent pipe and it ensures integrity between the source and destination hosts.

As suggested above, the transparent pipe may consist of a series of connections or links. Point-to-point protocols ensure that these individual links operate successfully.

Answer 12.7   Routers work on the Internet address as a means of forwarding PDUs. Bridges, on the other hand, work at the MAC layer and operate on hardware addresses.

Answer 12.8   The usual technique of using a bit pattern, such as all 1s, in the IP addressing scheme can be implemented.

Answer 12.9   A router is an addressable device. In Fig. 11.24, it can be seen that the router is connected to both LANs. Each LAN has its own IP (or Internet) address, and so the interface of the router (which is in itself addressable from that side of the network) must have its own ID.

Answer 12.10   255.255.240.0

Answer 12.11   128.10.129.64

Answer 12.12   Other protocols, such as the Novell, could be identified in this field. Indeed, within TCP/IP, there is a breakdown of a range of values that can be used.

Answer 12.13   The level of ease and confidence with which users can move between a range of applications should be directly reflected in the user's efficiency. A reduced level of training should be required, and detailed instruction may only be required for one package.

Answer 12.14   The SUN approach is indeed popular, and it has been licensed by SUN to a number of other network vendors. It is, however, a major item of software, and it may be more applicable to major sites where there is a significant amount of teamwork. Also, it would be of benefit where there is a significant amount of shared data. If, however, there is little shared data and each user keeps the majority of data generated to him or herself, then maybe the lightweight products such as Kermit have a function or role. This is, however, increasingly becoming less attractive, and network operating systems provide such simple mechanisms to share data that products such as Kermit need rarely, if ever, be used: I have not used it for many years.

Answer 12.15   System security is an important element in most environments (if not all of them). Having a common operating system does allow us to use the same access controls (e.g., read only, execute only) uniformly across the whole system. It is possible in a multi-operating-system site for some of the systems to be less secure than others. To embrace these into the LAN, compromises have been allowed.

13 Performance

1. Introduction

Before a LAN is initially selected, the network designer needs to have confidence that the proposed installation will be capable of meeting the performance requirements for the organization. If no LAN is currently installed then judging the volume of traffic that may be generated will be difficult. Alternatively, if an existing network is about to be extended, enhanced or replaced, then the network designer may be in a better position to determine the probable volume of future traffic levels.

In either situation the network designer needs to determine as accurately as possible the volume of traffic that will be generated. One method of obtaining a rough figure for this load is to use a traffic matrix (see Fig. 13.1). The rough figure may be more of an estimate when no LAN is currently in place.

Device ＼ Device	A	B	C	D
A				
B				
C				
D				

Fig. 13.1 Traffic matrix

We should enter each device that is to be connected to the LAN on the horizontal axis and the vertical axis. Then we fix a time interval, which may be a minute, an hour or other appropriate time slot. For this fixed time interval, the predicted volume of traffic between each pair of devices is entered at the relevant matrix position. The volume may be expressed in terms of the number of bytes expected to be exchanged per minute. An example is shown in Fig. 13.2. Device PC1 sends 780 byte/min to the file server, whereas device PC2 sends 980 byte/min. Here we have fixed the time interval to be 1 min and expressed the data volume in bytes. To determine the overall volume of data to be

222

carried in the specified time interval, we sum the data entries. It is frequently helpful to calculate the exchange volume over a longer period and in terms of activity types rather than a total number-of bytes.

Device \ Device	Unix A	Unix B	PC 1	PC 2	File server	Mac 1
Unix A						
Unix B						
PC 1					780	
File server						
Mac 1						
PC 2					980	

Fig. 13.2 Example matrix

The data exchange predictions should be considered in relation to the activities that are likely to be implemented, e.g., the downloading of system software, Internet access, file backups, listings to print servers, file transfers, e-mail exchanges, and straightforward terminal-to-host traffic. Each type of activity could be given a mean value, e.g., e-mails could all be assigned a mean value of 2 kbytes, and a file listing to a print server could be assigned a mean value of 3 kbytes. One observation is that any prediction will nearly always be significantly lower than the observed usage shortly after implementation.

Typically, the use of facilities such as e-mail, or conference facilities on hosts, or the introduction of network resource-demanding approaches such as client-server models (X-Windows) and CD-ROMs will radically change the figures. Users also become more proficient as they gain access to a larger and wider resource base. This proficiency creates an increasing requirement for even more network traffic.

Question 13.1 Why might proficient users create more network traffic than new users?

It should also be noted that the overheads of the network protocols contribute to the number of bits transferred across the network. In many networks, especially those supporting terminal-to-host traffic, this could easily double the number of bits that need to be transferred.

Question 13.2 A single character is entered at a keyboard and transmitted across a network in an Ethernet frame. What overheads are carried in order to transmit this byte?

It would be very unusual if a network remained static in size, since the number of connected devices rarely stays constant in most installations. Normally, there are incremental demands for further connections to be made. This is especially true as the range of services and facilities provided on a network is enhanced. Each separate facility added will create a whole new group of users who may then potentially wish to be connected.

The message to be firmly understood in this introduction to performance is simple. The traffic matrix will give a good guide to the minimum traffic requirement. This can probably be doubled to handle the protocol overheads and doubled again for the additional proficiency demands as users gain greater competence. At this point it may be prudent to double it again to be sure that future growth can be accommodated. It is therefore sensible to make sure that the initial load predicted is nowhere near the LAN's limit of performance. Plenty of spare capacity should be available to future-proof the investment. You can see that this is not an exact science. Leaving a lot of spare capacity is a wise investment.

Current LAN implementations often place specific devices such as servers in a position within the configuration, where traffic levels to and from the server is of greater importance than the overall traffic levels. For example, this would be particularly true of a major server attached to an ATM or Ethernet switch. In these cases the traffic on a specific link may be as important in the performance calculation as the overall traffic levels. Indeed, overall traffic levels are of importance only when the transmission resource is shared, such as in early Ethernet standards such as IEEE 802.3 or in the current wireless network standard of IEEE 802.11.

Question 13.3 What could we do if an installed LAN reached its capacity?

---

2. Throughput

There are a number of issues to consider in the area of throughput; it could be the topic of a complete book. A range of supporting mathematical techniques enable the network designer to model throughput. However, much of this modelling is complex, so the approach taken here does not require you to understand the detail behind this modelling, but simply to be aware of the facility. Modelling is often based on queuing theory. Anyone who is familiar with the technique will appreciate the difficulties involved in analysing an operating system which traditionally is a single server, multiple queue system. It could be argued that a LAN is a distributed operating system, and hence the extra complexity.

This has led us to an important point. The configuration of a LAN does not lend itself to very simple modelling. It provides a mechanism for transferring data between two points, hopefully quickly and reliably. To control access to a central facility such as a file server, and to provide security, access control, backup, etc., a network operating system needs to be resident over the hardware. The range of products is extensive, with the market leaders including Microsoft and Novell. Each of these has its strengths and weaknesses, but Microsoft has become the dominant NOS.

NOS products may provide both lightweight protocols for performance purposes and heavyweight protocols (e.g., TCP/IP) for interconnection and interoperability purposes. These alternatives will affect performance and this should be noted. Often, it is difficult to justify migrating to TCP/IP to accommodate interoperability for only 0.5 per cent of the generated traffic! Such a migration may reduce the efficiency and performance for the remaining users. Of course, the rapid increase in processing power of the server hardware is changing the conceptions that existed about using lightweight protocols in favour of heavyweight protocols. Hence TCP/IP has rapidly become the *de facto* standard. What is important is that the NOS selected should provide the full range of options and features required for use.

Question 13.4 Why should we change from Novell SPX/IPX to TCP/IP if only 0.5 per cent of the network traffic is internetwork and 99.5 per cent is intranetwork?

However, all of these NOS products sit on top of one or more of the hardware platforms and this area is fairly stable. It is therefore worth examining the performance characteristics of the leading hardware approaches, namely 802.3 and 802.5 LANs. Each have a declared nominal speed of operation, e.g., 4 Mbit/s, 10 Mbit/s, 16 Mbit/s, 100 Mbit/s, etc. In reality these are not fully achieved, especially for those networks which are built on a shared media access arrangement. It is important to know how great the shortfall is in practice.

The ideal situation would be if all the offered load was carried, without delay, up to the network capacity. Against this ideal condition, it is reasonable to expect a short delay before access is achieved. Any delay in allocating access means that some of the network capacity will be lost.

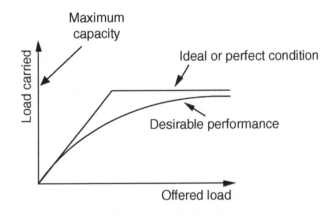

Fig. 13.3 Load performance on shared access network

Question 13.5 Under ideal performance conditions, why is the graph in Fig. 13.3 flat once the maximum capacity is reached?

The actual performance is likely to be worse than this. The observed performance will vary considerably depending on the type of traffic that is typically carried. Examples are simple character transmission for terminals, small data structures, or large volumes of data such as those generated by image processing activity. In general terms, it is possible that the observed performance may look more like that in Fig. 13.4.

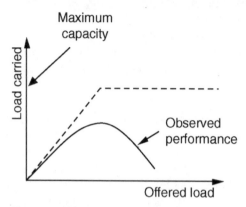

Fig. 13.4 Observed performance

It can be seen here that, after achieving only a percentage of the maximum throughput, the network gets congested and throughput is likely to degrade. This model is more representative of some networks than others. In particular, CSMA/CD LANs look like this, where the traffic is spread across a single 'collision domain' based on shared bandwidth.

To give a good idea of the performance expected, a network can be modelled using a simulation package. There are a number of such modelling or simulation packages available. This can act as an extremely useful confidence test for any network designer because the major network standards can be modelled. The designer sets up a typical workload condition, and the simulation package will indicate typical throughputs and delays.

Example ranges of loads and traffic types have been simulated, and the results are shown in Figs 13.5, 13.6 and 13.7.

Fig. 13.5 suggests that, for a single segment 802.3 LAN where traffic is typically light, several hundred users may be connected without adverse effects. With a medium level load, where each station makes a server request every second, the number of stations may comfortably reach 80. But with heavy loads, with each station making significant server demands every 100 ms, the performance peaks at ten stations and deteriorates rapidly thereafter.

Each of these figures relates to issues of a single collision domain. Many of the recent implementations, based on switches, have multiple collision domains. In the case of full duplex Ethernet connectivity, there is no CSMA/CD operational. For these cases, the issue on any individual circuit will be equivalent to the light/medium load case in Fig.

13.5. The load can rise almost linearly until capacity of the connection is reached or the capacity of the device itself is being reached (e.g., server bottleneck).

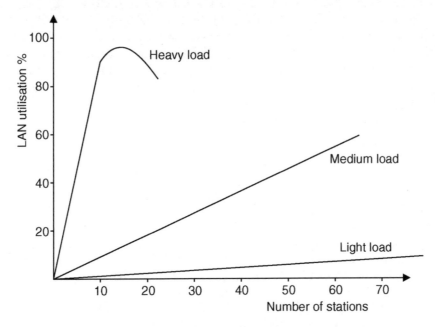

Fig. 13.5 Performance on an IEEE 802.3 LAN

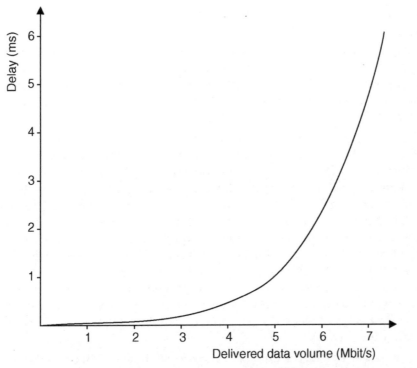

Fig. 13.6 Delay versus load on an Ethernet LAN

In Fig. 13.6, for a 10 Mbit/s shared Ethernet LAN with a mixed range of loads, and on a single collision domain, the graph shows that, once more than 5 Mbit/s of data is carried, the delay in delivery across the LAN increases rapidly. This indicates that a collision domain for an 802.3 LAN ought not to be loaded beyond 5 Mbit/s, since continuous traffic above this level will cause the performance to degrade rapidly. In comparison, a token ring reaches about 85 per cent of its capability before significant delays are experienced (see Fig. 13.7). However, at low loads there is no delay for an Ethernet system in accessing the network, whereas there is inherently some delay in a token ring network before access is achieved (perhaps half a token rotation time when no other traffic is being carried).

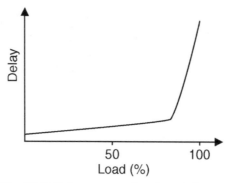

Fig. 13.7 Delay versus load on token ring

3. Trade-off

It is already apparent that the network designer has been faced with making compromises in the design of standards. At the selection and implementation stage, we are faced with a similar set of trade-off decisions to make. High on the list are the issues of speed versus cost versus cable types and structures. These are typical first thoughts, but careful and equal attention needs to be paid to future proofing the investment.

Consider an example where a bus topology network operating at 100 Mbit/s, but not conforming to IEEE standards, becomes available which costs one-third of the price of an Ethernet system. Of course this is an unlikely scenario, given the high volume low cost benefits enjoyed by Ethernet. However, as an academic point, this is worth pursuing. It may well be that the product has a range of interface cards for IBM-compatible PCs and a limited number of other devices such as a Unix workstation. Perhaps these cater for the existing range of equipment on site. On cost grounds, there may be a temptation to buy such a network system. If at some later stage you wish to add a new device to the network (e.g., a Sun Sparc workstation), a network interface card may not be available in this non-standard network product range. Alternatively, it is possible that network interconnection may become a requirement, perhaps because of corporate merger or a policy change. Bridge, router or gateway facilities may not be available for the network.

On this evidence, selecting a LAN which conforms to one of the standards is a good starting point. Otherwise, the difficulties that could potentially arise at a later stage may not be worth the savings that could be achieved now. Also remember that 'better than standard' or enhanced standards are non-standard. It is worth noting the enormous market penetration achieved by Ethernet networks, making it an almost automatic choice for most installations.

When considering cabling issues, it is important to remind ourselves of several major points. A 10baseT network may offer the opportunity of upgrading the speed at a later date, providing the right cable selection is made now (i.e., typically Category 5 UTP). However, given the low cost of 100 bit/s Ethernet cards, it may be that a 100baseT network is the first installation choice now. It maybe that IEEE 802.5 networks are favoured, especially in the case of IBM host installations. Since the expensive element of cable installation is the labour costs of installation rather than the cable materials costs, good quality cable should be selected at the outset. This issue will be revisited in Chapter 14. A point to remember is that upgrading of standards may continue for networks based on unshielded twisted pair cable.

Since network downtime needs to be minimized, the cable installation should also conform to a structured approach. This will make maintenance easier, help control the additional cabling requirements of the future, and provide an engineered cable base rather than a loosely defined arrangement.

Question 13.6 Why might we wish to add more cable in the future?

Question 13.7 How might we avoid the necessity of having to add more cable at a later date?

4. Reliability

Once a network has been installed, the user dependence on the facility gravitates quickly to it being an essential requirement. Whereas users of pre-LAN installations were prepared to accept a degree of isolation (e.g., working in terminal rooms and the associated lack of access to facilities), once dependence is established, the LAN access capability becomes a necessity. Indeed, most organizations structure their system developments predicated on the availability of LAN connectivity.

The network designer therefore needs to identify the reliability performance requirements. It is accepted that 100 per cent reliability is unachievable, and the LAN administration must agree with the corporate body of the organization as to what constitutes an acceptable reliability performance figure. The metrics in this area could be availability, the mean time between failures (MTBF) and the mean time to repair (MTTR).

The simple MTBF figures are quoted by the vendors, but clearly tend to represent the product at its best. If the figure is not available, it ought to be! A second critical figure is the MTTR. This will depend on the spares held locally, the level of the maintenance contract, the distance of the maintenance organization from the site, and the skill of the support centre and its staff. Each of these can vary quite considerably, and to get the clearest view of what the real situation actually is, attendance at the vendor's user group meetings can be extremely beneficial. At such a meeting, existing users will paint the picture as it actually is, warts and all.

Once the two metrics have been established, the fraction of time for which a component is operating, i.e., its availability, can be determined as follows:

$$\text{availability} = \frac{\text{MTBF}}{\text{MTBF} + \text{MTTR}}$$

Question 13.8 If a component has an MTBF of 6000 hours and a mean repair time of twenty hours, what is its availability?

Of course, in modern, large networks, with most components replicated many times, it is common to carry spares on site, or to have in-built redundancy in the network. Such approaches minimize the value of MTTR to the time it takes for simple swapping of the 'spare' kit.

It should be noted that, if a range of components are required to provide a particular facility, then it is the composite availability of each component that generates the facility availability:

availability of facility = availability component 1 × availability component 2 ×, etc.

Question 13.9 If six components, each with an availability of 0.95, are all required for a particular function, what is this function's availability?

A network designer should pay due regard to each component's availability contribution. If one area is critical for network uptime, then it may be that replication or redundant facilities should be installed. A good example is the contribution that a file server may make to a LAN. Without this device, little else may be achieved. Hence, the provisions of a file-server backup is a sensible plan. Indeed, NOS vendors are able to offer a range of file tolerance levels. For example, Novell offers duplicate files through to duplicate file stores. In between, duplicate spindles are offered.

The availability of data can be calculated for each component part, but the cable structure also has a contribution to make in this area. Because locating faults can be a time consuming activity, planning your system to help reduce downtime is a worthwhile investment. In particular, the investment in a structured wiring scheme, with wiring centres, will allow rapid identification for the removal of faulty cable 'conditions'.

Within the framework outlined, the designer may opt to build resilience into the planned network.

Question 13.10 If a switch in an Ethernet design was identified as a risk component, what resilience could be planned into the configuration?

Reliability may be enhanced by taking a proactive approach with respect to the following:

a) the help desk or network administration;

b) the monitoring of server resources;

c) the analysis of network loads and traffic patterns;

d) the anticipation of traffic loads for new applications.

Further questions

(There are answers to the questions marked with an asterisk at the end of the book.)

1. A department is currently planning to introduce a LAN operating at 100 Mbit/s. The installed equipment consists of ten PCs, each of which will exchange 100 kbytes with the file server in each 5 min period, and 150 kbytes with the print server in each hour.

    Construct a traffic matrix and check whether this is within the proposed network's capability.

2. *Why might Ethernet be a better proposition than a token ring for a network carrying low traffic levels?

3. *Consider an old network shown in Fig. 13. 8.

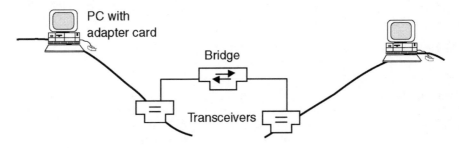

Fig. 13.8 Network for questions

The PCs are connected to a thin wire Ethernet network using the transceiver on the network card. The bridge requires external transceivers to connect to the cable.

What is the availability of the link between the two PCs if each component is separately rated as having an availability of 0.9?

4. *How do we improve the reliability of any network configuration?

5. What role does the cable structure play in enhancing the network reliability?

6. Modelling packages such as Lannet allow us to determine whether a proposed installation will work. Of what use could such a tool be once the network has been installed?

Answer 13.1   As a user becomes more familiar and proficient at using a system, greater demands are made on the facilities. Such a user is likely to exploit a greater range of facilities and network tools, and the outcome of this is that more traffic is generated on the network to service these demands.

Answer 13.2   The minimum size Ethernet frame is 64 bytes. The probability is that the receiving station responds with an ACK. Hence a single character transfer generates perhaps 128 bytes of network traffic, i.e., 64 bytes in both directions. If this character transfer resulted from a terminal sending data to a host machine, then the host would echo that character back for screen display. If that were the case, the echo back would double the previous data transfer estimates. Hence a terminal to host character transfer could generate 256 bytes of data.

Answer 13.3   If the shared LAN bandwidth capacity is reaching its limits, then the network should be partitioned. The network traffic being generated needs to be examined critically to ensure that the partitioning will isolate a reasonable volume within each partitioned area. It would not be sensible to partition the original network and then require all the traffic to flow through a specific link relay. It is not, therefore, a good strategy to place a file server on the other side of a link relay from the bulk of the file server requests. It is also worth noting that reaching capacity could mean that the peak performance for that network is being reached; further traffic would create performance degradation.

For networks with more dedicated elements, such as a switched Ethernet, if the capacity is being reached on the link to a key resource such as a server, then either multiple servers need to be deployed, or an upgrade to that device may be a good option. Alternatively, an upgrade in the speed of the link could be considered.

Answer 13.4 The network under discussion here has almost all of its traffic contained within the network. Only a very small percentage ever leaves the network. We should note that SPX/IPX is an efficient lightweight protocol, whereas TCP/IP is a robust, heavyweight product. However, with increasing use of the Internet, TCP/IP has a clear lead for interoperability, and the migration to ICP/IP is almost certainly worth the benefits gained.

Answer 13.5 Clearly, once the maximum capacity of the system is reached, this cannot be exceeded. In an ideal situation, once the capacity of the network is reached, no matter how much more load is offered, no more traffic can be carried.

Answer 13.6 Additional cabling may, in the future, be needed as the backbone cable system requires enhancement to handle higher backbone speeds. The direction of the future is towards FDDI or ATM backbones with local connectivity or towards 10 Gigabit/s Ethernet linking sub-networks together.

Answer 13.7 Since the cost of installation is significantly biased towards labour costs, it is a sensible strategy to flood-wire the areas from the outset. Whilst you are installing a single point at a location, additional point(s) will not add significantly to the overall cost. Since user mobility is high, flood-wiring will allow relocation without recabling. The use of patch panels, housed in wiring cabinets, is certainly supportive of such an approach.

Answer 13.8

$$\text{availability} = \frac{6000}{6000 + 20} = 99.667 \text{ per cent}$$

Answer 13.9 Not counting the PCs, there are six component parts making up the network function (NICs, bridge, transceivers and cable). $0.95^6 = 0.735$

Answer 13.10 We could add a second switch, each supporting half the connections. In the event of one switch failing, the connections can quickly be 'patched through' to the operational switch to provide a full service level.

14 Installation, management and security

1. Introduction

In Chapter 1 we described a LAN by including self ownership of the system within the definition. The implications associated with self ownership are hopefully clear. The responsibilities for installation and future maintenance and upkeep are not the PTT's; these are responsibilities that remain with the owner. In the early developments of LANs, this wasn't a particularly critical issue. The early 'pioneers' of networking were normally specialist networkers with responsibility for relatively small network systems. Hence, those early network systems were supported by enthusiasts.

This picture has changed rapidly over the years. The configurations have grown larger and more complex, and hence the general upkeep of the network requires considerably more thought. The supporting network management tools have consequently been an active product development area, and they have attracted significant attention from vendors and users alike. Interconnection to WANs and the general interoperability issues demand further action in an overall network management view. Network vendors have developed systems with the management of enterprise networks as their objective.

Question 14.1 Why should larger networks require better network management tools than smaller ones?

Question 14.2 Does the management of an enterprise wide network consisting of a number of LANs interconnected via a WAN create any more issues to worry about than a single LAN?

In this chapter we will examine the issues relating to both installation and ongoing management. Part of the installation will require tools for the work to be successfully undertaken. These tools will not be wasted, because they naturally form part of the network manager's upgrade and maintenance kit. Note that we have introduced the concept of a network manager. It is important that somebody is identified as carrying the LAN responsibility for anything but the very smallest of configurations.

Question 14.3 If nobody was identified as network manager, what sort of problems might arise?

---

2. Installation

The planning and testing stages start before the installation begins in earnest. Perhaps the most important decision is the choice of location for the wiring centre or wiring cabinets. The routes for the cabling need to be determined, and it must be ensured that the cable ducts or trays have the capacity to take further cable. The location and number of taps need to be identified, recognizing that it is important to plan for growth and some user mobility, e.g., to cope with movement and rearrangement of office furniture.

The proposed cable routes should be surveyed for hazardous environments, hence we must ensure that areas of high temperature, electrical radiation (including from fluorescent light strips) and heavy electrical plant are avoided.

Question 14.4 If one of these hazards is in the middle of the planned route, what can be done?

An installation toolkit may consist of a simple volt-ohm-meter (VOM) and a time domain reflectometer (TDR). The installation may cover three identifiable phases: pre-installation, installation and post-installation. A thorough pre-installation exercise can prevent a lot of possible fault-finding time post-installation. It is therefore useful to start at this point.

Pre-installation

Except perhaps in the very smallest of proposed installations, before any item is installed it should pass a pre-installation check. This might require the setting up of a small test rig so that the various devices can be checked as being operable before installation. Perhaps the most important item to check is the cable itself. We first check this while it is still on the reel or drum. A TDR should be calibrated for this medium (typically against a metre of cable if it is not pre-set). A pulse is then sent down the cable and the reflection of the signal is echoed back and inspected (see Fig. 14.1). Most TDR devices can produce hard copy. Any open or short circuits show on the trace and any non-conformance in comparison with good quality cable can be identified. Hence any poor cable can be identified and rejected prior to installation. Optical TDRs and unshielded twisted pair versions are also available.

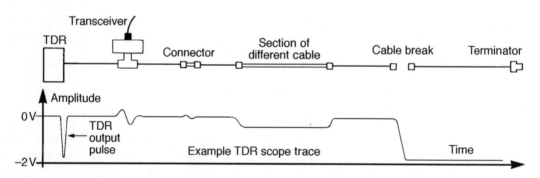

Fig. 14.1 Typical TDR trace
(© Layer One, reprinted with permission)

Fault-finding on installed equipment can be tedious and time-consuming, so testing the compatability and safe operation before installation can be a worthwhile investment. Once all the components are passed as satisfactory, the second phase of the installation can proceed.

Question 14.5 Checking all items prior to installation is time-consuming. If we installed everything and it worked, we would have saved a lot of time. Wouldn't this be a better strategy?

Cable installation

The first element to be installed is usually the transmission cable (or other appropriate transmission medium). Whilst installing the cable it is important not to stress or damage the cable by exerting too great a strain as the cable is pulled through the various ducts. Installation tools can include a cable puller, which can be set to prevent excessive tension being used. Each cable type comes with a specification which includes the maximum bend radius, and care must be taken not to exceed this figure, especially with fibre optic cable.

Indeed, fibre optic cable requires special care during installation. Although field kits are available to aid the splicing of fibre, special attention is required to avoid excessive signal loss at such points. A poor splice could lose half the signal strength or more. At the other end of the range, twisted pair cable is relatively easy to install, although IBM Type 1 cable is somewhat thicker than might have been expected, having a diameter of approximately $^3/_8$ in. Other IBM type cables are proportionally thinner.

During installation, it is essential to keep detailed records of exactly where the cable runs have been installed. These used to be largely paper records. Since cable structures were updated frequently, these cable plans became difficult to maintain. Facilities to keep computer records of such features are now common in the market place.

Question 14.6 What sort of advantages may emerge from having a cable layout computerized and online?

At each stage it is worth rechecking the soundness of the cable. Once again, the use of a TDR is required. When a fault condition has been detected, a TDR trace will identify its position on the cable to within a few feet. Because we have accurately recorded the cable runs, locating the physical point on the cable should then be easy, and corrective action to remove the offending area can be initiated. Hence if the TDR trace indicates a fault which is 20 m down the cable, we know where that physically exists.

When cable is spliced together with connectors, it is preferable to use identical cable, so keeping spare cable from the original installation is a good move.

Question 14.7 What are the benefits of having some spare original cable?

Multiple cable runs are typically brought out at a single location known as the wiring centre which houses the wiring cabinet, It is therefore imperative that we label the cable at both ends. Do not use sticky bits of paper; ensure that permanent marking with shrink ferrules or other appropriate marking techniques are used. When the appropriate connections are made to plugs, wall plate fittings, etc., a VOM can be used to check for short circuits, etc., With the current high speeds of 100+ Mbit/s, it is particularly important that connections meet installation specifications, including how many twists can be unwound before termination. This can be critical for the successful operation of the LAN, and installation is now normally left to installation specialists. They should certify that the installation meets the specification for high speed transmission. The installation of spare capacity is normal, and in the wiring cabinet all the cable is brought back to the patch panel.

Question 14.8 Sticky label attachments are quick to install, easy to read and cheap, so why are they not recommended?

Special testing tools are required for fibre optics installation and testing, as shown in Fig. 14.2.

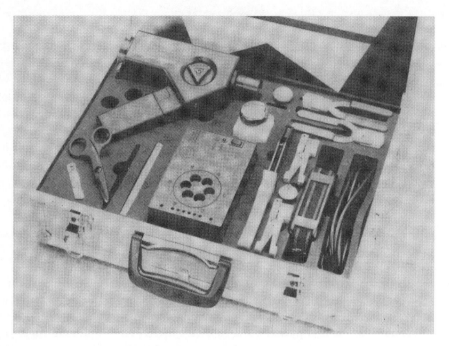

Fig. 14.2 Fibre optics cable kit
(© Layer One, reprinted with permission)

Network equipment installation

The wiring cabinet can house the Ethernet hubs or other devices such as switches, routers of MSAUs, as appropriate to the installation. For each user device that needs to be operational, the connection is 'patched through' with a cable connection from the patch panel to the hub, switch or router, etc.

Other devices can now be connected. It is recommended that this is undertaken in a staged manner. Perhaps the simple installation of two or three devices including the server supporting the network operating system would be sensible. A system build can then be attempted and the installed system checked using both a TDR and any software test to ensure operational functionality or integrity.

Question 14.9 Why might testing out a newly built system on a simple laboratory based network be a sensible strategy?

Once you have an operational network, complete a TDR test and keep the hard copy for reference. When a fault develops, it is helpful be able to compare a working environment with the fault situation. Up to 35 per cent of faults are cable related, so the wiring cabinet access is a core component in the ongoing network management. Many TDRs can only be used when the network is not in use. However, it is worth noting that devices called network quality analysers (NQAs) exist which can perform TDR routines on an operational LAN. This will ensure the physical infrastructure is secure.

Question 14.10 Why can't most TDRs be used on a live network?

An equally important part of the installation work is the correct installation of devices, such as routers, that need careful setting of their configuration. The correct installation of software drivers and other network system software is also critical, and is typical of the issues intended to be resolved in the pre-installation work.

Post-installation

It is worth undertaking a visual check of the entire installation to ensure that plugs and connectors are properly seated. Check that shrink tubing is placed around connectors to help secure them where appropriate, or that connection covers protect T connectors if still in use, etc., Poor connections account for a fairly high number of faults that develop on the network. Good installation checks now and at appropriate stages in the future will reduce the number of occasions when fault finding will be required.

Question 14.11 We have made a big issue of creating cable connections, securing the cable and mounting devices in wiring cabinets. A solid fault is easy to find on a network, so what's all the fuss?

3. Management and Security

Once installed, LANs will not manage themselves. It is important to have at least one identified person responsible for the management of a LAN. Even the smallest network really ought to have such an identified person. In the initial stages a heavy commitment of technician level support is also required. At the early stages in the life of a LAN, this may mean a ratio of one technician per 50 workstations, although clearly this ratio will change as a stable situation is achieved and good reliability of the network becomes the norm.

Question 14.12 Will the technician-to-workstation ratio change upwards or downwards under stable conditions?

There are a number of issues related to LAN management which can broadly be split into two main categories: technical issues and human-related issues. The latter category is sometimes overlooked in the quest for rapid introduction of technology, and this results in under-performance of the facility.

Technical issues

In any well managed LAN it is essential that an active maintenance policy be pursued, using some of the network management tools now available. It is in this area that the fastest developments have occurred in the past few years. Vendors have been striving to make their systems more attractive by offering the 'best' range of facilities in this area. Most networks do not operate independently, and interconnection and interoperability are increasingly a requirement. This has dictated that network management systems ought to be able to report on the integrated installation, hence the requirement for standards in this area. Unfortunately, at this time, more than one standard exists and this is likely to be the situation for some time to come. Having said that, there are some clear market leaders and it is on these standards that we will concentrate.

The Simple Network Management Protocol (SNMP) has gained rapid widespread acceptance and become a *de facto* standard with support from over 250 vendors. An attraction for SNMP vendors is the implementation cost, since MIB-1 agents are in the public domain. It is the ability to maintain such a management information base (MIB) that is critical, and this is maintained at the application layer (see Fig. 14.3).

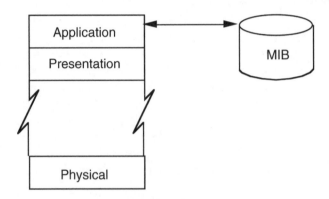

Fig. 14.3 Management information base

The result is that there are no licence fees when a system is developed. SNMP is based on UDP/IP with a limited number of primitives: 'get', 'set' and 'trap'. The SNMP standard evolved quickly, with the request for comment (RFC) route being used. In particular, RFC 1065, 1066 and 1098 contributed significantly to the evolution of the current standard.

Question 14.13 What is the request for comment system?

All devices, known as managed devices, which can be managed by SNMP are able to provide operational data when polled or requested for data by the network management centre. Typical of devices in this category are bridges; the code is referred to as the agent of the management station, and the station is called the client. The agent information which is created by a process running in the managed device, is in the form of counters or parameters, known as objects. Hence the client retrieves these objects in order to configure, fault report or gather statistics of the device being managed.

Generally speaking, only a vendor's agent and client can use its specific MIB. To address this particular issue, further updates on the MIB are in hand, with MIB-11 now having been introduced. SNMP is now the most widely used network management framework and is supported by most managed devices. The less favoured OSI offering is the

Common Management Information Service Element and Common Management Information Protocol (CMISE/CMIP). CMIP is a comprehensive network service and protocol tool (see Fig. 14.4) that supports what have become accepted as the major features required to maintain and operate an enterprise-wide network:

a) an accounting manager;

b) configuration management;

c) fault management;

d) performance management;

e) security management.

The MIB created is then controlled by a number of well defined primitives such as 'get' and 'create'. The result hopefully allows the integration of individual network management systems to be seen as a whole.

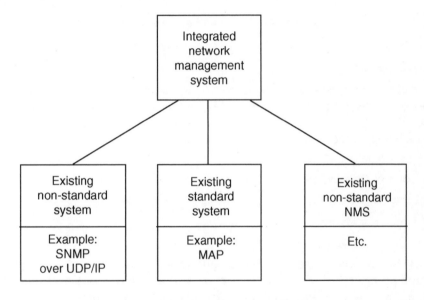

Fig. 14.4 Integrating capability of CMIP

Question 14.4 If all the LANs in an enterprise wide network use SNMP, does this make it easier to create an integrated network management system?

Examples of the range of network management systems currently available are given in Table 14.1.

The rationale for integration, given the continuing drive towards interconnection of LANs, is understandable. The Network Management Forum (NMF) has endorsed a programme named Roadmap, setting a standard called Omni-Point.

A number of features may be considered to be particularly desirable when selecting a network management system:

a) a graphical interface (including network maps);

b) remote control;

c) visual and sound systems (colour coding, audible alarms);

d) auto-discovery;

e) monitoring and analysis.

Vendor	Product
Cisco	CiscoWorks
Hewlett-Packard	Openview
3Com	Transcend
SUN	Solstice

Table 14.1 Network management systems

Network security

Perhaps the biggest change in emphasis for networks in recent years has been network security. This has partly been driven by the responsibilities placed on organizations to comply with the Data Protection legislation, and also by the recognition of the commercial value of information that could be compromised. Indeed, security threats are perceived as being:

a) loss of privacy;

b) impersonation;

c) denial of service;

d) loss of integrity.

Such threats may originate from unauthorized access, viruses and eavesdropping or wiretapping. The threats may impact on various aspects of LANs. Such impacts may highlight vulnerabilities in either policy, configuration or the technology itself. It is the role of the network manager to assess the risk of each threat against the vulnerable areas and take appropriate action. By appropriate, we should reflect the level of risk and the value of the 'asset' being protected. If the value and risk is low, the 'spend' on security levels may not be on an expensive solution or approach.

The policy area must encompass the risk assessment and covers access in terms of connectivity, performance, ease of use, manageability and overall availability. Equally, it must cover security policy issues such as authentication, authorization, accounting and confidentiality. Significant emphasis is placed on physical security of the network through the positioning and deployment of firewalls and access controls, with growing interest in intrusion detection and active audits to spot weaknesses.

User identification is often in the front line of securing authentication through the use of passwords. These can be held on a network access server (NAS) or passed to an AAA server. AAA represents Authentication (verifying identity), Authorization (configures integrity) and Accounting (audits), and is often called the triple A approach. It is based on a client–server approach, with a centralized security database, and frequently implements the RADIUS standards.

Other physical security approaches include the use of:

Access cards

Badge readers

Biometrics

UPS (un-interruptable power supply)

alarms

fire protection (detection/sprinkler)

safes and fire proof containers

CCTV

Finally, the use of digital signatures has been of rising popularity for systems needing high confidence levels. This is necessary when two parties want to communicate 'live' over the network, and need to be sure that authentication is robust. The authentication protocol for digital signatures starts with a message 'm' that needs to be sent. Using a private **decryption** key, d_k, the message 'm' is computed to be d_k (m). At the receiving end, the private **encryption** key e_k is applied to d_k(m), such that $e_k(d_k(m)) = m$. Because we are using private keys, the authentication confidence is high.

Unix tools

There are some basic network tools that offer low-level management functions within the Unix environment. These can be used to form the basis of a management suite. The tools are as follows.

a) *Ping*: This checks whether the destination address is running and is free and able to receive data. This can also be run from a windows environment and typical data looks like:

```
C:\WINDOWS>ping www.aber.ac.uk
Pinging www.aber.ac.uk [144.124.16.237] with 32 bytes of data:
Reply from 144.124.16.237: bytes=32 time=44ms TTL=250
Reply from 144.124.16.237: bytes=32 time=30ms TTL=250
Reply from 144.124.16.237: bytes=32 time=27ms TTL=250
Reply from 144.124.16.237: bytes=32 time=23ms TTL=250
Ping statistics for 144.124.16.237:
Packets: Sent = 4, Received = 4, Lost = 0 (0% loss),
Approximate round trip times in milli-seconds:
Minimum = 23ms, Maximum = 44ms, Average = 31ms
```

b) *Traceroute*: This can determine the various routes available for a destination to be reached and various features about such routes (e.g., the route status).

c) *Etherfind*: This is available on system machines to analyse TCP packets.

d) *Netstat*: This can analyse and display host information relating to connections, routing, tables, etc.

e) *Nslookup*: This can search the domain name server to determine IP addresses from a known generic name.

f) *Rdist*: This automates the distribution of files throughout the network.

Equipment

A number of devices offer facilities to support the management of LANs. Such network management centres (NMCs) provide the facilities of configuration management discussed earlier, allowing device dependent parameters to be installed (see Fig. 14.5). The NMC should offer support for a topology map to show the current status of all the LAN nodes.

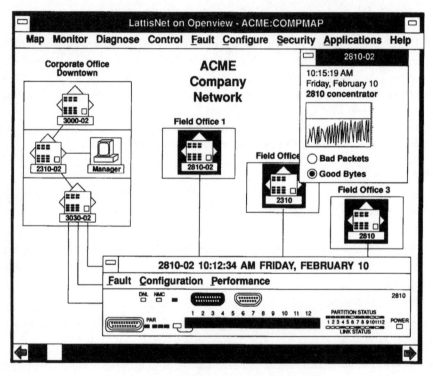

Fig. 14.5 Network configuration
(© **Layer One, reprinted with permission**)

This requires status monitoring to be implemented. It is also important, especially if the network is heavily loaded, to undertake performance management. Such data will indicate the source and destination of traffic, and sufficient data will be presented to enable the topology to be redesigned where appropriate.

Question 14.15 How might the recorded data on an NMC be helpful in redesigning the topology?

An example of a NMC output is shown in Fig. 14.6.

If detailed recording of the packets protocol is a requirement then protocol analysers can be a helpful tool. They are able to analyse the protocols on the network and display the analysis in a convenient format. Most analysers, having captured the transmitted data, are able to interpret a range of protocols. The display will recognize the individual protocols being used and present the information in a meaningful format with the protocol fields correctly interpreted. Filter criteria and trap conditions may be established such that packets that are not wanted will be ignored, and only the selected data will be recorded for analysis.

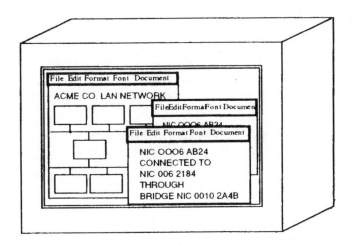

Fig. 14.6 Typical NMC display
(© Learning Group International, reprinted with permission)

There are many devices in this product range; they may be either specialist boxes or cards, such as the Excelan Analysis Card, that fit into PCs. The functionality of such devices partially overlaps that of NMCs, but it operates at a more detailed level. Most products are also able to generate pseudo-traffic when attempting to fault find, and to carry out basic diagnostic tests that check the operability of transceivers, etc., Typical outputs are shown in Fig. 14.7, and typically the products are able to count the number of errors and loading on the network at specific time intervals.

Human-related issues

There are several aspects that have to be addressed which broadly fall into the human-related category. Firstly, every network needs a network manager to take responsibility for maintaining the configuration, allocating any necessary disk space, ensuring that the correct releases of systems software are maintained, checking that the relevant security measures are adhered to, and generally overseeing the development and growth of the LAN installation. In a very small network, this may be a part-time thankless task, but it is a critical role in any size of network. One observation is that users quickly become

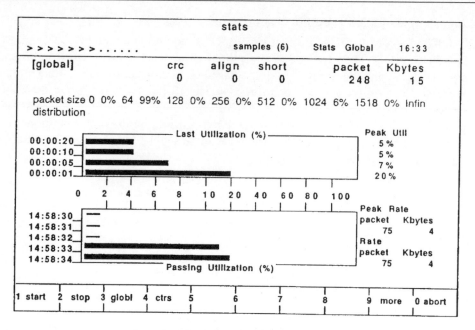

Fig. 14.7 Protocol analyser output
(© Learning Group International, reprinted with permission)

very dependent upon LAN services, to the extent that many jobs could not be tackled without the LAN being operational.

Therefore, it is important to have a contingency plan to offer a service to the users if the network should suffer a major disaster. If a structured wiring scheme has been implemented, then any major catastrophe in the cable infrastructure should have a limited impact on the services. At least a degraded service ought to be available. All other components should be individually analysed to see what impact the disaster would have on the user groups. Could the basic functionality be carried for a short time without major impact on the organization?

Each set-up will be unique, and the user population will have different expectations and demands for each one. It is therefore useful to consider the 'loss' of network facilities as it relates to the users together with network performance and availability. This becomes part of the policy that was raised earlier in the chapter.

Question 14.16 If loss of service could critically affect the users, what action should be taken?

To get the best out of the installation, the users need to be both comfortable and competent with the facilities offered.

This dictates that a user training programme be implemented. The planning of such an activity also needs to take into account the training requirements as new users appear on the network. In other words, training is not a one-off activity. It needs planning for continued operation at relevant periodic intervals.

Another issue for the network administration to resolve relates to file-server activity.

Many network users were previously users of free-standing workstations and had responsibility for making their own file backups. Once they are using a central facility, the expectation and requirement is that the file server will be secured regularly. Hence a strategy needs to be implemented that establishes the frequency and method of backing up the file server. This may include having a strategy for systematically rotating tapes (or whatever).

Finally, the network administration is responsible for paying attention to the various events that may occur or exception reports that may be produced. There is no point in monitoring and recording events on the network if nobody pays attention to the outputs. This is especially true with respect to maintaining network security.

Question 14.17 What sort of outputs may be notified to the network manager?

It is this last aspect that will enable the administration to begin to exercise preventative maintenance. If errors are identified whilst they are intermittent or developing, and where natural error recovery procedures have been invoked, then the fault may be corrected before any downtime occurs. In this arrangement, the user is largely unaware of any incidents having occurred.

Further questions

(There are answers to the questions marked with an asterisk at the end of the book.)

1. *Projects invariably get behind schedule and the pressure is always on the activities at the end of the project cycle to try to recover lost time. Let us assume that this situation has just arisen and senior management have suggested to you that the time for the network installation phase (that is now scheduled to begin) should be halved. What case would you put forward for not skimping on the planned LAN schedule of work?

2. *Why is it seen as important by many large vendors to arrive at a standard network MIB?

3. Research the range of facilities offered by several of the leading NMCs. Compare and contrast the provisions and facilities that they offer, and suggest what are now considered to be essential features and those which may be viewed as nice to have but not essential.

4. One of the noticeable aspects of equipment that offers multiple features is the limited range of facilities that are actually used. Are we in danger of reaching that point in the development of NMCs?

5. *How do we sell the benefits of being part of a network community to a user who has always enjoyed his or her independence and freedom and feels that conforming to network user regulations are an imposition?

Answer 14.1   In the case of a small network, it is likely that the network manager will know the detail of the cable layout, the exact detail of each connected device, each of the users and their levels of skill, and the applications and versions of software being used at each station. However, as soon as the network grows in size beyond perhaps twenty users, this level of knowledge cannot be sustained, and a formal network management policy is absolutely essential. Of course a formal network management policy should be in place for all networks, including small configurations.

Answer 14.2 At the simplest level, the network manager has to manage the interconnecting devices as well as the individual networks. In addition, the internetwork places demands upon the naming conventions and hardware addresses, etc., If different standards are in place in each LAN, then the problem becomes more difficult. Some of these issues will be addressed later in this chapter.

Answer 14.3 If nobody is identified as the network manager, who will take the responsibility of initiating corrective action when an error condition arises? Who will take the lead role in making changes to the network? This could be undertaken by an enthusiastic user who changes the LAN to his or her own benefit without consultation with the other users. Hence, there is a real possibility that the LAN could become obsolete, misused or remain broken once a fault developed.

Answer 14.4 Either we have to find an alternative route, or we have to change the transmission medium. For example, if we are going past a heavy electrical workshop, then we can simply put a fibre optics run through that section.

Answer 14.5 The probability of everything working straight away in anything but the very simplest of networks is slim. If you have to find a fault that exists in a large configuration (or indeed there may be multiple faults), this is more difficult than if only a small incremental change has been made since a known working state. Indeed, checking individual items can save a lot of disassembly that might be required in a fraught attempt to identify a faulty component at a later stage. The reliability of some components, like network cards, has reached such a level that individual testing is not necessary. Equally, if the cabling infrastructure is certified, this should not be an issue. Finally, with the level of management tools being very effective at fault identification, provided this functionality is operational, the intermediate testing during a build may be less of an issue now than 10 years ago.

Answer 14.6 There is the obvious answer, which is that the quality of the document after several updates is likely to be more presentable if it is an edited online copy rather than hard copy which has had several amendments. A second point is the availability of an online document, which can be coupled in with the network management system and hence updated automatically with each change of status of the device.

Answer 14.7 If we need to splice in a piece of cable to bypass a fault (or whatever), having a section of the original cable is useful since the electrical characteristics and the cable properties will be identical to those of the installed cable, and will not adversely affect the ability of the transmission medium to carry the signal.

Answer 14.8 Sticky labels get grubby very quickly, and can become unreadable after a while or can 'fall' off. Then you have no markings!

Answer 14.9 Building a system is not without its problems. It may well be that, in the first instance, not everything is correctly installed. By having a simple testbed, we are able to secure the system build and developments in a safe and controlled environment. This enables the system to be built and software compatability and configuration details to be resolved.

Answer 14.10 A TDR is connected to one end of the cable and the terminator removed at the other end. The terminator of an Ethernet network cannot be removed in a live network, and a logical ring cannot be broken to undertake the TDR test. Hence it is necessary to use the device when the network is down.

Answer 14.11 It is quite correct that a solid fault is easy to find, but intermittent faults are quite difficult to find. The majority of connection faults tend to fall into this category of being intermittent. Well installed infrastructures which conform to specification make the job easier.

Answer 14.12 Hopefully, when the network stabilizes, fewer technician staff will be required. On the other hand, the level of demand may increase as the experienced user makes use of an increasing range of facilities and services, which in turn generates a requirement for more technician support instead of less. Each site will have its own characteristics, but few will have the level of technician support recommended here. The reason will probably be that there will have been an underselling of the number of staff support needed in order to make the case for a network installation more attractive and more likely to get senior management approval for the go-ahead.

Answer 14.13 Effectively, it is the equivalent of a bulletin board dedicated to the development of a particular standard. Interested parties are able to make comments on draft proposals, and the fact that the system is electronic allows wide access and very quick development (in comparison with the necessity to call rounds of meetings with the various interested parties).

Answer 14.14 Yes. If they all use the same standard then the integration is straightforward.

Answer 14.15 If an NMC is showing that the total load on a network is approaching a threshold point and that further loads may lead to a downturn in performance, then it is a good strategy to partition the network and rejoin it with a bridge. The statistics gathered by the NMC will indicate where the data is being originated and where the destinations are. Armed with this data, we can take an informed decision about where to place the bridge to maximum effect.

Answer 14.16 If there is a critical service requirement, then this should have been identified as part of the specification and alternative provision made (e.g., maybe redundant or spare kit should be installed). It may be that the policy identifies the need for standby arrangements which are off-site if the service levels identify the need as critical.

Answer 14.17 Alerts, alarms and violation of any predetermined thresholds should be notified. The output of routine data should only be recorded for analysis when required. Network security and attempts to breach the security are obvious areas of interest to the network manager.

Appendix – ASCII code table

Low 4 bits	High 3 bits							
	000	001	010	011	100	101	110	111
0000	NUL	DLE	SP	0	@	P	`	p
0001	SOH	DC1	!	1	A	Q	a	q
0010	STX	DC2	"	2	B	R	b	r
0011	ETX	DC3	#	3	C	S	c	s
0100	EOT	DC4	$	4	D	T	d	t
0101	ENQ	NAK	%	5	E	U	e	u
0110	ACK	SYN	&	6	F	V	f	v
0111	BEL	ETB	'	7	G	W	g	w
1000	BS	CAN	(	8	H	X	h	x
1001	HT	EM	)	9	I	Y	i	y
1010	LF	SUB	*	:	J	Z	j	z
1011	VT	ESC	+	;	K	[	k	{
1100	FF	FS	,	<	L	\	l	|
1101	CR	GS	-	=	M	]	m	}
1110	SO	RS	.	>	N	^	n	~
1111	SI	US	/	?	O	_	o	DEL

Glossary

Acknowledgement Notification of the correct receipt of a message.

Addressing Specifying the source or destination location.

American Wire Gauge (AWG) System for classifying cable thickness.

Amplitude modulation Modifying the carrier's amplitude to indicate a data signal.

Appletalk Proprietary network of Apple Macintosh equipment and compatible devices.

Application layer Layer 7 of the OSI model.

Arcnet Proprietary network of Datapoint Corporation.

Asynchronous transmission Transmission system which allows variable time gaps between characters.

Bandwidth The range between the lowest and highest frequencies that can be transmitted on a system or channel.

Baseband The frequency band occupied by a signal before the point where signals are modulated on an analogue carrier.

Baud rate The rate at which signalling changes.

Bridge A data link layer relay device.

Broadband System using frequency division mutiplexing to support multiple channels on the media.

Carrier Sense Multiple Access (CSMA) A technique which listens for a period when no other transmissions are active before 'talking'.

Carrier Continuous frequency which can be modulated.

Cheapernet Thin-wire Ethernet.

Checksum A form of error checking.

Circuit switching Opening a fixed route/path for data transmission.

Coaxial cable A cable with two conductors separated by a dielectric. The conductors form concentric circles.

Connection-oriented A connection or route must be established before data transmission.

Connectionless No connection or route needs to be established before data transmission.

CSMA/CD Carrier sense multiple access with collision detection, i.e., CSMA operates but the system listens while it is 'talking' and aborts in the event of hearing a corrupted transmission.

Cyclic redundancy check A number of check bits appended to the data to facilitate the detection of transmission error.

Data link layer Ensures the reliable transfer of data across the data link, i.e., between two nodes.

Data Communication Equipment (or **data circuit-terminating equipment**) DCE PTT device to attach DTE to the network.

Data Terminal Equipment (DTE) User device connected to a network.

Datagram A data packet switched independently through the network.

Drop cable Cabling from the distribution cable to the wall outlet, or equivalent.

Encryption Making data intelligible only to authorized readers by modifying its data pattern.

Error rate The ratio of corrupted bits against total transmitted.

Ethernet LAN implementation using CSMA/CD and following the IEEE 802.3 standard.

Ethertalk Ethernet implementation of Appletalk.

File Transfer Protocol Delivers file structured information from one host to another.

Flow control A technique to restrict the flow or number of messages between two nodes.

Fragmentation Breaking a message into smaller units for ease of transmission.

Frequency Division Multiplexing (FDM) A method of dividing a transmission medium bandwidth into discrete channels.

Frequency Shift Keying (FSK) Modulating a signal by varying the frequency of the carrier.

Gateway Allows the interconnection of two networks.

Half repeater Device to extend a LAN over another medium.

Headend A device on a broadband network which translates incoming frequencies into separate outgoing frequencies. Also provides power boost to the signal.

Idle RQ A stop and wait for response protocol. If no response is received, then retransmit and wait again.

International Standards Organization (ISO) Standards body.

Jamming Intentional interference with a signal.

Local Area Network (LAN) A shared communication facility allowing interconnection of devices over a localized area.

Localtalk Appletalk over twisted pair cable.

Logical channel A virtual call (X.25).

Manchester encoding A method of signalling digital data with an embedded clock.

Modem A device for converting (and reconverting) digital data into analogue data for transmission on an analogue carrier (and the reverse at the receiving end).

Modulation Conversion from digital to analogue format.

NetWare Novell application protocol.

Network layer Covers layer 3 services, particularly routing.

OSI Open system interconnection providing a reference model or framework for network development.

Packet assembler/disassembler This allows character mode devices to be connected to a packet-switching network by assembling asynchronous characters into packets and vice versa.

Packet switching This allows small self-contained units of data (packets) to be forwarded across a network.

Phase modulation Modulation by changing the phase of a carrier.

Piggy-backing ACKs are returned in the same packet as a data transfer in the opposite direction.

Presentation layer Layer 6 of the OSI model.

Protocol A set of rules to control the exchange of data between two points.

PTT The main telecommunications company in any country.

Repeater A device which extends the transmission distance limits by regenerating a signal (amplifying and retiming it).

RG58 Thin coaxial cable.

Ring A network with a circular logical topology.

Router A relay device working on the network layer.

Session layer Synchronous data transfer, operating at layer 5 of the OSI model.

Structured wiring A cable design technique which attempts to reduce the amount of recabling.

Switching A method of getting data across a network.

Synchronization This allows timing to be recognized.

Timeout When a device gives up after attempting data transfer for a predeterimined time.

Token A data structure which contains control information.

Topology Network structure or layout.

Transceiver A device allowing transmitting/receiving of data on the transmission medium.

Transport layer Host-to-host communication function, operating at layer 4 of the seven-layer model.

Virtual circuit This provides sequenced, error-free delivery between two nodes.

Wide Area Network (WAN) A network over a large geographical area.

Window The range of sequence numbers of packets or messages that can be sent.

Work area A cluster of workstations in a small area.

X. series Digital standards (CCITT).

Answers to further questions

Chapter 1

Question 1

    D is 44_H, i.e., 11000100 with odd parity

                         01000100 with even parity

    F is 46_H, i.e., 11000110 with odd parity

                         01000110 with even parity

Question 2

200 characters is 10×200 bits = 2000 bits

To send 2000 bits at 9600 bit/s will take

$$\frac{2000}{9600} = 0.206 \text{ s}$$

Chapter 2

Question 1

$x^5 + x^3 + 1$ is a polynomial generator represented by 101001

Hence the modulo 2 division becomes

```
101001 | 10110100000
         101001
         _____
           100000
           101001
           _____
             100100
             101001
             _____
              01101
```

The CRC is 01101. Remember that it has to be five digits because the highest power of the polynomial is x^5, and so we keep sufficient leading 0s to ensure that the CRC has five digits.

Question 3

With Idle RQ, the sequence will be iterations of

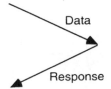

    Data

    Response

To send one data block of 512 bytes and get a response will take

(data transfer time + propagation delay) + (response transfer time + propagation delay)

$$= \frac{(512 \times 8)}{(64 \times 10^3)} s + 2ms + \frac{(128)}{(64 \times 10^3)s + 2ms}$$

$$= 64 \text{ ms} + 2 \text{ ms} + 2 \text{ ms} + 2 \text{ ms} = 70 \text{ ms}$$

If 10 kbytes needs to be sent 512 bytes at a time,

$$\text{total number of packets sent} = \frac{10 \text{ kbytes}}{512}$$

$$= 20 \text{ packets}$$

Therefore, time to send 10 kbyte file = 20 × 70 ms = 1400 ms or 1.4 s

This represents the minimum time since it assumes the following:

a) a response is immediate and no delay occurs on receipt at the destination;

b) the next packet is transmitted immediately the response is received with no delay;

c) no errors occur and hence no recovery action time is involved;

d) no overheads are associated with each data device.

Chapter 3

Question 5

It is unlikely that, for a parallel cable of length 20 m, the skew problem discussed in the Chapter could be avoided. Hence we would not normally expect to see such a connection.

Question 6

With an RS232C connection, we can transmit in both directions simultaneously because the Tx and Rx are separate wires. Hence this is a full-duplex connection.

Chapter 4

Question 4

Because 3000 Hz is the bandwidth that is normally allocated to human voice, and 64 kbit/s was the PTT channel capacity that was originally established to carry voice traffic across the telephone network. Given that voice traffic represents the majority of the PTT traffic, it is not surprising that data networks were initially designed to fit in with the existing voice networks.

Question 5

3	2		3	2			2		3	2	1

Chapter 5

Question 1

It is usual for an organization to enclose pre-prepared documents in an e-mail message. If these enclosures have been prepared with a particular word-processing package, if the document is to be viewed at the destination in the same format as it was sent, this requires the system to have the same (or compatible) word processing environment.

Question 2

First, using a server-based repository for the word-processing package means you are more likely to get everyone using the same product and the same version number of that product. This achieves the objectives in Question 1. It also allows the number of active word processing sessions to be monitored to ensure that software licence restrictions are not being violated within the organization.

Chapter 6

Question 3

Star topology

Advantages:

a) Cable damage has a limited impact.

b) It is possible to use existing cable.

c) It is suited to dumb devices.

d) Mixed transmission speeds can be accommodated.

e) Fault detection and isolation is easy.

f) It supports the new fast LAN standards.

Disadvantages:

a) It has a central point, which could bring down the whole network.

b) If it is a PABX style, then the speeds may be low.

Bus topology

Advantages:

a) The layout is simple, and there is a relatively cheap range of devices.

b) It is easy to attach new devices.

c) The system is suited to 'bursty' traffic.

Disadvantages:

a) There are no automatic acknowledgements.

b) There is a potential security risk, since anyone can listen in.

c) Intelligence is needed in the interfaces.

Ring topology

Advantages:

a) The transmission capacity is shared equally amongst all attached stations.

b) Error rates are low.

c) Access is guaranteed under heavy loads.

d) Routing on a single ring is trivial.

Disadvantages:

a) It is more difficult to add new stations to a pure ring than other topologies. However, this is easier with a structured cabling system.

b) Repeaters are required in each station interface.

c) One station interface could break the whole ring if it was faulty.

Fully connected or mesh topology

Advantages:

a) There is a multiple choice of routes.

b) It is robust and able to withstand cable breaks.

Disadvantages:

a) Significant cabling is required.

b) Adding more stations becomes increasingly more expensive.

Question 6

The maximum length of any transmission medium is normally dictated by the distance a signal can travel on that medium without the quality of that signal degenerating to a level at which the signal cannot be recognized.

Chapter 7

Question 1

The answers may be quite varied. It is true to say that any new and innovative idea will take perhaps a number of years to become an accepted standard. Sometimes an organization will launch into the marketplace and hope that the standard will follow at some later stage. However, the major point to remember is that most sites either already have, or are likely to have at some point in the future, a range of different computers and peripherals. A firm standard for network connectivity is a major advantage when connecting a disparate range of vendors' equipment together and letting them 'talk' to each other. Without this standard approach, the future developments of interconnected systems will be hindered, and so perhaps the price of slower development on the network connections is a price worth paying.

Question 2

In order to achieve a worldwide network addressing scheme we need a standard which specifies how addresses are allocated or interpreted. Without such a standard, it would be a significantly harder job to set up a worldwide network. At the hardware level, the address may be the address allocated to the network board, and these are the addresses used at the level 2 operation. However, an international addressing scheme needs a conceptual mechanism, and that requires a means of allocating network addresses from a single point. These addresses are allocated to the network level which operates at level 3.

Question 3

Although in the bottom three layers the protocols may well have a mechanism for acknowledging the receipt of a packet of data, such a protocol need not necessarily be in place. However, there is a requirement in most networks to know that data has been successfully delivered. This is achieved by putting a piece of software at the sender's and receiver's interfaces to handshake the data across. Such software resides within the station being connected to the network, and it is part of the level 4 software.

Chapter 8

Question 1

In the development of data communications we have seen the data components enveloped within a framework which allows the receiver to be alerted to the arrival of the start of the flow, and the data component to be recognized within such a frame. At the low transmission speeds for which such arrangements were developed, it was fairly easy for the receiving station to remain in synchronization with the sender for short bursts of data.

In LAN situations, the transmission speeds are several orders of magnitude faster than this, and the length of the data frames is also much larger to assist with the efficiency (i.e., the percentage of red tape bits in comparison with the actual data is reduced). Hence, a system has been designed to send the clocking signal embedded with the data signal such that the receiver can use this clocking signal to remain locked onto the transmitted signal and remain in synchronization for long periods of time.

Question 2

No. Baseband components are cheaper than their analogue broadband counterparts. Also, the necessity to have expensive devices such as a headend is eliminated.

Question 3

Yes. If we do this then each side of the headend can sustain the maximum length cable run and so the length of the system is effectively doubled. Of course, the more devices connected to a single segment that we have, the greater is the risk of contention on the transmission medium.

Question 4

Typically, we would use four adjacent channels. A 10 Mbit/s data signal would require a 20 MHz channel for signalling (to accommodate the embedded signal for clocking purposes).

Question 5

If we implement CSMA, then stations wishing to transmit will listen to the transmission medium to ensure that there is no other dialogue present. Provided that it is quiet, the station can start to transmit. Clearly, in this scenario, it is possible for two stations to start talking almost simultaneously. In such an arrangement, all such transmitting stations will continue to do this until their message is complete. This could have been avoided if the stations had realized that there was a problem and had aborted the transmission. Without such an arrangement, time is spent in transmitting garbled data. If we could abort the attempts immediately then this wasted time would be reduced considerably. The mechanism used to detect such conditions is CSMA/CD.

Question 6

Structured cabling allows the LAN to be extended and maintained with the minimum of effort.

Chapter 9

Question 1

In an IEEE 802.3 LAN, no station should be able to send a transmission that collides with another station's transmission and not be aware that this has happened, otherwise we cannot support CSMA/CD as a media access control technique. To ensure that this condition is met, we need to make sure that every transmission is sufficiently long for the transmitting station to be able to detect whether another station has also transmitted during that time. The time taken should not be so short that the station has finished sending data before it can be alerted to the fact that such a collision has occurred. Consequently, the standard was set that no packet should be shorter than 64 bytes. A consequence of setting this part of the standard was that the maximum length of a LAN from extremity to extremity such that the detection rule would always hold true was also established.

Question 2

If we are sending data on a network to a particular station, it is important from the security point of view that only that specified receiving station should attempt to receive it. If this were not true and every station were always to respond to every message sent, then the LAN would be of limited value.

Question 3

The first thing to note is the distance between the offices, which is beyond the normal transmission range of a single segment unless it is a fast fibre optics cable run. This scenario matches the needs met by the configuration shown in Fig. 9.26. The link between the switches does not need to be a high speed link, but the topology is typical of the approach taken.

Chapter 10

Question 1

If we look at applications such as voice and video, it is no use delaying the transfer of such data content if it is to be useful at the destination. For example, can you imagine talking to someone on a telephone where the communications system supporting the data transfer is variably delaying elements of the conversation? Hence we need to get data transfers under way very quickly from the time the data is available to send. To get a continuous and even flow of data that supports voice, we need to take each small data element and send it quickly. This pushes us in the direction of creating small cells of data and rapidly sending them (or switching them) across the network.

Question 4

QOS metrics include an administrative weighting field. The feature that can be addressed in the field is the line speed. This ability to change the figure from a default setting is vendor dependent at this stage.

Question 5

When ATM was being developed for LAN implementation, it was a clear route for sites to follow. Given the 'seamless' integration with future WANs that it offers, it was the obvious way forward. The recent Ethernet developments have offered a much cheaper alternative with 'the friend you know'. The result is likely to be that existing Ethernet sites will stay with the Ethernet upgrade paths, at least for several years, rather than there being the rapid migration to ATM that one might have predicted at the launch of ATM.

Chapter 11

Question 1

Although the full range of interconnection relay devices could be considered, including repeaters, it is more likely that, if there are LANs already in existence, higher order relays will be required. If the LANs are in close proximity to each other, then bridges may well suffice, provided that each of the LANs conforms to one of the well established standards. If the LANs are remote from each other, then we may be able to use remote bridges, but the more favoured option is likely to be interconnection using the services of a WAN. Provided, once again, that we are using standard LANs and protocols, we would naturally select a router to provide the connectivity to the WAN. If non-compatible systems are to be interconnected, then a gateway device will be required.

Question 2

If the volume of traffic being carried on a single collision domain LAN rises above a given level, then the performance of the LAN may well deteriorate or not meet the required specification, and users may experience unacceptable delay.

Alternatively, there may be a group of users for whom there is a security requirement that their local group traffic should be kept isolated from the rest of the LAN user community, whilst at the same time this 'isolated' group is provided with the organization-wide services for all of the rest of their work. Equally, it could be that the network is being split to make both halves more robust, with each half being capable of supporting itself independently of the other in the event of a fault occurring on the network.

If servers are being used to support identified workgroups, it may well be helpful to separate out each workgroup and server onto a separate entity and reconnect to the total network via a router. This will have the advantage of providing good local performance, containing the server traffic to just that workgroup area, and not loading the rest of the network heavily. At the same time, we still have the full network interconnection for all the traffic that needs to access stations more remote than the local workgroup. More typically it is a series of LANs connected to a backbone using routers that is implemented.

Question 3

In such a building, the probability is that each part of the office block can be reached by a relatively short run or a daisy-chained segment. In such a situation, it could be a sensible strategy to bring all the wiring back to a single point on each floor of the building (this is part of a structured approach to wiring). Having got that local concentration, rather than use a whole series of interconnection relays, it would be better to use a single multi-port repeater to provide the connectivity.

At the time that multi-port repeaters were used, it allowed multiple segments to be linked at a single point. In a multi-storey building, each floor could have had a multi-port repeater to link all the segments on that floor.

Question 4

If two bridges have been used to provide the added resilience such that there should always be one operable bridge, then we have to be certain that we don't create a loop. If that were to happen a data packet could circulate around and around such a loop and never be killed off. Hence the way in which each of the two bridges learns (or is configured) to forward packets from one bus to the other bus must prevent such a looping situation. The learning algorithm employed does just that. It allows both bridges to construct a relevant table, but only one of the bridges will assume responsibility for forwarding particular traffic. The other bridge will stay in standby mode, and it will only take over responsibility if a fault develops and it determines that data packets are not being forwarded when they ought to be. Note, the use of bridges is no longer a frequent occurrence.

Question 5

Remember that the bridge in an 802.3 network is transparent and works on the basis of a spanning tree algorithm, whereas a bridge on an 802.5 network implements source routing. Bridges between an 802.3 LAN and an 802.5 LAN, where they exist, need to note the different MAC packet structures as they try to implement STA. It is now normal to place a router, rather than a bridge, between two different 802.x networks.

Chapter 12

Question 1

Interconnection is a means of providing the physical connection between two or more networks with the result that data packets can be sent from any station to any other station. For that data packet to be recognizable at the receiving end it is possible that some reformatting or protocol translation of the originally despatched frame is required. If that is so then devices such as gateways, etc., are utilized. This second aspect is providing interoperability.

Question 2

The range of network approaches that have been adopted by the plethora of vendors is vast. A comparison may well be the range of dialects used in the English language. As an example, it may well be that each network uses an Ethernet framing structure and physical connection, making interconnection an easy activity. However, sorting out the contents of each of the various protocols adopted and making those contents understandable to the intended recipient could involve significantly more 'translation' work. Hence interoperability is much more difficult to achieve.

Question 3

In attempting to achieve interoperability, if you select a transport protocol that is widely used by the majority of other network users, then the problem is reduced somewhat. TCP/IP falls into the category of such a protocol. It enjoys a wide penetration of the network market and is readily available in vendors' products.

Chapter 13

Question 2

At low data traffic levels it is probable that the LAN is idle at the given instant at which any individual station is seeking to gain access. With an Ethernet network, the access method is such that this sending station is able to gain access immediately. With a token ring LAN, to access the transmission medium, a station needs to be holding the token. On average, even in a no-load network, this will require the token to rotate halfway round the network. Hence access is not quite so immediate as in the Ethernet case. At higher levels of traffic a token ring is more able to sustain the traffic levels, giving each station its fair share of the network capacity. Ethernet, on the other hand, can't sustain continuing high levels, and the performance at traffic volumes constantly above 5 or 6 Mbit/s will deteriorate.

Question 3

The network availability between these two stations relies on the four network cards and the bridge all being operable. If any one of these is faulty, the link will be broken. Hence the availability of the link is 0.9^5. This equates to 0.59 or 59 per cent availability. Clearly, if you were investing in a network, you would want the system to be available for a lot more than just over half the time. We therefore need each of the individual components to have an availability that is a lot higher than 0.9.

Question 4

First, we need to include well proven and standard products that are multiple sourced so that the availability of the component is high, and if the supplier is no longer able to supply the component, an alternative supplier is able to provide it. Second, we need to examine the network and identify the potential major risk points. It might well be that a faulty interface card on any individual station will have a limited impact on the network at large (even though it has a major impact on the user whose station it is). However, if the faulty interface card is on the server station, then that will have a much larger impact, or if the router between two LANs becomes inoperable, that could reduce the network functionality. In such cases, it is prudent to carefully consider the affect of such an outage and make appropriate standby provision. This could include the addition of a redundant component within the network, or simply having a spare readily available.

Chapter 14

Question 1

The concepts behind the answer to this would almost certainly be the same for any project. If we take short cuts on the cable installation, it could take a long time to fault find at a later stage. The connection of devices to the system is also an activity which needs to be undertaken with great care and in a controlled manner. By doing a step by step installation with full testing at each stage, we are likely to get a successful installation, without problems occurring later when the network is up and live. Equally, the correct configuration of devices such as routers and the establishment of network security measures are serious issues. Fault-finding can be a really expensive exercise that involves downtime for all the users. Whilst it might be attractive to try to save time now, beware of the trade-off you may be entering into.

Question 2

Increasingly, we are seeing sites consisting of several different LANs that are interconnected to form a large, integrated network. In order for the system to be effectively managed in its entirety, each part of the network needs to be able to contribute its data to the central monitoring function. Since this is based on a single database, a standard MIB is a desirable feature. This would allow the network administrators to inspect and monitor the operation from a single management station.

Question 5

Being a user on a centrally controlled LAN system brings with it a range of disciplines that may not be welcome. It may be that control of your own backups is lost and handed over to the server. It may be that standard versions of the software are imposed or that a central decision to standardize on particular word processor packages or spreadsheets is imposed. This may mean the loss of your favourite piece of software.

This has to be measured against the potential benefits to the organization at large. The transportability of information between any individuals within the LAN community becomes easier under such centrally controlled situations. The latest releases of the standard software are likely to be made readily available, and all users will then be working with compatible versions.

There are also a number of facilities that were not usually available to stand-alone users, such as e-mail and access to servers such as fax servers and laser printer servers. Equally, access to the Internet may be offered. These additional facilities, the inclusion within the perimeter of the network security offered in the installation, plus the standardization benefits, ought to more than make up for any perceived loss.

Index